W9-AGV-699

HELPING VICTIMS OF SEXUAL ABUSE

HELPING VICTIMS OF SEXUAL ABUSE

LYNN HEITRITTER
& JEANETTE VOUGHT

BETHANYHOUSE
Minneapolis, Minnesota

Library of Congress Cataloging-in-Publication Data

Heitritter, Lynn.
  Helping victims of sexual abuse : a sensitive biblical guide for counselors, victims, and families / Lynn Heitritter and Jeanette Vought. — Updated ed.
    p. cm.
  Summary: "Includes documentation of abuse of children and adults and the work of the support group BECOMERS in restoring victims to normal, productive lives through relationship with Christ. Covers nine steps to mental, emotional, and spiritual wholeness"—Provided by publisher.
  Includes bibliographical references and index.
  ISBN 0-7642-0228-6 (pbk. : alk. paper)
  1. Sexually abused chi' ' ̄ 2. Adult child sexual abuse victims—Pastoral c‹
  BV4464.3.H44   200‹
  261.8'3272—dc22

We wish to acknowledge our families
for their unfailing support,
encouragement, and prayer
during the preparation of this work.
We thank you and we love you.

We wish to dedicate this book
to the courageous women and men
who have "fought the good fight" into recovery
and shared their lives with us
so that together we might encourage others
to come out of the darkness into the Light.

About the Authors

LYNN HEITRITTER, RN, PhD, has been a faculty associate in Marriage and Family Studies at Bethel Theological Seminary and was the founder and former director of BECOMERS Sexual Abuse Support Group Program. Together with her family, she has provided licensed foster care to physically and sexually abused adolescents. For nearly a decade she promoted strategies for abuse prevention through family wellness workshops and seminars to equip clergy and laypersons in acquiring skills needed to break cycles of shame in families and churches. She and her husband spend much of the year in Africa, currently serving with The Love of Christ Ministries, a South African orphanage that cares for babies abandoned due to HIV/AIDS. She and her husband maintain a home in Minnesota and have two adult daughters.

JEANETTE VOUGHT, PhD, LP, is the executive director and founder of Christian Recovery Center in Minneapolis. She is a licensed psychologist, licensed marriage and family therapist, a licensed social worker, and a certified criminal justice specialist. Former president of the Minnesota chapter of the North American Christians in Social Work national board, Vought has extensive experience in counseling sexual abuse victims (including child, adolescent, and adult) as well as sexual abuse offenders; she has extensive experience in conducting BECOMERS sexual abuse workshops and group leaders training sessions, and she has several years' experience in the field of social work and group home coordinating. For ten years she conducted in-prison inmate seminars as a volunteer for Prison Fellowship. She and her husband have four grown sons and make their home in Minnesota. Vought has also written the book *Post-Abortion Trauma, Nine Steps to Recovery*.

Anyone wishing to contact the authors to schedule training seminars and workshops, to request BECOMERS "start-up" packets or additional resources, or for assistance in developing a local BECOMERS group, may contact them at the following address:

BECOMERS
Christian Recovery Center
6120 Earle Brown Drive, Suite 200
Brooklyn Center, MN 55430
(763) 566-0088
www.christianrecoverycenter.org

To Our Readers

Sexual abuse is not only prevalent in society at large but is occurring within the church as well. Sixteen years ago we began the introduction to the first edition of this book by stating that we recognized a need to inform the church about sexual abuse. As well, we wanted to provide specific materials that would enable people within the church to develop effective ministry to adults who had experienced sexual abuse as children. Over the years, while many have been helped, many continue to bear scars of childhood abuse and desperately struggle with hidden trauma that interferes with spiritual growth and relationships with others. The revised edition builds on our earlier vision of equipping members of the body of Christ to promote healing and restoration of women and men who have been victims of sexual abuse.

Our purpose is fourfold. First, we hope to provide Christian counselors, clergy, support group leaders, and those involved in ministries of care with increased understanding of the experience of childhood sexual abuse victims and to provide resources that can be used as tools in the recovery process of adult survivors and those who love them. Second, we want to help adult survivors of childhood sexual abuse to identify areas of damage resulting from sexual abuse, to feel strengthened as they participate in their individual journeys of recovery, and to be encouraged that many adult survivors have experienced restoration and are living satisfying and successful lives. Third, we wish to help friends, relatives, and spouses in their efforts to be supportive to loved ones who have been victims of sexual abuse. Fourth, we offer current perspectives about ministry to adult survivors of sexual abuse over the past two decades.

The book is divided into five sections, each with a particular focus.

Section One acquaints the reader with sexual abuse as seen through the eyes of children, including life histories of adult survivors sharing some of the trauma of their childhood experiences. Special attention is given to the effects of abuse from childhood, through adolescence, and into adulthood. This section describes physical, emotional, psychological, and spiritual damage of sexual abuse.

Section Two gives an overview of sexual abuse within the family, with guidelines for intervention in incest within families.

Section Three offers insight into some of the spiritual and psychological influences affecting sexual abuse offenders. A description of different types of offenders is presented with treatment issues that need to be addressed.

Section Four presents the BECOMERS Sexual Abuse support group recovery program, including teaching materials, illustrations, and individual homework exercises.

Section Five offers a reflection of Second Thoughts from the authors. Nearly two decades ago, we collaborated on research and preparation for writing *Helping Victims of Sexual Abuse*. At the present time, we write a new chapter from our individual perspectives to share with our readers ways in which God has shaped parallel ministry paths since the first edition of the book.

To the fullest extent of our knowledge, we have given credit to all the authors and other sources of materials that have been used in our research and writing. We appreciate each of these contributions to our work.

With the first edition of this book, we wrote to share our deep concern for adult victims who needed acknowledgment of the truth of their experience. Our continued prayer is that God might use this revised edition to empower the church to recognize, understand, offer hope of restoration, promote healing, and, ultimately prevent child sexual abuse.

Contents

Section One

Understanding Abused Children

1

Messages . . .

They cry in the dark so you can't see their tears
They hide in the light so you can't see their fears.
Forgive and forget all the while . . .
Love and pain
Become one and the same
In the eyes of a wounded child. . . .[1]

We all receive "messages" in childhood that have an effect on our adult life, messages transmitted to us primarily through relationships with others. These early transmissions have a powerful influence on our concept of being loved, being valuable, and belonging. The messages received by children who are sexually abused can have a devastating impact on them.

We cannot know the actual number of children who are being impacted by destructive experiences of sexual abuse. However, in recent years, the number of reported cases of sexual abuse has risen faster than the number of reported cases of other forms of child abuse and neglect.[2] Perhaps the clearest picture of the scope of childhood sexual abuse comes from national surveys in which 27 percent of women and 16 percent of men disclosed a childhood history of being sexually abused.[3] Research suggests that only about 10–15 percent of incidents of sexual abuse are actually reported by child victims.[4] [5] Whatever estimates are cited, there is consensus that sexual abuse is vastly underreported. The following life histories are from adult survivors who have courageously spoken out about their childhood sexual abuse. Through their stories they offer a glimpse into some of the harmful messages transmitted to children who are sexually abused.

FATHER-DAUGHTER INCEST

Julie's Messages

Grown-ups had told Julie that as a baby she was her father's pride and joy—his little red-headed sweetheart. But while still a preschooler, she began to feel apprehensive in his presence. At the end of the day, he would pick her up and rub his bristly beard on her soft face and demand, "How about a kiss for your dad who's been working hard all day?" As his burly strength trespassed the boundaries of her uneasiness, she began to "hear" a nonverbal message: *His feelings are more important than mine.*

Vague uneasiness grew into fear as Julie and her brother experienced their father's unpredictable and explosive anger. Her mother's form of discipline was the continual threat, "You just wait till your father gets home!" Beatings with a belt left bloody stripes on her frail body. Over time, having to lie at school about facial bruises and black eyes was enough to eventually convince Julie: *I am worthless and unlovable.*

She cowered in her room one night, writhing in emotional pain as she heard her brother screaming during a beating. Frozen in fear, she raged with hate for her father—yet he was her security. Julie knew children were supposed to love their parents, and also that she was completely dependent on them. She eventually turned her choking hatred for her father against herself, which translated into an indelible message of self-reproach: *I am bad because I hate my father.*

One evening just before her mother went out, she asked nine-year-old Julie to shower before going to bed. About half an hour later, her father sent her brother to bed and suggested that because he, too, needed to take a shower, they should shower together to save water. Feeling acutely embarrassed, Julie replied she'd rather shower alone. Her father's suggestion soon became a command, and he pulled her into the bathroom. Her stomach knotted with fear and her heart pounded furiously as he ordered her to undress. He "explained" how stupid she was for feeling embarrassed. After all, she was "his little girl." He had changed her diapers and had seen her undressed for years; in fact, until she died he would have that right! Julie wished she could crawl into the wall to escape his prying eyes.

Then he approached her in an unusually nurturing way and began to fondle her as he explained "where babies come from." He seemed to be actually caring for her!

A surge of conflicting feelings erupted all at once. Her experience of some physical pleasure and this newfound closeness with her father clashed violently with the disgust, shame, and fear at what was happening to her. She felt dizzy.

When she passed out from the intensity of the physical and emotional distress, a new message began taking root that would shape her life with devastating effect: *Bad love is better than no love at all.*

Julie's experience is not unusual. Though incest was once thought to be rare, "recent estimates of incestuous experience run as high as 10–20 percent in the general population."[6] Children seem to be most at risk of family incest between the ages of seven and thirteen years old. It is important to note that in the eyes of children, a sexually abusive relationship with an offender who is an ongoing caregiver, such as a foster parent, stepparent, or live-in nanny, might also reflect dynamics of "family incest" even though such a relationship might not be considered "family" in legal definitions related to incest in families.[7] While accurate statistics on incest are impossible to compile due to the many undisclosed cases, the problem is much more prevalent than most of us would care to admit.

In addition, Julie's father was not some sort of easily identifiable "pervert." Like many men who abuse their children, he was a well-respected, wealthy member of his community and, in this case, a deacon in his church as well. The church must not ignore the reality that sexual abuse exists within church families.

CLOSE ACQUAINTANCE MOLESTATION

Laurie's Messages

Laurie's parents divorced when she was nine. Laurie's father had no further contact with the family. Her mother became depressed. Grieved and hurt over the divorce, Laurie's mother became emotionally unavailable to Laurie and her siblings. Laurie had a sense that she was not to have conversations with her mother about any of her feelings, especially about the "loss" of both parents in different ways. Over time, Laurie perceived this lack of connection meant that neither her mother nor father cared about her. She concluded: *If people I care about reject me, then I must be unlovable.*

To fill this empty place, Laurie started spending more time away from home with a new friend, a thirty-nine-year-old man named Joe. He worked with cars just as Laurie's father had. Joe's companionship brought back memories of the few special times she had enjoyed with her father at his auto body shop.

Joe became a father figure to Laurie. He took her everywhere with him, bought her gifts, and gave her anything she wanted. It all seemed too good to be true. He told her she was "his girl" and that their relationship would always be special. She gladly gave him the hugs he asked for and enjoyed being cuddled on his lap. For the first time she could remember, she felt loved and cared for.

She spent more and more time at Joe's home; it became her favorite place to be. One afternoon, however, while she was sitting on Joe's lap as they watched TV, he started fondling her. She became uneasy and scared. She wanted to be loved, to be special to someone, to have nice things like the other girls had, but something was going wrong. Joe was her special friend, but his touching didn't feel good. She tried to move away from him, but his grip remained firm.

As he continued, confusion overwhelmed her. He had been so good to her and had given her so many gifts. He said he loved her, in spite of the fact that she had concluded she was unlovable. Surely he wouldn't do anything bad; there must be something wrong with her. At the age of nine, Laurie had become convinced that she was so worthless that she should let others decide what was best for her, even if she didn't like it. A silent message of disregard for herself began to set in: *I should depend on others because they are wiser and stronger than I am.*

This was the beginning of Laurie's nightmare of sexual abuse. Though she was fearful and confused, her desperate need for love drove her deeper into dependence upon Joe. She continued going to his house, even though his actions became increasingly bizarre. She felt like two persons—one willingly participating in the abuse, the other filled with shame and fear. It seemed as if she were standing outside of herself watching this happen to someone else.

Gradually, over time, Joe led her into all kinds of sexual perversion, eventually making her view pornography, destroying the last remnants of her childhood innocence. Hating who she was and what had happened to her, she turned away from God and her family, drinking to numb the gnawing pain within and using drugs to forget the terrible things that had happened. Finally, at age thirteen, Laurie could take no more. She ran away from home. Alone, frightened, deeply wounded, and chemically dependent, she began working the streets of Minneapolis as a prostitute. It had become the only way she knew how to take care of herself and try to be loved.

Abuse situations like Laurie's are all too prevalent, with very destructive results. In the United States, the average age of girls entering prostitution is thirteen to fourteen years old, with 60–90 percent of juvenile prostitutes reporting a history of childhood sexual abuse, particularly incest.[8] One woman's metaphor for the connection of sexual abuse to prostitution is that "incest is boot camp" for prostitution.[9] Even though Joe was not Laurie's biological father, he was a father figure in her life and, as such, the abusive relationship was in many ways equivalent to father-daughter incest. Another facet of Laurie's experience was Joe's use of pornography in the progression of escalating abuse. In one study, 50–80 percent of recovering prostitutes reported that pornography played a "significant role in teaching them what was expected of them as prostitutes."[10]

While Laurie's story may seem like an extreme case, the progression from sexual abuse to prostitution is tragically familiar. Even in cases where abuse victims do not engage in prostitution, many still end up "prostituting" themselves by trading their bodies in exchange for someone to care about them.

Nearly 50 percent of violent crime rape victims are under eighteen, with 15 percent of rape victims being children younger than twelve.[11] However, in Laurie's case, as in countless others, her offender did not use physical force to initiate sexual abuse. Instead, offenders, such as Joe, manipulate children over time with premeditated "grooming behaviors," such as gifts and affection, to build a trusting relationship with the intentional goal of sexually exploiting them.[12] A recurring theme from stories such as Laurie's is that most such cases are never reported because child victims feel guilty, ashamed, and are deeply fearful of rejection and abandonment.

PEDOPHILE ABUSE

Jim's Messages

When Jim's father died, Jim was two months old, the youngest of three children. His mother soon began to work full time, and from about age two, Jim was cared for by a series of baby-sitters. The sudden shift from a consistently nurturing relationship with his mother, coupled with the loss of his father, created a home situation where Jim developed increasing feelings of insecurity and emptiness.

Jim's older brother responded to the family's losses with rebellious behavior. Jim thought his brother was causing his mother to have even more problems. Jim resented the amount of attention his older brother received because of his misbehavior, and yet he continued striving to be the "good boy" he thought his mother wanted. A message of conditional approval was forming within Jim: *If I am good, I will be loved.* Jim felt his duty in the family was to try to make his mother's life easier, and, without really realizing it, he began setting aside his own feelings to try to take care of hers. A powerful message of over-responsibility was taking root: *I am responsible to take care of the behavior and feelings of those around me.*

When Jim was eleven, his mother married a university professor, a charming and handsome man with a PhD in psychology. Soon after their marriage, the couple began to argue frequently, and Jim had difficulty trusting this stranger who had become his "father." Jim was already sensitized to take responsibility for the way those around him felt, but another message began building on that foundation: *I am responsible to bring about change when I see it is needed.* He reasoned that if he could be "extra good," he could stop the arguing between his mother and stepfather and they would all be happy. He decided to try harder to get along with his stepfather.

Jim's stepfather liked to hunt and fish. He began spending a great deal of time with Jim, seeming to show genuine care. On camping trips, Jim's stepfather encouraged the seeds of insecurity to grow within Jim by suggesting that Jim's mother was the cause of all the problems in the marriage and that his mother did not truly care for either him or Jim. When Jim's mother would discipline Jim, his stepfather would use the incident to prove to Jim that his mother did not understand or love him.

At the same time that his stepfather was sabotaging the relationships between Jim, his mother, and his brothers, he behaved like a "buddy" to Jim. His stepfather painted a picture of himself as a poor, beleaguered man whom Jim should feel sorry for. As a sensitive young boy, Jim had long since incorporated a belief that: *If someone does not approve of me, that means I am not worthwhile.*

Sensing a lack of approval and love from his mother, Jim felt alone and rejected and began to withdraw from her. Feeling alienated from his mother and family, Jim tried to put up a defensive wall between himself and others based on a new message: *I should try to be independent and protect myself because others are untrustworthy.* However, in spite of his resolve not to trust anyone, Jim proved no match for the insidious dependence fostered by his stepfather, who had positioned himself to be Jim's only source of care and acceptance. The groundwork had been laid. It was a very short step from the exploitation of Jim's tenderhearted innocence to sexual exploitation.

During a particularly difficult time of conflict between his parents, Jim's stepfather was sobbing, telling Jim he might have to leave the home. He threw himself against eleven-year-old Jim, weeping and embracing him. Jim felt sorry for his stepfather and tried his best to comfort him. In the next few days, the hugging became more frequent and more sustained, until his stepfather began kissing him. Acutely embarrassed and ashamed, Jim felt this was wrong. He was deeply confused but had no one to talk to.

When they went hunting together and had to sleep in the same tent, Jim awoke to overt sexual advances by his stepfather. The relationship with his stepfather was the only significant relationship Jim felt he had in his life, but it was growing into something dirty and scary. Jim felt a suffocating oppression, as if he was being absorbed by his stepfather, losing his identity. He couldn't bring himself to talk about it. He was certain that no one would believe him even if he did tell, and he was sure everyone would think he was a total "jerk." Jim experienced great shame and an ominous sense of guilt, feeling as he imagined a woman would feel who had been raped. He had a sense of being destroyed, used up, with no place to hide.

What happened to Jim happens to thousands of young boys in the United States each year. Researchers suggest that one in six boys will be assaulted by age sixteen.[13] [14] However, even though the sexual abuse of boys is common, it is "underreported, under-recognized and under-treated."[15] In Jim's case, he was deeply confused about what it meant to be a "man." He tried to "forget" the abuse, wanting to protect his family from further disruption. Jim maintained his silence about his stepfather's abuse until his adult years, as do about 20 percent of boys who are sexually abused. In national surveys, about one-third of male victims reported that they had never disclosed their abuse to anyone.[16] Jim's stepfather was a pedophile—that is, an adult sexually attracted specifically to children. Pedophiles often prey upon young children lacking a father figure. Young boys (and girls) deeply needing male attention and love will often feel a deep sense of loyalty toward this type of offender and not report the abuse. According to the U.S. Department of Justice, 250,000–500,000 pedophiles reside in the United States.[17] In a National Institute of Health survey of 453 pedophiles, pedophile offenders were collectively responsible for the molestation of over 67,000 children—an average of 148 victimized children per individual pedophile.[18] In Jim's case, the pedophile offender actually married Jim's mother in order to have access to him, and the abuse continued for years without intervention. This is a tragic illustration of what some researchers have begun to suspect: "It may be the case that a growing number of stepfathers are really 'smart pedophiles,' men who marry divorced or single women with families as a way of getting close to children."[19]

SIBLING INCEST

Diane's Messages

When Diane was born, her mother was overwhelmed by the birth of this sixth child and descended into a severe depression for over a year. The younger children were passed around from relative to relative and, as a result, felt they didn't belong anywhere. When Diane's mom reentered the family after a lengthy hospital stay for postpartum depression, she was functional but unable to connect emotionally with her children. Feeling emotionally distanced from her mother, Diane perceived her father to be cold and detached. With stony silence and cruel indifference, it seemed as if he was punishing his children for existing. In a family environment of emotional neglect, family members felt uncared for and isolated from one another.

Diane tried desperately to earn her parents' approval by being good, being extra vigilant to try to match their moods by monitoring and stifling her feelings. She was so well-attuned to the family atmosphere that she imperceptibly noticed when, on the rare occasions when she was angry, her parents expressed their disapproval with greater distancing. At those times, she felt even more rejection from them. She would soon come to internalize a message about experiencing feelings: *I am bad if I feel angry.*

There was no verbal or physical affection shown between

Diane's parents or between the parents and their children. The children were often left in the care of their older brother, who was aggressive and demanding. Diane soon learned that resisting her older brother's rules brought hostile punishing silence from her parents. To avoid the painful rejection that came from standing up to her brother's aggressive behavior, she began to believe a new message: *I must keep the peace at any price.*

When she was six years old, her brother approached her with a "game" that he insisted would be fun. She participated in "the game" in which he fondled her, teaching her to manipulate herself to "feel good." From a six-year-old's frame of reference, the game seemed mostly harmless, especially because it was the only time her brother treated her nicely or that anyone had paid any nurturing attention to her. The game became their "secret."

The game continued with increasing frequency, and her brother began to demand more sexual involvement. On the farm where they lived, there were many isolated places available. He began to force her to cooperate with his new "games," threatening to tell their mother that Diane had been "fooling around with herself" and that she had taken her clothes off and crawled into bed with him. What could she say? Those things were true—but not as he made them out to be.

Frustrated, alone, with nowhere to turn, Diane continued as her brother's passive partner in the sex "games." Believing the message that she was *trapped and could never change,* she suppressed her feelings of humiliation and disgust for her brother and maintained her act of passive accommodation. She tried not to think about the game, hoping that if she ignored it, it would go away. A sense of inferiority and helplessness engulfed her.

She compared herself to the other girls at school and was convinced they knew something was wrong with her. She painfully did her utmost to achieve perfection, hoping flawless performance would cover up the nagging guilt and shame within her. The fear of making a mistake nearly paralyzed her, and without realizing it, she believed the message that *mistakes just confirmed her worthlessness.*

Diane's experience of relationships with male role models had been extremely wounding. The sexually coercive relationship with her brother and the remote and distant relationship with her father contributed to intense anxiety around males in general. Sermons at church aroused intense internal conflict in response to the pastor's portrayal of God as a loving heavenly Father. She questioned what she had done to cause bad things to happen to her. Maybe God was punishing her for being bad, and that was why her brother kept hurting her. Perhaps she had seduced her brother after all. Maybe what he said about her was true.

In desperation, she took measures to protect herself as best she could. Her brother once remarked that she had pretty hair, so she cut it, thinking short hair would protect her from further abuse. She began eating to comfort her pain and calm her anxieties and gained eighty pounds. She wore boys' clothing. She built walls of silence, withdrawal, and isolation, spending many hours in her room alone. At the age of ten, Diane developed a somber message that would powerfully affect her future relationships: *No one will ever get close enough to hurt me again.*

Sibling sexual contact is considered to be the most widespread form of incest, though it often goes unreported, even when discovered.[20] Sibling sexual contact can simply be developmental curiosity about the body parts of the opposite sex. However, the context in which sibling sexual contact occurs is significant to its impact on child victims. While different families might define "normal" childhood sex play in different ways, there are general parameters as to what distinguishes sex play from sibling abuse. Sibling sexual contact is generally considered abusive if there is a three-year age difference between siblings, because of developmental differences in vulnerability between children three or more years apart. Sexual behaviors, such as oral-genital contact, intercourse, or vaginal-anal insertion also distinguish sibling sexual abuse from exploratory sex play. Sexual behaviors that involve coercion or force and/or secrecy are considered abusive.[21] In Diane's case, abusive elements of sibling incest were intensified within a family atmosphere of emotional deprivation, insecurity, isolation, and rejection.

These brief glimpses into the lives of four sexually abused children illustrate some of the destructive messages that were incorporated into their worldviews from each abusive situation. These children believed these messages to be true about who they were, their value as persons, and how they should be treated in relationships.

With different levels of conscious awareness, sexually abused children often carry such damaging messages into their adult life. One adult survivor of sexual abuse stated, "When somebody sexually abuses you, they don't just invade your body . . . they invade your soul." The very core of personhood can be affected by abuse trauma: physically, emotionally, intellectually, psychologically, and spiritually. Adult survivors of childhood sexual abuse will continue to live their lives based on damaging messages and will most likely pass them on to others . . . unless someone intervenes.

2

Through the Eyes of Child Victims

Children are referred to as "victims" because children are always victimized by sexual abuse, even in situations where they appear to be "willing" participants in sexual behavior. Offenders sometimes try to rationalize sexual acts by claiming that a child was being "provocative," when, in fact, children might be displaying age-appropriate exploratory or stress-related, acting-out behavior. The appropriate adult response to such behavior in a child would be to set limits or redirect the child's behavior—not to sexually abuse them. Children lack the developmental capacity to cope with premature introduction of sexuality by an adult or someone significantly older than they are.

Children are victims because they are exploited by abusive power and control dynamics between offender and victim. *Power* in interpersonal relationships can be simply defined as the capacity of one person to influence another. Control, on the other hand, is the flip side of power; that is, *control* can be defined as the capacity to resist or restrain influence from someone else.[1] In healthy relationships, there is a balance between power and control, so that persons in relationship with each other have a sense of reciprocity or mutual give-and-take.

Sexual abuse is a destructive distortion of power and control because offenders exert power over child victims, who have little control or capacity to resist them. Offenders exert powerful influence over child victims in many ways, such as through force or threats of physical harm, intimidation, or manipulation through seduction or enticement. Imbalances in power may be reflected in an offender's larger physical size, position in family or church, life experience, or position of authority.[2] Offenders exert power over child victims by the knowledge that their behaviors are sexual in intent, while children are victimized by the lack of that knowledge. Child victims have no control over power abuses by sex offenders. That is why children are always victims.

IMPACT OF ABUSE: AN OVERVIEW

Children are victimized not only by betrayal of their vulnerability but also because they have few resources or references against which to evaluate and understand complex effects of sexual abuse. Impact of sexual abuse on child victims depends on many factors that combine to either promote more positive outcomes or increase negative outcomes. Because effects can vary dramatically from child to child, impact of abuse should be understood through the eyes of each child victim and from the context of their individual experience.

Due to the complex range of effects of childhood sexual abuse, it is generally helpful to think about the impact of sexual abuse as clusters of effects that are experienced over time—from initial reactions of victimization, to ways of coping with ongoing abuse, to longer-term outcomes.[3] The following section provides an overview of several potential effects of sexual abuse on children.

INITIAL EFFECTS: A RANGE OF RESPONSES

We define early reactions to sexual abuse as *initial* effects rather than *short-term* effects because most of us tend to think of "short-term" as something that is quickly resolved or that goes away over time. Researchers have defined "initial effects" as children's reactions that usually occur within two years after the abuse ends.[4] Unfortunately, without intervention, many initial effects of sexual abuse will continue to grow right along with the children.

Surprise and confusion might be initial reactions of some child victims to sexual abuse. A child might wonder, "What is going on?" "What is happening to me?" "Is this right or wrong?" "Will it happen again?" "Should I tell someone?" Child victims can experience intensely conflicting emotions all at once. Some parts of an abuse experience may seem pleasurable if the context of the abuse includes closeness, nurturing, or special attention from the offender. Other emotions might be extremely painful and often frightening, such as guilt, fear, anger, or shame. Emotional confusion increases a child's vulnerability to being further manipulated and used by an offender.

Some victimized children might believe that the abusive behavior is "normal" because the offender tells them it is "okay." Sometimes children are confused because they are too young to understand that the actions of the offender are sexual in nature. Or, they are confused when an offender tells them the abuse makes them "special" and, at the same time, warns them not to tell anyone. When five-year-old Susanne's grandfather began fondling her while she was sitting on his lap, she was so pleased to be his special girl but also confused about why he was touching her "that way." When he replied that all grandfathers showed their love to their granddaughters like this, she became all the more confused. Her other grandfather never touched her like that. Did that mean he didn't love her?

When children experience sexual abuse that overwhelms them with feelings of fear, helplessness, or horror, those experiences are termed "traumatic" in a specific sense. In such scenarios, children's initial response to sexual abuse might include symptoms related to post-traumatic stress.

The Baylor College of Medicine publication, *Post-Traumatic Stress Disorders in Children and Adolescents*, outlines the three main clusters of symptoms in children who meet diagnostic manual criteria of post-traumatic stress disorder: (1) reenacting the traumatic event in play, dreams, or behaviors; (2) avoiding cues/reminders associated with the trauma, or general withdrawal or emotional "numbing"; and (3) a physiological state of hyper-alertness that disrupts sleep, generates anxiety, and creates cardiac reactivity (racing/pounding heart rate).[5] Research indicates that 80 percent of child sexual abuse victims experience some post-traumatic stress symptoms, such as trouble concentrating, impulsiveness, or aggression.[6]

Very young children don't often display symptoms of post-traumatic stress disorder (PTSD), partly because several of the symptoms require children to have well-developed language skills in order to be able to describe feelings and events associated with the traumatic experience.[7] However, young children may express post-traumatic stress as sudden fears, reenactment of the sexual abuse trauma in play, or by reverting to an earlier developmental level, such as regressing in toilet training or thumb-sucking.[8]

Although many adults with PTSD experience flashbacks (distressing, intrusive recollections of trauma), clinical reports suggest that elementary school-age children may not experience flashbacks. Instead, elementary-age children may have "memory deficits" similar to amnesia and therefore have unclear recall of the original trauma, or they may recall trauma-related events in a disordered way, out of sequence.[9] [10] Children with posttraumatic stress symptoms tend to believe that if they had been "alert" enough, they would have been able to prevent the abuse from happening, so their physical bodies and their minds become "hyper" alert trying to avoid anything associated with the abuse in an effort to prevent being abused again.[11] Some children might compulsively replay some part of the trauma to try to ease anxiety. A forty-year-old man recalled his childhood compulsion to tap his foot three times before he entered the door of his bedroom and three times after closing the door. It was his "good omen" to try to keep his sexually abusive uncle from coming into his room.

Guilt

Almost universally, child victims feel responsible for sexual abuse. This sense of being responsible is most often experienced as feelings of "guilt." Children will believe the abuse was their fault for many reasons: because they believe they did nothing to try to stop the abuse, because the abuse was sometimes pleasurable, or because they received special favors or rewards.

Children may feel they did something to cause the abuse or that they are so bad that they deserved the abuse. A forty-five-year-old woman had lived most of her adult life with an overpowering sense of "guilt" for causing her childhood abuse. When she was nine, her mother became very ill and went to the hospital. During one night of her mother's hospitalization, she woke up fearful that her mother might die, and went into her parents' bedroom for comfort and reassurance from her father. However, rather than comfort her, her father sexually abused her. At that point, the nine-year-old girl concluded that she had "caused" the abuse by going into her father's room. Thereafter, he came into her room at night. Because she was convinced of her "guilt" in causing the abuse to happen in the first place, she felt she "deserved" to have it continue.

Child victims feel guilty for feeling both love and hate toward the person who abused them and toward other family members who did not protect them. Victims are convinced of their "guilt" when other family members blame them for reporting the abuse, blame them for being "responsible" for a divorce, or blame them for "causing" the imprisonment of an offender. An eight-year-old girl was accused of causing her father's death after she inadvertently told a teacher about the incest. Shortly after the father was confronted about the abuse, he became ill with cancer. The family told the young girl that she "caused" her father's cancer by telling about the abuse and "making so much trouble."

Children will almost always experience or interpret the overwhelming sense of blame, of feeling "dirty," of worthlessness, of being "different" from everyone else as feelings of intense "guilt." However, these feelings are actually components of shame—not guilt—which can become a crippling bondage. Significant differences between shame and guilt are discussed in chapter 10.

Fear

Child victims have many fears. They may fear that they have been physically damaged in some way because of the abuse. An abused teen had stopped having her menstrual periods due to extreme stress and fear. She mistook the absence of her menstrual flow as confirmation that her father's abuse had "broken" her inside. Children may fear being found out by others or that others can tell by looking at them that they are "bad."

Fear of family disruption is often an overarching fear that causes many children to remain silent and continue to be abused. Fear of rejection by both the offender and the non-abusing parent can make the child feel there is no way out. Fear of abandonment causes children to go to great lengths to deny their abuse to others and even to themselves.

A child may be intensely afraid of physical injury by the abuser, especially if the abuser has made threats. The very real danger of personal harm must not be discounted by those who work with child victims. A thirteen-year-old girl was threatened with death if she ever told anyone that her father was abusing her. Her father was later picked up on abuse charges for abusing another young girl. At the trial, his daughter was persuaded to testify against him to confirm the other victim's case; he was found guilty and sent to jail. After the trial, the daughter felt safe from him for the first time in her life. However, a few weeks later, a car deliberately tried to run her down while she was walking home. She was able to jump out of the way, but she found out later that her father had actually hired someone to kill her. She left the state to live with relatives but continued to live with tremendous fear.

Helplessness

In addition to fears about violence, children can experience an almost incapacitating sense of helplessness. Researchers suggest that chronic feelings of helplessness come from the fact that children are neither physically nor psychologically able to defend themselves from their abuser, leaving them with a sense of being in constant danger but without options for escape.[12] A twelve-year-old girl felt complete helplessness in the face of repeated and unpredictable sexual assaults from her father. Whenever she heard him come home, she would curl up into a ball under her bed to try to hide, but he always found her. For some children, the unpredictable nature of their sexual abuse causes such a constant sense of imminent danger that an immobilizing helplessness becomes a "complete surrender" to the reality of being abused.[13] This kind of helplessness also contributes to a sense of hopelessness about the future.[14]

Anger

In Ephesians 6:4, fathers (and mothers) are instructed to "provoke not your children to wrath, but bring them up in the nurture and admonition of the Lord" (KJV). The English word *provoke* comes from the Latin *provocare*, "to call forth." To provoke someone to "wrath" suggests a repeated, ongoing pattern of treatment that "calls forth" a response of deep-seated anger that can escalate into outward or inward hostility. Provoking children to anger by repeated abusive acts not only violates guidelines for parental discipline in the first section of this verse but also violates the principle of nurture in the second section. Sexual abuse can be the soil where seeds of "provoked anger" and lack of nurture contribute to destructive forces that damage a child's spirit.

Child victims often experience intense anger but have few outlets for expressing it. They feel anger at what the abuser has done and often feel angry toward non-abusing parents who do not protect them or stop the abuse. Children may appear outwardly passive or compliant but inwardly may experience intense rage and hostility. A fourteen-year-old abuse victim said she "wished the situation" on girls at school that she disliked. "Why should they be happy, and why should I have to go through this awful thing with my stepfather?"[15] Children may turn anger inward against themselves, where it can present itself as self-hatred or depression. Or, they may express anger outwardly in aggressive actions, such as bullying or even victimizing other children.[16]

Philip was being sexually abused by his priest, who bribed him not to tell about their "secret." When Philip's parents encouraged him to spend more and more time with their priest, Philip grew increasingly hostile and angry. Without an outlet for his anger, Philip began expressing an uncharacteristic cruelty toward his pets in an expression of inner rage. His parents finally sought professional help after he drowned the family cat. Through therapy, it was discovered that being sexually abused in combination with not being protected from continued abuse were two aspects of provoking Philip to wrath.

Anger may also be a symptom of PTSD. Children who are subjected to force and coercion may experience such incredible stress from a hyper-alert state of anxiety that they behave aggressively toward others, show signs of uncontrolled irritability, or react with anger and hostile outbursts to those around them.

Loss of Trust

Building blocks for developing trust are formed throughout infancy as children experience their needs being met through consistent patterns of nurture within a safe environment.[17] Childhood sexual abuse in infancy seriously disrupts the development of trust, while abuse later in the child's development is more likely to erode trust that might have been established earlier.[18] Children, such as Philip, lose trust in their parents when parents do not intervene and stop the abuse. Even when parents are unaware that someone outside the family is abusing their child, children often assume that parents "know" or "should know" about the abuse. Because parents are powerful people in children's eyes, a lack of intervention by a child's "powerful" parents can precipitate a loss of trust in them.

In her book *Sexual Abuse*, Adele Mayer writes, "Victims' loss of trust in authority figures is one of the most devastating effects of incest. Their parents are the first adults children learn to trust, and incest represents the ultimate betrayal of that trust."[19] Because of violations of parental trust, children might tell peers about sexual abuse occurring in their family before they will tell another adult, because their abuse experience tells them that adults are untrustworthy. However, most abused children tell no one.

The erosion of trust is often progressive over time, as seen in the following case of revictimization from childhood into adult life. Between the ages of five and ten, Marie was fondled by two different male baby-sitters who frequently baby-sat for her. During

those same years, she watched her father in his bedroom masturbating while he viewed pornographic magazines. Her older brothers also noted their father's use of pornography, which prompted
them to do the same. Concurrent with viewing pornography, both
brothers began sexually abusing Marie. By age ten, Marie had concluded that she could not trust anyone older. As a teenager, she
turned to peers, thinking she could trust peer relationships to be
safer. When she was raped by a group of boys from school, she was
devastated and withdrew, feeling there were no peers she could
trust. As a young woman, Marie met a man who seemed trustworthy, and married him. She was hopeful that she had found security
for the first time in her life. But within the first year of marriage,
she endured several incidents of physical and sexual violence. In
light of such a pattern of abuse, she was convinced that she could
never trust anyone ever again.

Early violations and continued erosion of trust, along with
many other factors, contributed to a pattern of repeated victimization for Marie. Researchers have found that children who are sexually abused early in life have a greater chance of being victimized
and exploited over time. It is a heartrending prediction that two
out of three persons who were victimized as children will be victimized again as adolescents and/or as adults.[20]

EVALUATING THE IMPACT OF SEXUAL ABUSE: CONSIDERING THE CONTEXTS

Building on the previous overview of potential effects of sexual
abuse, we now look into some factors that might influence individual impact of those effects—both on child victims and on adult survivors of sexual abuse. Effects of abuse are experienced differently
by children according to the contexts in which abuse has occurred.

Many variables work together to influence the impact of abuse
on a particular child. In *The Silent Children,* therapist Linda Sanford writes: "Every victim of child sexual abuse needs sympathetic, professional intervention, even if it is just one visit to a
social worker to clarify that the child is not responsible for the
crime."[21] Her point is well taken. Children need to be reaffirmed of
their value by persons that they love and trust, in addition to
repeated reassurance that the responsibility for the abuse lies with
the offender.

Even though children are resilient, sexual abuse *does* have an
effect on them.[22] Parents, counselors, and those who work with

children will need to discern when they might be minimizing a child's experience of sexual abuse because the abuse seems to them to be "insignificant" or, conversely, when they might be intensifying the impact. If we allow children to define the impact from their own experience in their own words, we will be less likely to project more or less trauma onto the child than the child is experiencing. Here are some factors that are helpful in evaluating the degree of effects from sexual abuse.

Child's Relationship With Caregivers: Bread and Stones

When children have a sense of stability and security in relationships with their caregivers, they develop feelings of self-worth that build on a foundation of trust.[23] Both clinicians and researchers tell us that a child's early attachment ("bonding") to their caregivers can significantly affect the child's response to any abuse that might occur later. In Matthew 7:9, Jesus asks his followers, "Which of you, if his son/daughter asks for bread, will give him/her a stone?" From earliest experience in families, children have a developing sense as to whether they are more likely to receive "bread" or "stones" in family interactions.

Prior to any sexually abusive experience, children situated within loving families and connected to other caring people develop a deep sense of being loved unconditionally. In such settings, after abuse occurs, children who need "bread" are given bread; families are able to provide sustenance and a safe place for restoring damage from sexual abuse. When a child's family setting includes characteristics such as substance abuse, high levels of aggression, and/or shaming and unrealistic expectations of children, these factors may not only interfere with early bonding but also make abuse recovery much more difficult for a child.[24] In such settings, when a child asks for "bread" and receives "stones" instead, the stones add weight to the child's burden.

Age and Developmental Level

A child's perception of sexual abuse is likely to vary according to age and developmental level. The naïveté of a younger child may sometimes offer some buffering from abuse trauma if, for example, the child is not developmentally old enough to be aware that her uncle's fondling "tickling game" is anything other than a game. However, an older child with a greater understanding of sexuality might be more negatively affected by the uncle's fondling. An older child knows something is "wrong" with fondling and may feel violated or even responsible for the sexual contact. Overall, however, research indicates that the younger the child, the more vulnerable she or he is to trauma from sexual abuse.[25]

Child's Relationship With Offender

When compared with abuse by all other types of offenders, sexual abuse by fathers or father figures is consistently reported to inflict the most trauma on children. Dynamics of incestuous abuse can present catastrophic consequences for children.

A sexual crime committed by a stranger often has less impact on a child than a sexual crime committed by a trusted parent. When evaluating the child's level of trauma, whether an offender is actually a relative or not may not be as important as other factors in the child's relationship with the offender. For example, abuse by a trusted neighbor might be more devastating than abuse from a distant grandfather. Abuse committed against a child by someone they trust involves significant betrayal; abuse by a stranger or someone more distant to a child might involve more fear and, in that regard, might be viewed by the child as more traumatic.[26]

Sometimes an offender who began as a stranger to a child becomes a loved and trusted person in the child's eyes. Charlie was a stranger to his victim and her parents, but over a period of time he manipulated himself into a close friendship with the child. Charlie's eight-year-old victim says, "I kept on trying to get my parents to understand that Charlie was my friend. They didn't know him, but they wanted to get him fired at his job in the school. I didn't want that because then Charlie wouldn't have any food to eat."[27]

The relationship of the child to the offender must be assessed by understanding the relationship through the child's eyes.

Type of Sexual Activity

One central variable in assessing the impact of abuse on children is related to the type of sexual act. In circumstances where physical force is used and a child is subjected to deliberate humiliation, the crime is more accurately defined as a crime of violence committed through sexual means.[28] The effects of severe trauma cannot be easily measured or accurately described. However, Judith Herman, author of *Trauma and Recovery*, writes that "the salient characteristic of the traumatic event is in its power to inspire helplessness and terror" in the victim.[29] This kind of abuse experience is often associated with outcomes of post-traumatic stress disorder.

When a child is both physically and sexually abused, two dynamics of trauma converge. The trauma of physical abuse may even initially overshadow the sexual abuse. One eleven-year-old victim explains, "When I was in the hospital, they were stitching up my face where he had hit me so hard. I forgot to tell them about the sex part until later. I was more worried about my cut-up face."[30]

In light of such horrific crimes against children, it is essential to be reminded that most sexual abuse is not violent but rather involves multiple forms of coercive manipulation. Some people assume that sexual abuse involving more invasive physical contact, such as vaginal or rectal penetration or oral sex, is more traumatic than less invasive contact, such as touching and fondling of the breasts and genital area. However, both researchers and clinicians who work closely with sexual abuse victims report that non-penetrating abuse frequently has an equally serious impact on child victims. Penetration is one among many other components of abuse that must be evaluated when trying to determine the severity of an abuse experience.[31]

Some people assume that non-contact abuse is "insignificant." However, a child's personal and emotional space can be violated through words or being exposed to a variety of non-contact intrusions that are sexual in nature.[32] The author of *Secret Shame: I Am a Victim of Incest* invites us to step into her third grade context. She helps us to understand the violation of her father's penetrating stare.

Third Grade Teacher

Dear Third Grade Teacher:
You found me daydreaming today.
Usually I work real hard,
 finish on time,
 read lots of books,
 write poems that rhyme,
and act like a very good girl.
You scolded me
again
because I was dreaming.
You didn't know that
yesterday
when no one else was home,
Daddy made me lie on the couch

with all my clothes off.
He just sat in his big chair
and looked at me,
smiling a smile I can't understand.
I was ashamed,
embarrassed and afraid.

Today I couldn't remember
my "times eights,"
and I spent the April afternoon
daydreaming.
You didn't understand.[33]

Non-contact abuse also includes "flashing" (exposing genitals), especially while masturbating; verbal pressure for sex or lewd, overtly sexual remarks; and victimization by voyeurs. In years past, children were victimized by observing openly displayed pornographic materials. In contemporary culture, it is likely that a new category of non-contact sexual abuse poses a greater threat to children—pornography via the Internet.[34] A nine-year-old girl discovered that her twenty-seven-year-old half-brother had been taking digital photos of her in the shower through a hidden camera, storing the photos on his computer, and then posting them online at child pornography Web sites.[35] Children not only feel humiliated and ashamed, but are placed at risk of further exploitation by having their photos uploaded onto pornographic Web sites where they are more vulnerable to be re-victimized by other Internet offenders.

Duration of the Abuse

Perhaps the age at which abuse begins is less significant than the stages of abuse through which the abuse continues.[36] The longer the abuse has continued, the greater the impact. Repeated trauma across childhood erodes a child's normal development by forcing her or him to develop incredible strategies for survival. Effects will be measured by the degree to which children use such necessary defenses. A child may deny the abuse is occurring, both to themselves and others, or rationalize the abuse to make it seem more acceptable, such as the child who says, "My dad never meant to hurt me. He only abused me when he was drinking and didn't realize it was me."

Sally pretended to everyone that she had the most wonderful dad in the world. They spent time together and seemed to have a happy family. She told no one, especially not her mother, about the times that her father forced her into sexual submission. The abuse began when she was seven years old and continued throughout Sally's high school years. Sally's reality had been so distorted by the solitary suffering of long-term abuse that, as an adult, she recalls being shocked in her junior high health class when she realized that not all fathers were having sex with their daughters. Surviving abuse over such a span of childhood development forces children who are unable to escape their traumatic reality to find ways to escape it in their minds.[37]

Parental Reactions to Disclosure of Abuse

It is rare for a child to tell anyone about sexual abuse. Most children are warned not to tell, so it is at great risk and with great courage that they do tell. If a child is living with or emotionally close to their offender, disclosure will be very difficult. Children may fear that no one will do anything to intervene in the abuse and they will have to suffer retribution from their offender for telling.[38] Children often keep silent to protect their parents from knowing about the abuse. Children also maintain silence out of fear that a parent or special person will think they are "bad." In light of many barriers to disclosure that a child faces, the reaction of parents or other significant adults to disclosure can radically influence the child's adjustment. In her parent's guide to abuse prevention, Linda Sanford writes that a parent's initial reaction to abuse disclosure by a child "is the single most important factor in preventing the abuse from becoming a life-destroying event."[39] Research indicates that believing the child, supporting the child's experience, and taking some protective action decreased the number of symptoms suffered by the child, whereas children who were not believed or, even worse, were punished for telling suffered increased psychological trauma.[40] Studies indicate that the closer the relationship a male offender has to the child's mother, the less likely the child is to feel supported by the mother.[41]

Unfortunately, many children are not believed when they tell about their abuse but instead are doubted or, even worse, accused of lying.

Christian therapist David Peters writes:

> A further example of our desperation to ignore the sexual abuse of children is the totally erroneous statement often heard: "It may not be true. After all, children lie about many things and could fantasize about having been sexually abused." Of all the cases I have investigated and seen investi-

gated, I know of only one instance of a child lying about sexual abuse. Furthermore, every authority in the nation, as far as I am aware, reports the same conclusion. Children have neither the inclination nor the information necessary for false reporting.[42]

Children are subjected to increased suffering by parents or others who don't believe them. Failure to believe the truth a child is telling destroys trust, compounding issues that will later have to be resolved. Some parents have gone to great lengths to test the truthfulness of their child's disclosure of sexual abuse.

An adult victimized as a small child recalls such a situation from his childhood:

> My parents dragged me over to the coach's house. I was screaming and crying the whole way. He was the last person I wanted to see, but they were intent on this big confrontation. Of course he denied it—said I was trying to get him into trouble because I didn't make the team. . . . They believed him. I don't know which was more traumatic—the molestation or that scene.[43]

Because of parents' disbelief, children have been forced to endure the humiliation of facing their abuser, who then discredits them and accuses them of lying. Through a child's eyes, the ultimate betrayal may be parents' believing the offender at the child's expense.

On the other hand, parental reactions can also intensify a less-intense experience by their response to a child's disclosure. An adult woman was fondled on the school bus as a young child and told her parents as soon as she got home. She recalls that for weeks after the event, her parents hovered over her, fretting about her. From her point of view, the molestation involved a pervert on the bus and it wasn't that big of a deal. Her parents finally got over it, she said, but a long time after she did.[44]

EVALUATING "TRUTHFULNESS"

Researchers suggest that one of the reasons that people question children's reports of abuse is that there are few helpful stereotypes that accurately identify sexual perpetrators. The general public may expect the majority of sex offenders to "be" a certain way. However, when those perceptions cannot be confirmed in actual fact, people are more likely to be skeptical of a child's report because the offender "doesn't seem to be the type who would do such a thing."[45]

Several factors help evaluate the validity and accuracy of a child's disclosure of abuse. First, a child will often be able to give particular details about the abuse. These details would include information that is explicitly sexual, or of a sexual nature, and that is beyond the child's developmental age. Generally, a child will need to be three-and-a-half years old or older to have the language skills to be able to reliably respond to questions about where, what, who, or how an abuse episode may have happened.[46]

Second, a child who has experienced abuse will often exhibit some of the symptoms listed in chapter 3. The onset of symptoms might coincide with the timing of the reported abuse or might not appear until later.

Third, a child may have risk factors that make her or him more vulnerable to abuse, such as low self-worth, little accurate sexual knowledge, a highly stressed family with a lack of close relationship with one or more parents, or the experience of previous abuse.[47] However, it is essential to remember that sexual abuse occurs in all types of settings, with all kinds of children and offenders. When a child gives any indication that he or she might be experiencing abuse, the child's story needs to be treated with sensitivity, concern, and respect until the full measure of that situation can be discerned.

HELPING AN ABUSED CHILD

1. When a child discloses sexual abuse, try to remain calm. This will be difficult in light of many feelings that will surface, but your feelings must be vented away from the child's presence. Do not overreact in front of the child.

2. Allow the child to describe, in her or his own words, what has physically happened. Ask "directed" questions rather than "leading" questions. Leading questions are questions that can be answered with yes or no. Directed questions are different from leading questions. Directed questions help the child focus on the *content* of the question without putting undue influence on the *response* to the question. For example, a leading question might be "Does your daddy touch your privates?" A directed question might be, "What happens to a girl's privates?"[48] Do not suggest to the child what might have happened, such as, "You didn't like that,

did you?" Instead, "What was that like?" Keep the number of persons talking to the child about the episode to a minimum, both to protect the child from repeatedly having to expose the events of the abuse and to protect the clarity of the details of the case, should it go to court.

3. Believe the child. Let the child describe the feelings resulting from the abuse, and refrain from minimizing what has happened.

4. Assure the child that it was right to tell, and that she or he will be protected from the offender, if that is a threat. Protect the child's confidentiality against further trauma from peers or others at church, school, or the neighborhood.

5. Reassure the child repeatedly that the abuse was not her or his fault, that she or he is not to blame, and that she or he is not "bad" because the abuse happened. Reinforce that the offender is responsible for the abuse. Many times a child has a special relationship with the offender and has some positive feelings for him/ her, so a child may defend the offender if you express intense or negative feelings about the offender.

6. Follow regular home routines and daily life schedules. Under normal circumstances, children do not usually like changes in the routines of daily living. When major changes, such as moving away, follow sexual abuse incidents, it may appear that the abuse is bigger than the family's ability to cope with it. This might have the unintended outcome of increasing stress on the child for disclosing the abuse.

7. Preserve normal physical affection. Returning to typical patterns of affection is important in helping children reestablish trust in adults and feel reassured that they are loved and cared for. Ask the child how much physical affection she or he wants; don't assume you know. Respect the child's boundaries. Normal displays of affection may help a child who is trying to cope with fears about affection and closeness.

8. Provide the child, and each family member, with support and counseling. When a child stops talking about the abuse after disclosure, it is often perceived by parents and others as a sign that the issue has been resolved or forgotten. Often, family members whose lives have been seriously disrupted by the disclosure of sexual abuse would like to forget the sexual abuse and move on with their lives. However, if the strategy used to "move on" involves requiring a child to simply "forgive and forget" without sufficient time for a process of healing, then the family's distress may only be

temporarily soothed and the child will have a greater burden to bear.

RECOVERY IN YOUNG CHILDREN

In *Sexual Abuse of Young Children,* child therapist Suzanne Long offers indicators of recovery for young girls who have been victims of incest. Even though the female pronoun is used here, these guidelines highlight significant areas addressed in professional counseling with young children, both male and female, and offer ways to think about assessing progress of children who are in recovery from abuse. When a child has been able to accomplish many of the changes mentioned here, or has made significant progress in that direction, she or he may have reached a stopping point in counseling. This is especially the case when children have consistent, nurturing support at home as well as from other caring adults in their social network. The child's family setting is a crucial piece of the restoration process.

INDICATORS FOR TERMINATION OF THERAPY

- Has she dealt sufficiently with her feelings of guilt, fear, anger, confusion, and depression?
- Has she dealt specifically with the nature of the molestation, the methods of coercion, negative and positive feelings about it, secondary gains? [*Author's note:* Secondary gains are "benefits," such as conditional love in exchange for the abuse, peace in the home if the child goes along with the abuse, or earning rewards for sexual favors.]
- Does she feel less responsible for the sexual behavior, the storminess following disclosure, and the disruption to her family?
- Has she dealt with her anger and hostility at both her mother and the perpetrator for the molestation and the lack of protection from it?
- Does she demonstrate trust in her mother and see her as a protector (or have another trusting relationship with another significant adult)?
- Is she aware of earlier confusion between sex and affection?
- Is she able to set limits on sexual advances?
- Is she able to seek help in the event that she is approached again?

- Has she developed an increase in overall social skills?
- Has she developed outside social contacts and activities?
- Is she more age-appropriate in activity than at the beginning of treatment?
- Does she feel better about herself?
- Is she more trustful?[49]

It would be realistic to expect that future therapeutic intervention might be important as a child continues to mature and progresses through life transitions, such as developmental milestones of puberty, during dating, engagement, or marriage, or bearing and raising children.

If it is necessary for a child to reenter counseling along the way in her or his life, this should be viewed as simply another step in the healing journey. It does not mean that the older child or the adult survivor of sexual abuse is not "right with the Lord," or did not do the "work" involved in counseling, or that God was not faithful in the healing process. It means that another point in life has been reached where some of the distortions from past abuse have come up against normative issues such as intimacy, sexuality, or closeness with significant others. At times of personal growth and life transition, a trusted counselor or spiritual mentor might be helpful to reinforce one's identity in Christ and reaffirm one's value to God and to others.

3

Indicators of Sexual Abuse: "Telling" Without Telling

Indicators of childhood sexual abuse present themselves differently across time as children grow through adolescence to adulthood. An important key to uncovering sexual abuse is to look for clusters of indicators to provide a clearer picture about abuse rather than considering any one indicator by itself to "prove" that sexual abuse has (or has not) occurred. While these indicators are *potential* indicators, the list has been compiled from the collective "telling" of child sexual abuse victims themselves.

The following section is an overview of some of the tragically creative ways that victims of childhood sexual abuse have used to try to "tell" us about their abuse. These indicators might be thought of as "inventive strategies" for communicating that sexual abuse has been, or is, occurring. The children are "telling" us; we must actively listen.

EARLY CHILDHOOD INDICATORS

Physical Symptoms

In most cases, there are no physical indicators of the crime of sexual abuse. However, some of the more overt physical signs of abuse in young children might be vaginitis, persistent bladder infections, sexually transmitted diseases, or pain in urinating or defecating. One church discovered that an adolescent boy, working in their church nursery over a two-year period, had systematically abused more than sixty children between the ages of six months and twenty-four months. The physical symptom of some of those children was pain while having bowel movements. When one mother took her child to the doctor for an examination, the doctor told her the small lacerations in the rectal area were probably due to the child being constipated. When several children were discovered to have rectal enlargement or lacerations, however, the sexual abuse occurring within the church nursery was brought to light.

Persistent sore throats or unexplained gagging can be a symptom of abuse, due to forced oral sex, especially with younger children. Having bowel movements in underwear (encopresis) or bedwetting may signal a child's distress.

Sexualized Behavior

Children often end up coming through abusive sexual experiences with an inappropriate "collection" of sexual behaviors, along with distorted emotional associations with sexual activities and with specific body parts.[1]

Children sometimes indicate abuse by remarks in conversation that indicate sexual knowledge that is inappropriate to their age. For example, while watching TV, a young child saw a couple kissing and said, "That man is going to tickle her wee-wee." Children sometimes indicate abuse trauma by drawing pictures of adults' or children's genitals, especially with details like pubic hair.

Sexual interaction with others can be a behavioral way that children "tell" others about their abuse. Sexual aggression toward younger or more naïve children may indicate the child is acting out to others what an offender has done to her or him.

If a young child has experienced some degree of pleasure from abusive activity, such as "tickling games," the child may "tell" about that abuse by initiating sexual activities with peers.

If a child makes sexual gestures or overtures to adults, this may indicate that the child has been taught to expect sexual activity as a "normal" way to behave with adults.[2] When Tom and Edna Smith went to visit Edna's sister, one of the sister's day-care children crawled up onto the couch where Tom was sitting. When the four-year-old girl reached over nonchalantly and unzipped Tom's pants, Tom was horrified; he and Edna left the home almost immediately. Unfortunately, his surprise and disgust did not motivate him to pursue the incident further. Ten years later, when that little girl was fourteen and pregnant, a crisis pregnancy center discovered that she had been sexually abused by her stepfather for several years as a child. By her nonchalant unzipping of an adult man's pants, she was "telling" Tom that she was being abused.

Masturbation might be another type of sexualized behavior indicating abuse. Although children might touch and explore their bodies at different stages of development, there are patterns of masturbation that might be an indicator that a child is "telling" someone about being abused. A likely sexual abuse indicator in young children would be masturbation that is to the point of personal injury, many times a day with a seeming inability to stop, or making groaning noises or sexual movements while masturbating.[3]

Changes in Behavior

Behavioral changes may indicate abuse, especially if changes occur rather abruptly or dramatically. A young child may have appetite changes, changes in sleeping patterns, nightmares, or a sudden onset of fears or anxieties. A child's behavior may indicate abuse by regressing in one or more developmental areas, such as bed-wetting, thumb-sucking, or baby talk. Sometimes children indicate abuse trauma through self-injurious behaviors such as biting themselves or others.

Changes in School Performance

Children may show behaviors that seem consistent with learning disabilities or attention deficit disorder, such as poor concentration, daydreaming, being unable to sit still, finish tasks, or be fully aware of what is going on around them. However, these same behaviors may be indicators that a child is under the chronic stress of an abusive situation and is "telling" about abuse through symptoms of post-traumatic stress.

Fears

A child may fear playing alone, fear strange men or women, strange situations, or a specific person or situation. A twenty-five-year-old woman told of being molested by her godfather—a close friend of her parents—when she was eight years old. Thereafter, every time her parents wanted to visit the godfather, she threw a temper tantrum and refused to go. She was punished by her parents for being "disobedient" to them, but her fearful tantrums were trying to "tell" her parents that she was being abused by her godfather.

Refusals

Sometimes a child resists a previously favorite activity or refuses to be with a previously favorite person. Such a change in attitude should be explored to discover underlying reasons for a child's actions. The following case is a poignant example of a child using a refusal to "tell" his parents he was being abused.

Timmy's father owned a local auto service station. Mr. Thompson, one of his regular customers, came over and asked if Timmy, age seven, would like to go swimming with him and his son that evening. Timmy loved to go swimming, so he gladly collected his swimsuit and went with Mr. Thompson and his son. Mr. Thompson took the boys out for pizza, then swimming, but later anally raped Timmy behind the Kmart before taking him home.

The next week Mr. Thompson came by and asked Timmy's father if Timmy would like to go swimming with him again. Timmy's father recalled that when Timmy had come home the week before, he had been quiet and said he didn't have a very good time. Timmy looked at the floor and said he really didn't want to go. His well-meaning father insisted that Timmy go swimming because he liked it so much, and assured Timmy that he would have a good time once he got there. That evening Mr. Thompson anally raped Timmy again. Later, an investigation was begun after one of the other children being molested by Mr. Thompson reported being abused. When the investigation expanded, Timmy's abuse was discovered.

Timmy's parents were devastated. They had not "heard" what he was trying to "tell" them through refusing to participate in his favorite activity of swimming. After several months of counseling, Timmy disclosed some of his feelings of betrayal. He had told his father that he did not want to go with Mr. Thompson, but when his father encouraged him to go the second time, Timmy not only concluded that his parents knew about the abuse but, more tragically, that his parents actually condoned the abuse.

Feeling "Bad" and Looking Good

Children betrayed by a trusted person have received many messages that convince them they are "bad." Children may be extremely conflicted with feelings of guilt and shame that coexist with any positive feelings they might have for the offender. One way of not "telling" about sexual abuse is pretending on the outside that everything is fine. If practiced long and hard enough, children may "convince" themselves that the abuse is not happening.

A widely held image of an abused child as a withdrawn loner with low self-esteem contrasts sharply with the image of a high-achieving "perfect" child, overly compliant in trying to please adults. Both outward appearances may be concealing sexual abuse.

"Spacing Out"

If a child is under severe duress in an abusive situation, one coping skill they might discover is that of dissociation—"spacing out." A child can separate themselves, in a sense, from physical feelings in their body, from their emotions, from the reality of what is happening during abuse. The ability to dissociate is very high in school-age children[4] and can be a symptom associated with post-traumatic stress.

Loss of Being "Me"

In healthy families, there are clear "rules," or boundaries, governing what family members can expect from their interactions with one another, such as respecting each other's privacy and being able to say "yes" or "no" to requests.[5] In situations of sexual abuse, children's boundaries are violated; they may feel as though their body does not belong to them but to someone more powerful. A child may come to feel that she or he is merely an "extension" of the offender—an "other" not a "me." Being made to feel responsible to meet the needs of an offender, children are forced to comply with abuse at the expense of personal boundaries and may end up losing a sense of identity as an individual. When children are not allowed or taught to discern between reasonable and unreasonable requests from others, they are set up to be re-victimized in later stages of life—often without understanding how it relates to loss of identity, violations of boundaries, not having a "no" or a "me."

INDICATORS OF ABUSE IN ADOLESCENCE

Adolescents may display many of the same indicators that are seen in older childhood. However, some children don't show any effects of abuse until they reach adolescence (or even adulthood) when they encounter severe challenges and distress in trying to form close relationships.[6]

Physical Symptoms

In addition to presenting some of the same physical indicators that younger children do, adolescents may "tell" us about their abuse through sexually transmitted diseases or pregnancy. Traumatic emotional pain of undisclosed abuse may present itself through physical symptoms such as chronic abdominal pain, gastric distress, or headaches. Bed-wetting could continue from childhood to adolescence as an indicator of abuse. One woman reported wetting the bed until she was twenty years old and wondered why no one had ever thought to ask why.

Eating Disorders

Anorexia, bulimia, or other eating disorders can reflect an adolescent's painful way of "telling" about their abuse. Eating disorders may reflect personal attempts to regain some kind of control over their own bodies, to alter body image in some way in order to "protect" themselves from further abuse, a reflection of self-hatred or a way to "punish" one's own body or a way of trying to assert some type of control through starving oneself. Eating disorders or overeating may be an adolescent's only outlet for stress in an abusive family system where rigidity and emotional suppression are major "rules" governing family interactions. (See also chapter 17.)

Withdrawal and Isolation

Children with poor concentration may become even further withdrawn and emotionally constricted as adolescents. They may exhibit a marked lack of insight due to developmental deficits created by an abusive relationship. An inability to interact emotionally with others may severely impair abused adolescents in trying to have meaningful relationships with others. One sixteen-year-old incest victim, even though placed in a loving and secure foster home, was so withdrawn that she did not speak for three months. At night, she would wedge her bedroom dresser against the door to prevent intrusion. She would place coat hangers on the doorknobs in the hallway leading to her room so they would make noise signaling anyone's approach. Withdrawal, fear, distrust, and/or the building of walls of isolation can be "telling" responses to abuse.

Children who build defensive walls inside to protect themselves from others may progress into adolescence concluding, "I don't need *anybody*!" Withdrawal may lead to a pattern of unintentionally setting others up to reject them, which protects them from intimacy but reinforces isolation.

Dependency and Re-victimization

An overly compliant child may become a dependent "needy" adolescent who feels unable to withstand any type of rejection and who will follow peers at any cost. Because personal boundaries have been violated during abuse, dependency for an adolescent may come in the form of being sexually used. Or, a younger child who earned favors for being sexually abused may become what appears to be a manipulative, seductive, sexually active adolescent who views him or herself, as well as others, as sex objects. Church youth workers need to seek God's discernment in ministry to teens who are sexually acting out. There may be many reasons for such behavior, but sexual abuse is certainly one of them.

Adolescents and adults are especially vulnerable to re-victimization because they are often unaware of having a "self" to protect (that is, they have lost a sense of being "me"). Thus, they may appear to be gullible to wrongful requests or suggestions from others or appear to be "irresponsible" in not protecting themselves from risky situations.

Running Away

Running away can be a "red flag" indicator of abuse in adolescence. If running away from home is not possible, adolescents often find other creative ways to run away, such as running away into a room or a closet, or "running away" into dissociation to escape reality and intense emotional pain.

Distrust

Loss of trust can result from many levels of betrayal experienced through sexually abusive experiences. Betrayal can be thought of as a process of increasing awareness that someone who should have provided nurture and care has instead caused harm.[7] As children develop greater ability for abstract thinking during adolescence, a sense of betrayal of trust might take on new dimensions. Coupled with a forced silence not to disclose abuse, an adolescent may grow increasingly distrustful of adults or authority figures. Messages of shame and guilt from childhood may continue to build within the soul of an adolescent who lives with an inner anguish and sense of inherent worthlessness.

Role Reversal

A preadolescent child may show a pseudo-maturity and seem remarkably capable of handling adult responsibilities, especially in areas of home management and child care. This, in itself, may be an indicator of an inverted parent-child relationship in which responsibility shifts from parents to children for meeting family needs.[8] Unspoken role reversal may be a risk factor for, or an indicator of, sexual abuse in families where a child has been pushed into a parent's caregiver role in the home. In cases of incest, the role reversal has extended into the marital sexual relationship, where the child is grievously wronged and forced to function as a "spouse" instead of a child.

Acting Out and Acting In
Adolescents might display "acting out" behaviors as ways of coping with their sexual abuse. Adolescents might present an array of indicators to "tell" others about their abuse, such as rebellion against authority figures, running away, arson, violence, stealing, cruelty to animals, precocious sexuality and possible pregnancy, having intentional "accidents," substance use/abuse, physical aggression against others, vandalism, or other negative behaviors. Male victims, in particular, may have severe and complex outcomes to being sexually abused, such as aggressive criminal behavior, poor performance in school, truancy, and sexual acting out.[9] As self-destructive as these behaviors are, they are often ways that adolescents use to try to "anesthetize" tremendous inner pain, regain some sense of control over their lives, fill up empty spaces within their hearts, or ways they "tell" us of their self-hatred—a legacy of sexual abuse.[10]

"Acting in," or internalizing behaviors, may be associated with depression. Researchers find that child victims are four times more likely to experience major depression than children who are not abused.[11] Severe depression may lead some teens to attempt or complete a suicide. Self-abusive behaviors of childhood can intensify during adolescence. Cutting the flesh, slitting wrists, burning the body with cigarettes, especially in the breast or genital areas, can be desperate ways of trying to "tell" about abuse. One adolescent melted the skin on her forearms with a hot iron as an indicator of her distress. She said that at least it gave her a reason to "hurt." Inflicting harm to the outside of her body temporarily brought relief from inside pain. Destructive and self-abusive masturbation can continue from childhood into adolescence and can become an obsessive preoccupation.

Confusion About Sexuality
In a healthy development of sexuality from childhood to adolescence, children gain an increasing awareness that sexuality is not only related to genitals or biological aspects of procreation.

Healthy sexuality is experienced as one part of a person's entire personality that contributes to personal identity and self-esteem—especially related to being female or male created in the image of God. However, sexual abuse violates a child's personhood in many ways and greatly distorts a victim's sense of sexual identity. It is not uncommon for abuse victims of any age to despise their gender or specific body parts. Degrading messages of abuse warp body image and distort what it means to be male and female in relationship with each other.

IMPACT OF ABUSE ON ADULT SURVIVORS

We began the previous section by explaining why children are always the victims in instances of sexual abuse. In this section, we make a transition to the term *adult survivor* of sexual abuse. Diane Langberg, author of *On the Threshold of Hope,* suggests that the word *survivor* speaks both to the experience of sexual abuse and to the recovery process.[12] On the one hand, "survivor" speaks to the *experience* of sexual abuse because it underscores the idea that survivors have endured a most grievous offense and have continued on in spite of overwhelming odds. On the other hand, "survivor" speaks to the necessity of a *recovery process* because sexually abusive experiences can shape lives in such damaging ways.

Long-Term Effects of Sexual Abuse

From the groundwork already in place from childhood and adolescence, the impact of sexual abuse on adult survivors may continue to deepen and intensify. As survival strategies (defense mechanisms) take up "permanent" residence within adults who have not yet entered a recovery process, adult survivors may feel defeated in many areas. In everyday life, adult survivors may wrestle with distress both within themselves and within important relationships. Countless adult survivors have recalled being completely unaware of dark shadows within their souls that needed to seek the healing Light.

Depression

Researchers tell us that the most commonly reported symptom of adult survivors of abuse is depression. In one psychiatric emergency room, 66 percent of the women who were adult survivors had made suicide attempts, compared to 27 percent of the non-abused women coming to the same emergency room for help.[13] Our ministry experience leads us to the same conclusions that are documented in research studies. Untreated depression in adult survivors can be a matter of life and death.

Substance Abuse

There is a significant link between childhood sexual abuse and substance abuse. One crisis center for women reported that women clients who were sexually abused were ten times more likely to have a drug addiction history and twice as likely to be alcoholics than were the non-sexually abused women who came to the same clinic.[14] Boys who are sexually victimized begin drug use earlier and typically use more than one kind of drug, likely as a way to try to "medicate" their underlying distress, especially if there are no other outlets for help.[15] The probability for problems with alcohol in adulthood is nearly 80 percent for sexually abused men, which compares to 11 percent for men who were not sexually abused.[16] Such challenging evidence points us to a need to understand the underlying anguish of adult survivors who use chemical substances to medicate inner pain, and to offer effective intervention resources.

Dissociation

Dissociation is also closely linked to the experience of sexual abuse. While therapists and counselors are familiar with this symptom, education about long-term effects is reaching into other helping professions. For instance, dissociation is currently listed as one of the two most common symptoms that family physicians are advised to be aware of in caring for their sexually abused patients.[17] Adult survivors report feeling as if they are outside their body, have a sense of not being "centered," lose touch with reality, or "watch" themselves from a distance. If dissociation has provided a way of psychological escape during earlier abuse, it is even more likely that survivors will wrestle with it as adults. Unfortunately, even though dissociation was once protective in childhood, it can be very dangerous in adult life. Dissociation leaves adult survivors "distanced" from, and less aware, of their surroundings and is a significant reason why so many adult survivors of sexual abuse are re-victimized.[18]

Denial and Minimizing

When adult survivors see no connection between their present situations and a past history of abuse, denial is probably functioning to block the pain of the past: "That happened so long ago. It has no effect on me now." Minimizing serves to downplay the abuse: "It really wasn't a big deal. I shouldn't let it bother me anymore," or "He made a mistake and didn't know it was me in the bed; he thought it was Mom." Statements like this indicate that adult survivors are fighting to deny that the abuse was painful or significant in their lives.

Shame on Me/Shame on You

Shame can be emotionally crippling and convincing enough to make adult survivors believe that they are bad, worthless, and of no value. Shame is so powerful and insidious that it motivates many "cover-up" kinds of behaviors from behind the scenes in the minds and hearts of adult survivors. Essentially, these cover-ups have a common theme: to put forth great efforts to earn approval from God and/or others. Or, perhaps more fundamentally, expending great efforts to avoid abandonment by God and/or others. Many adult survivors have come to believe dark lies, such as *You will never measure up; You're defective; You're unlovable and were unwanted; Your feelings are not important; You are bad for having needs.* The lies are endless and require endless energy to try to keep them at bay. A desire to combat shame by appearing to be perfect may push adult survivors into "over-proving" themselves.

On the other hand, an attitude of contempt for and shaming of others may be another way to defend against residual shame from abuse. Defending against shame may surface as a need to always be "right." Rage and violent outbursts of anger sometimes hide shame and effectively keep others at a distance.

Temporary "Fixes"

Adult survivors may employ temporary "fixes" to suppress a sense of worthlessness associated with shame. In addition to substance abuse, mentioned before, many "over-the-top" behaviors temporarily suppress shame: over-achieving at work, over-volunteering at church, overeating, overspending. Also, over-involvement in sex. Researchers tell us that adolescent and adult survivors are vulnerable to bouts of frequent short-term sexual encounters with different partners, putting them at great risk for sexually transmitted diseases and pregnancy.[19] Adult survivors sometimes alternate between two extremes in sexual behavior: complete aversion to sex or compulsive sexual activity. Many adult survivors have told us that indiscriminate sexual activity was used at some time in their lives to partially "distract" them from inner pain. Both female and male survivors tell us that compulsive sexual behavior has very little to do with enjoying or desiring sex but rather is an attempt to overcome painful isolation and/or seek affection.

Because sexual abuse takes place within interpersonal relationships in childhood, it follows that being in interpersonal relationships in adulthood can create fears and ambivalence about what "intimacy" might mean and what it might mean to be "vulnerable." Adult survivors may use sexual activity, however brief, in an attempt to meet needs for closeness and intimacy that were lacking in earlier life experiences. Fearing intimacy and lacking trust, adult survivors may be unable to form stable relationships. Casual sexual encounters can seem "safe," because the more intimate a relationship becomes, the more frightening it is.

The truth of Proverbs 22:6 can be brought to bear on the long-term effects of child sexual abuse. This scriptural principle speaks to the training of children, instructing parents to train children in "the way [they] should go," so that when they are old, they will not turn from that training. Unfortunately, children "trained" by sexually abusive relationships may not turn from that training when they are adults.

Over-Responsibility

Adult survivors may appear to have everything "together" and be "on top of things." However, this can be an outer reflection of a pervasive inner sense of unworthiness or inadequacy. Denial and depression are often connected to various expressions of a "performance syndrome."

A forty-seven-year-old woman was viewed by church members as the perfect pastor's wife. She gave selflessly to others, listened to and cared about everyone's problems—any time, all the time. In addition, she desired to be a faultless example of "submission" to her husband and the ideal mother as a role model of the Christian faith. She felt that others expected a higher standard for her as the pastor's wife, and she tried to live up to what she thought the congregation expected of her. What she never shared with anyone was her chronic depression, for which there was "no reason," and her paralyzing inner fears of inadequacy as a wife and mother.

In her late forties, she tentatively shared with a close friend about a "few incidents" of sexual contact initiated by her father against her. However, she quickly followed this disclosure by saying that she loved her father, had forgiven him, and subsequently there were no effects of sexual abuse in her life. How fortunate she was that her initial disclosure was met by a friend who responded with grace and with informed compassion about the potential long-term effects of child sexual abuse. Her friend encouraged her to see a counselor, where denial was gradually replaced with insights into some of the destructive and shaming messages that she had been carrying with her since childhood.

Through her journey of recovery, she was able to discern ways that fears of being "found out" had motivated her to "perform" and to look perfect *at all times*. Her counselor helped her to recognize how her well-intentioned views about her roles in family life and in ministry were, in many cases, over-responsibility and feeling a need to be in control of every outcome. She began to see how depression had been a signal that she was being crushed under the load of her unrealistic expectations of herself and how that, in turn, was connected to the legacy of shame from past sexual abuse. In a season of life where she was now "ready" to begin the healing journey, God used a wise friend as a tangible expression of Proverbs 25:11, one who offered the right word of encouragement at the right time.

Staying in Control

Adult survivors have experienced devastating consequences from being in situations earlier in life where they were not in control. In adult life, one of the only ways to feel safe may be the impossible task of trying to be in control of all things all the time. A sense of needing to be in control is deeply rooted. It is not often in conscious awareness, and may emerge in many disguises in vastly different ways. Situations in which adult survivors feel at risk of failure or vulnerability can trigger an intense fear of not being in control. A contemptuous attitude toward others can be a way of being in control, as can careful attention to appearing "all together" in front of others. The need to look good may influence adult survivors to choose relationships with people who will "help" them look good. In contrast, under-responsible adult survivors are "in control" when they find others to take care of them.

Under-Responsibility

In contrast to feeling over-responsible for everything and everyone, some adult survivors are under-responsible in their relationships with others. Experiencing overwhelming helplessness as children, some adult survivors have come to believe that they are also helpless as adults. They have given up many areas of personal responsibility and want others to take care of them. They may often feel overwhelmed by "just everything" in life, and most things seem like too much to deal with.

Feeling they are powerless to control anything, adult survivors with this perspective may feel helpless to change things in their lives and therefore look to others to take care of them. In both verbal and non-verbal ways, they communicate to others some form of *I am helpless, I am weak, I can't make it without you, I desperately need you.* Some adult survivors may feel it is safer to let others take most of life's risks for them, and they live their lives vicariously through others.

There is an underlying passivity to this kind of neediness. Others around them might initially respond by trying to help or "rescue" them. However, passive dependency is a barrier to forming intimate relationships because those who try to get close tend to feel "used" and "drained dry" over time. This is yet another tragedy of sexual abuse: Some adult survivors continue to live as adult "victims."

Neither over- nor under-responsibility can foster healthy trust and intimacy in relationships. In principle, Galatians 6:5 offers some insight into distortions of "responsibility" in intimate relationships: "Each one should carry [their] own load." For survivors who lean toward over-responsibility, this verse contains a gentle reminder that an individual can only take responsibility for oneself, and offers release from burdens of over-responsibility for others. For survivors who lean toward under-responsibility, this verse contains a gentle reminder that only an individual can truly take responsibility for oneself, and offers release from burdens of dependency. Finding a balance of mutual responsibility within relationships is a challenging part of the healing journey for adult survivors.

Damaging Effects on Sexuality

Adult survivors have experienced damaging effects on their views of sexuality resulting from childhood sexual abuse. Researcher David Finkelhor has been on the forefront of concerns about child victimization for nearly thirty years. With regard to sexual abuse, he describes a process of "traumatic sexualization" through which a victimized child's sexual feelings and attitudes about sexual activities become distorted and damaged in many ways.[20]

Children are left with confusion about what is "normal" and what is "love" when they are repeatedly rewarded for sexual behaviors that are not appropriate for their age and developmental level. The process of traumatic sexualization is particularly destructive when an offender intentionally tries to evoke a sexual response from a child or entices the child to be involved sexually. Many adult female survivors feel that sex is dirty, immoral, or bad, and some are unable to accept or experience sexual pleasure within a marital relationship. They may feel intensely shameful for experiencing any type of pleasure during the abuse, not realizing that they were too young to know that the offender may have been intentionally manipulating them into a sexual response. If an adult survivor was stimulated against her will in abusive acts, it is sometimes difficult for her to relinquish control and respond sexually to her husband because of past abuse. A tragic outcome of this kind of exploitation might present itself as a reflexive response that "shuts down" pleasurable feelings.

When an offender exchanges affection or gifts or privileges for sexual behavior, children can learn to frame sexual behavior as a way of manipulating others to get needs met. An adult survivor may feel she has sexual "power" over men in her body, but she may view it as destructive. Many have seen how sexual feelings have taken control of others, and those feelings can be frightening. Conversely, some survivors—both male and female—are involved in prostitution, which they tell us allows them to get paid for doing what they are good at. It also confirms their belief that they are "damaged goods" and not good for anything else.

When certain body parts of a child are given distorted importance by sexual actions of the perpetrator, children can develop negative associations with those body parts. Personal violations of body space may contribute to negative views of the body, in general. Some adult survivors have become convinced that their bodies are ugly or untrustworthy, and some believe their bodies "caused" their abuse. Some adult survivors have recalled deliberately trying to appear unattractive, such as one woman who wore thick glasses, feeling safer to be behind her glasses than to be noticed by men. Or, another woman, five feet tall, who achieved a weight gain of 235 pounds to make her body a "barrier" of protection against closeness with others.

When force is used, traumatic sexualization results in tremendous fear being associated with sex in a child's experience. In adult life, the linking of violence with sex can have dangerous consequences. In addition, adult survivors may fear being forcibly hurt in some way, or fear being "used." Sometimes wives cannot "unfreeze" themselves even within a loving sexual relationship due to patterns of dissociation from childhood, in which they "numbed" themselves physically and emotionally during abusive sexual acts. Some researchers have found that 60–87 percent of adult survivors in clinical settings report fear or anxiety-related symptoms during sexual contact.[21]

The experience of "flashbacks"—vivid mental images of past events—is often triggered by something in the present circumstances. Flashbacks are very distressing to abuse survivors because the triggering event activates painful memories that wash over the individual with a wave of intensity. Flashbacks are also distressing to a spouse, because the spouse is likely to receive an intense negative response that seems inappropriate to the situation. A thirty-six-year-old woman found herself intermittently reacting with revulsion to her husband prior to sexual intimacy. Her spontaneous reaction seemed out of her control and caused her intense shame and guilt for having such hostile outbursts toward her husband at these particular times. Neither the husband nor the wife understood the reaction, and it confused and hurt both of them deeply. In counseling, a trigger event was discovered. The smell of a certain brand of soap triggered the memory of the wife's abusive father, who always showered with that soap before he abused her.

Even though many abused single women would like to be in stable marriages and have children, they may not have been able to overcome fear, repulsion, and distrust of men. Adult survivors who are single tell us they often feel as if they don't fit into a "couple's mode" in society or in churches, which adds to a sense of isolation.

Adult survivors might continue to wrestle with issues related to sexual identity and sexual orientation as they perhaps did during adolescence. Adult survivors may struggle with meanings of "maleness" and "femaleness" as it relates to their adult sexual identity. For example, there may be hidden bitterness and feelings of betrayal toward females in general due to the experiences of adult survivors who felt betrayed by mothers who did not protect them from male offenders. As well, both female and male adult survivors may struggle with gender issues as an impact of being abused by mothers or other female offenders, such as baby-sitters or female relatives.

Adult male survivors who have been sexually abused by female offenders, especially mothers, have been some of the most silent victims. When the perpetrator of abuse is a woman, people sometimes do not take a male victim seriously. Even some male survivors minimize abuse by a female offender by calling it a "sexual initiation," even though they may suffer significant emotional trauma as a result of the exploitation.[22] Some adult male survivors have suffered great anguish because a father committing incest can "force" his victim, but a mother committing incest generally "seduces" her son in order to maintain sexual arousal and/or an erection. The pseudo-tenderness makes it difficult for male survivors to recognize emotional pain. Some men report feeling "betrayed" by their bodies for having a sexual response against their will. Adult male survivors of female perpetrators may even feel like an "accomplice" rather than a victim.

The occurrence of sexual intercourse in mother/son incest is less common than emotional seduction and fondling of a son by a mother or mother figure. While this sexually abusive experience may seem less overt, it is abusive and emotionally destructive to male survivors and can contribute to insecurity, extreme self-consciousness, and discomfort around women. While some men who are victimized by female offenders do become offenders themselves due to underlying rage against women, most male victims of child sexual abuse do not grow up to become sex offenders.[23]

Adult survivors of father-son incest can feel deep depressive symptoms of self-loathing, sexual identity confusion, and have difficulty in relationships with both men and women. If the male survivor hates his father, who is his role model, he hates a large part of himself. In U.S. society, boys and men are generally taught that men are to be strong and self-reliant; thus being victimized means they are "weak" and not "real men."[24] Male survivors of male offenders may struggle with a need to "prove" their masculinity by having multiple sex partners or being involved in risky "macho" behaviors. Some may fear that being sexually abused by another male means they must be gay or that the abuse might cause them to develop a homosexual orientation. Because so few people have a knowledgeable understanding of the incredible stigma felt by male survivors, abused men may experience nearly insurmountable stumbling blocks in pursuing restoration and healing.

Reading through this section of potential effects of child sexual abuse is sobering. However, a principle from Luke 14:28 guides us along our path. Jesus posed a question to a group of his followers: "Suppose one of you wants to build a tower. Will he not first sit down and estimate the cost?" As an essential first step in ministry, we must first "sit down" and listen to the voices of children and wounded adults in order to hear what they have to tell us. Part of "the cost" is the discomfort of increasing our awareness, broadening our understanding, and gaining substantial knowledge about the damage experienced in the lives of those who have been victimized. If we want to "build a tower" of refuge for adult survivors within our Christian communities, we must continue to count the cost.

4

Spiritual Damage

Elizabeth was brought up in a Christian home; all of her family members were professing Christians who attended church whenever the doors were open. She made a decision for Christ at an early age and experienced a normal, uneventful childhood until the abuse began. Elizabeth's Uncle Phil, himself a professing Christian, had always been affectionate with her. But when she was ten years old, he began to French kiss her and fondle her. He warned her not to tell anyone—it would just be their "little secret." He threatened her that if she did tell, Aunt Mary would divorce him and her parents would be very upset with her.

Elizabeth had been repeatedly taught that a good Christian girl must obey her elders, so she was very obedient. She didn't tell. Once, early in the abusive relationship, Elizabeth tried to tell her mother that her uncle was putting his hand down inside her blouse. Elizabeth's mother became angry with her for attempting to show her mother what Uncle Phil was doing. Her mother said, "Oh, his hand must have slipped. He would never do anything wrong." Elizabeth never talked to her mother—or anyone else—about it again. The abuse continued.

Elizabeth's uncle used his Christian faith as a means to abuse her. He lived out-of-state but made frequent visits to Elizabeth's family. During his visits, at mealtimes, he always wanted Elizabeth to sit next to him. While he was praying, he would be touching her under the table. Sometimes at night he would come into her bedroom, telling her, "Say your prayers like a good girl." And then he would fondle her after she prayed. Elizabeth was very confused about God. Is this what he wanted for her? She prayed, "God, stop Uncle Phil!" But the abuse went on.

Her uncle became more forceful in his expectations of her. He started demanding to have sexual intercourse with her and forced her to perform oral sex on him. The guilt, shame, and confusion were indescribable and agonizing. Didn't God care about her? Was he powerless? Why didn't God answer her prayers? Elizabeth didn't understand how Uncle Phil could be a Christian and do these things to her. She became very angry with God and didn't want to go to church. When she did go, she felt guilty and dirty and fearful that others could see right through her and know her terrible secret.

Elizabeth became concerned about her younger sisters. She was afraid that if she did not submit to her uncle's abuse, he might begin abusing her sisters. So to protect her sisters from harm, she deliberately sacrificed herself, continuing to endure the abuse and remain silent.

The abuse continued for seven years. Finally Elizabeth could no longer keep silent. She told a Sunday school teacher about the abuse. The secret was out. What would happen now? Would all those bad things happen that he had threatened? The police were called in. Uncle Phil was taken to jail and had to have some brief counseling sessions. That was all. Aunt Mary did not divorce him.

Elizabeth's parents reacted to the abuse disclosure by telling her it was "all over now." She was to "forgive and forget," to "put it behind her." Injustice raged within her. Why hadn't her Christian parents protected her from him in the first place? She had never even been told anything like this could happen. Why hadn't her mother listened to her when she first tried to tell her about the abuse? Why couldn't her parents understand how much pain she was going through now that her horrible shame was exposed? Why wouldn't they support her by at least *trying* to understand the intensity of the pain she had been enduring in silence for so long?

New information came to light after her uncle's arrest. Elizabeth discovered that Uncle Phil had also been abusing two of her sisters. He had told her sisters he was doing this to Elizabeth and that because she submitted to him they should submit to him, also. Elizabeth's emotional pain and shame increased enormously. She realized she had been unable to protect her sisters from Uncle Phil; now she felt responsible for what had happened to them.

At this point, Elizabeth was not only enraged with a powerless, absent, unfair God, but with her parents, her uncle, and most of all, herself. She rebelled against everything familiar; she started drinking and using drugs to numb the incredible inner pain. Confused about her sexuality, she became sexually active with both men and women. Her intense anger at God came out sideways. She unconsciously tried to "get even" with God for her uncle's immoral violations of her by "immoral violations" of her own—against God. To Elizabeth, God had become a punitive parent/judge, a cruel taskmaster who delivered punishment for every wrong thought, feeling, and action. She wanted to die. After an attempted suicide, she ended up confined in a psychiatric ward for a week, seeking to find some way out of the darkness her life had become.

Not long after her release from the hospital, Elizabeth met a Christian young woman who showed her love, care, and acceptance. Elizabeth felt like this was the first person who had ever really loved her just for herself. Elizabeth's inner anguish and extreme emptiness led her to become unhealthily dependent on her new friend. Within months, the young woman had transitioned from being a friend to becoming a lover. Elizabeth felt she was making wrong choices, but inner neediness overpowered her decision-making. She was inwardly divided between the head knowledge of what she had been taught about same-sex relationships and the emotional intensity within her heart. Above all, she feared abandonment and felt that that the only "source" to meet her needs for security and worth was her lesbian lover.

Elizabeth began attending a Christian college, somehow hoping that being in a Christian setting would help her become a "better" Christian and help quiet the dark memories of her past. Her past torment did not go away, however, nor did the guilt from involvement in her same-sex relationship. She felt like a hypocrite. The required Bible classes only increased her sense of guilt. Her secret inner turmoil again mounted to an almost unbearable level. She was at a turning point in her life.

She sensed there was nowhere else to go and nothing more to lose, so she made a remarkable decision: She would attempt to discover what God was really like. She was unsure whether he could, or would, help her but she took one step in that direction. She began attending a Christian sexual abuse support group in conjunction with individual counseling. Over time, her intense inner pain dissipated just enough for her to begin to see God in a new light. Her image of a punitive, cruel, uncaring God softened in the face of his empathy, compassion, and unconditional acceptance of her. She experienced his grace, reflected to her through those who came alongside and supported her in her healing journey. She began to experience stirrings of God's presence in her daily life. It may take years before she will be able to experience substantial restoration from the extensive damage of such grievous abuse, which was compounded by denial and rejection by her parents. She has, however, taken the first steps toward relief of the heavy burden she has carried for so many years.

The emotional and spiritual damage in Elizabeth's life was devastating, crippling. It brought her to the brink of taking her life. Her questions were intense and valid and needed answers. How could she trust the God of her uncle who prayed while he sexually abused her? How could she trust the God of her parents, who didn't protect her and then, when the abuse was revealed, didn't understand or support her? How could an all-loving God allow a little girl to suffer abuse for seven years?

VIOLATIONS OF PERSONHOOD: SPIRITUAL EFFECTS OF SEXUAL ABUSE

Elizabeth's story speaks of many levels of spiritual damage caused by the sexual violation of a child. In deeply hidden ways, sexual abuse can bring a sense of death to the soul. Sandra Flaherty, author of *"Woman, Why Do You Weep?"* is also a survivor of incest. She writes of insight she gained when reflecting on Mary Magdalene at the tomb after the death of Jesus. Finding the stone rolled away and fearing the body had been stolen, Mary begins to weep: "They have taken my Lord away and I don't know where they have put him." She turned around and saw Jesus standing there, but she did not realize it was Jesus. "Woman," he said, "why do you weep?"

Ms. Flaherty writes that for her and many others, the answer to Jesus' question is that they are weeping from the wounds of childhood sexual abuse.[1] She continues: "It is interesting to note that Mary did not recognize that it was the risen Christ who asked her, 'Woman, why do you weep?' She did not realize that even at the tomb, hope and resurrection were within her immediate grasp."[2]

Distorted Images of God

Distortions about God became an integral part of the human condition in the Garden of Eden. Adam and Eve became afraid and hid from God after their first image of God had become distorted by sin. God suddenly looked "different" to them from their fallen state.

When providing a remedy to this fallen state, God did not send a mature adult. When "the Word became flesh and lived among us" (John 1:14 NRSV), he came as an infant. Jesus grew through each phase of a child's development, knowing the love of earthly parents and experiencing the fullness of childhood. By entering into human history as a child, Jesus demonstrated, among many things, how much God values children. When Jesus discovered that his disciples were shooing children away, he was indignant, because the disciples were hindering the children from getting close to him. He then took the children in his arms and blessed them. In addition, Jesus admonishes us in Matthew 18:6–7 that hindering children in their faith is a serious offense to God.[3]

Children are introduced to a relationship with Jesus through the primary relationships they have with their parents and significant caregivers. Parent-child interactions are a preliminary introduction to God's grace. Parents and caring adults are to shape children's views of God by reflecting his unconditional love to them within intimate settings—integrating love and limits with affection and guidance.

When parents abuse or neglect children, their actions become tools of destruction instead of a means of grace. As happened to Elizabeth, children are sometimes even abused in God's name, being told it is God's will for them to submit to abuse as a function of being "obedient" to their parents. What a travesty of grace! Viewed through Elizabeth's eyes, it is understandable that her "God" was a punitive and cruel parent and judge whose only involvement in her life was to punish her.

Distortions about God can take many forms: God is dead or nonexistent, God is impotent, an impossible taskmaster, a celestial "kill-joy," or perhaps a "Santa Claus" in the sky keeping track of whether we're naughty or nice.[4] But those who have been sexually abused—especially those violated by professing Christians or clergy—do not just view God "through a glass, darkly" (1 Corinthians13:12 KJV), but rather they see God *as* dark.

A forty-five-year-old woman recalls early memories of her father exposing his genitals to her and forcing her to touch him. As she got older, he systematically abused all her brothers and sisters, following the abuse by reading Bible verses about honoring your father and "loving" one another. She viewed God as a punitive, inconsistent Father figure who always demanded more from her than she was able to give and then punished her for not measuring up. Similarly, Elizabeth's uncle was an elder in his church. He used religious practices, such as prayer, as opportunities to abuse her—at the same time that he was representing God to her.

In cases where children are abused by someone outside the family, spiritual damage can be reflected in images of God as inept, undiscerning, or powerless. In such situations, it is understandable that God is viewed as neither caring nor protective. A twenty-five-year-old woman recalls feeling very afraid to tell her parents about being abused by a teenage neighbor boy when she was a child of seven. As a child, she was convinced that her parents would blame her for causing trouble. Only "happy Christian feelings" were allowed in her home. Other feelings were considered sinful (ungrateful/selfish) and "not appropriate for Christians." In her late twenties she sought professional counseling for depression.

As she slowly unraveled her thoughts and feelings, she began to understand the effects of the shame, anger, fear, and pain she had buried inside. Not only did she experience trauma from the abuse, but the absence of support from her parents was deeply wounding. For the first time, she became aware that deep inside she had come to a dark conclusion: Only a "jerk" would allow a little kid to *be* hurt and then be mad at them for *feeling* hurt. Based on the role-modeling of her parents and their denial of feelings, she had long ago decided that God must be a "jerk" too, someone who was detached and inept. Her concept of God had effectively isolated her from being able to relate to him on a personal level, even though, ironically, she was actively involved in ministry.

Distorted Images of Self

Our concept of God is a composite of theology (what we believe about God and what we believe God thinks about us) and our experiences in interpersonal relationships (what we believe about ourselves and what we believe others think of us). Thus our concept of God is the sum total of our life experience.[5]

Elizabeth learned many things about God at church that were not reflected in her daily life experience. As the abuse continued, she felt increasingly negative about herself and felt somehow responsible for causing the abuse. She became more and more angry with God for not protecting her from the abuse. Her self-hate and her hate for God became one.

Elizabeth's experience is an example of how incredibly difficult it is for victims of sexual abuse to respond positively or freely to

God's grace. More often than not, God is perceived as being absent when needed instead of present and available; of being unjust and unfair instead of being holy and just; of being a punitive parent/ judge who hands out condemnation rather than a God of unconditional grace.[6]

A twenty-six-year-old woman recalled trying to please God by attempting to increase her own suffering during the years of her abuse. She believed, as she had been taught, that "suffering makes Jesus like you better and means He loves you more." At age ten, she knelt for five hours on broken pieces of hard macaroni—the closest thing to broken glass that she could think of. She begged God not to love her anymore. Who would not experience fear, bitterness, or anger toward such a God?

Just as disrupted interpersonal relationships create emotional damage, so a disrupted interpersonal relationship with God creates spiritual damage. Our emotional and spiritual well-being are inextricably linked. Even sincere adult believers can harbor a warped inner childhood image of God and be unable to *feel* personally intimate with or unconditionally accepted by him. Being sincere often worsens the struggle because many adult survivors devoutly study Scripture and pray steadfastly, compiling intellectual truth but not experiencing a sense of relationship or closeness with God. They may be aware that "something" is wrong but, because they don't recognize the effects of spiritual damage from sexual abuse, they once again blame themselves for somehow failing to please God.

"What did I do so wrong that God let this happen to me?" wept Janice in one of her first counseling sessions. "I try so hard to make up for being a bad little girl, and I really do want to be a good Christian. But, somehow, I always end up letting God down." Janice interpreted her emotional struggles as spiritual problems, without realizing that her view of God from childhood abuse was so damaging that trying to have a relationship with such a judgmental God as an adult caused great inner turmoil.

Another area of spiritual damage may emerge through teachings about being "dependent" on God in order to be "used" by God. The meaning of such terms might be vastly different when "heard" by adult survivors of sexual abuse. Adult survivors have told us this: Relinquishing control of their lives to God is fearful because they have learned that dependent vulnerability is the essence of victimization. A necessary path for most adult survivors on their healing journey lies in asking the questions: "Where was God during the time the abuse was happening?" and "What part does God play in the healing process?'' After having been sexually "used" by someone older and more powerful, one woman reacted with rage to the idea of going through a painful healing process in order to then be "used" by God. It is important to realize how frequently the "good news" can become the "bad news" to adult survivors of abuse.

An insightful sixteen-year-old girl in one of our sexual abuse support groups came to grips with this issue by defining victimization as "when you have no choice" and dependence on God as "when you can ask for help." For her, the difference between victimization and dependence on God was a perspective of choice. A person who is dependent on God has the freedom to choose that dependency, she told us, rather than re-experiencing the helplessness of victimization where there were no choices. God gave to her that personal insight, and it soothed her soul.

HELPING ADULT SURVIVORS

Many survivors of sexual abuse have tremendous anger toward God, their parents, and other Christians who did not understand the deep pain of the abuse they endured. Many pastors and other Christians are personally uncomfortable or unfamiliar with such intense pain. Wanting to "rescue" others as well as to avoid experiencing their own pain through personal involvement, some people may tend to give "formulas" or "pat answer" solutions: "Just trust in Jesus and everything will be okay."

However, such superficial advice may simply increase pain and confusion that adult survivors are already experiencing. Trivializing the trauma with simplistic formulas implies that adult survivors don't have enough faith, that they should be "fixed" by now, or that they are not pleasing God in some way if they aren't yet "healed." Sometimes when an advice-giver admonishes someone to "Just give it to the Lord," what is really meant is "Don't give it to me! I don't want to be involved."

In our experience, restoration from childhood sexual abuse often involves a lengthy journey. As Christ invites abuse survivors into his presence, he also waits to be invited into their healing process. There is no "quick fix" to the deeply rooted pain of sexual abuse. A relationship with God must often be re-formed along a pathway that includes trusted counselors and a supportive network of caring relationships. As Christ has assured us, where two or three are gathered in his name, there he is with us.

Understanding Sexual Abuse in the Family

5

Incest: The Ultimate Betrayal

There can be many hurtful patterns within families, but one of the most devastating and damaging family experiences is that of incest. Scripture states that "a little yeast works through the whole batch of dough" (Galatians 5:9). This principle provides a parallel to the pervasive damage of incest—the "family secret" of incest affects the entire family. Accordingly, "if one part suffers, every part suffers with it" (1 Corinthians 12:26). Thus, when incest occurs in families, all persons in the family suffer. When incest occurs in Christian families, the whole body of Christ suffers.

This section will acquaint the reader with the reality that incest does occur in Christian families and will offer insights into ways that hurting families might be helped.

While the church is becoming more aware of the occurrence of incest, there are sometimes broad generalizations made about "incest families," such as all incest families are "enmeshed" or all mothers are in denial, which "allows" sexual abuse to occur. As researchers learn more about the complexities of incest within families, it is important to note that incest involves very complex groupings of destructive patterns. There are some common themes as well as distinctive differences. The following case history is shared with permission from an adult survivor of incest. (All names have been changed.)

In the Taylor family, the first incident of incest occurred when Melanie was seven. Her father phoned from work in the afternoon, telling her he was coming home to see if she had obediently completed her household chores. She quickly finished cleaning the kitchen for his approval. When her father arrived, he sent her brothers out to play. He took Melanie into the bedroom, put a knife in the lock on the door so no one could come in, fondled her, and digitally penetrated her while he masturbated. From that time forward, he routinely came home in the afternoon to abuse her while her mother was at work. The abuse intensified, including attempts of intercourse, which were unsuccessful because of her small stature. He often took her in the car with him, alternately fondling her and masturbating while driving. One continuous threat maintained Melanie's silence: "Don't tell your mother; it will kill her. If she finds out, she'll die, and it will be your fault."

How did incest happen in this Christian family? Examining multiple factors influencing the development of incest provides insight into intervention and possible restoration.

MULTIPLE MOTIVATIONS UNDERLYING INCEST

Different types of incest offenders can be characterized by their motivations for abuse.[1] Two questions are particularly useful for counselors to consider when confronted with complex factors of incest: (1) What was the offender thinking/feeling during the abuse? and (2) What meaning did the abuse have for the child victim?[2] Four types of incest offenders are discussed here.

Affection-based offenders are primarily motivated by a lack of nurture and physical affection displayed in the family. The offender usually comes into the family with deficits of lack of nurture and care from childhood. When affection-based offenders are asked what they were thinking/feeling when involved in sexual contact with a child, they make statements such as *"I wanted her to feel loved."* The child victim's interpretation of meaning about this kind of incest might be reflected in statements such as *"He makes me feel special when he touches me."*[3]

Incest committed by *erotic-based offenders* is more likely to be motivated by a desire for sexual contact. When asked what they were thinking/feeling when involved in sexual contact with a child victim, these offenders make sexually oriented statements such as *"I enjoyed watching her feel good when I touched her."* The child victim may make meaning out of this situation by assuming sexual contact is a normal way of relating in families, reflected in statements such as *"This is just the way dads show they love their kids."*[4]

Aggression-based incest offenders are often violent and want to dominate their victim. Incest is an expression of focused anger. Negative anger toward the offender's own parent or a spouse is expressed indirectly through abusing a child victim, such as a father reporting that during the abuse of his son he was thinking about getting even with his ex-wife and wondering how he could take the boy away from her. Child victims of aggression-based offenders, such as Julie from chapter 1, reflect their experience with fear: "*I knew he was going to hurt me,*" or "*I was scared and cried but he wouldn't stop.*"[5]

Rage-based, violent incest offenders may be life-threatening to child victims and are deeply damaged psychologically, usually acting out of a long-standing history of personal abuse, shame, and rage. The terrified and traumatized response of a child to this horrendous abuse might be "*I was sure he was going to kill me.*"[6]

From these examples, it is apparent that for intervention to be effective, the underlying motivations must be addressed with appropriate treatment. Churches should identify therapeutic resources and referrals that are most suited to address different underlying motivations of incest. One approach might involve family intervention.

A "family systems" approach is a process that has developed since the 1980s and is sometimes used in *very specific* kinds of family incest situations. This approach focuses on the family, as a unit, with the goal of identifying destructive family interaction patterns and underlying interpersonal boundary violations. A family systems view holds that even though removing the offender and treating the victim stops sexual abuse in the family, at the same time, other physically, emotionally, and verbally abusive interpersonal dynamics might remain "embedded" in family interactions.

The goal of family-focused intervention is to stop all forms of abuse in the family and increase the likelihood that the family might survive the devastation of incest and achieve a much higher level of functioning in their relationships with one another. When the entire family is the focus of treatment, the complexity of the process involves a rigorous regimen of long-term intervention.[7]

ADDRESSING FAMILY ISSUES: OVERCOMING SHAME WITH GRACE

Shame is an underlying dynamic within incest families, which might be characterized as empty circles:

The inner circle represents an inner void that yearns for love, acceptance, value, meaning, and purpose. This kind of inner life, at its core, is spiritual in nature. Inner spiritual life cannot be earned, bought, or discovered but can only be *received* as a gift of God's grace, based on Christ's work on the cross. God's love flows out from his fullness rather than being allotted/withheld based on "performance" or good behaviors. (See also chapter 11.)

The outer circle in the diagram represents behaviors used to cover emptiness and reduce exposure of "defectiveness" to others. External behaviors may be positive or negative, depending on the particular group that the behaviors are intended to please/impress. External behavior motivated by an inner sense of not "measuring up" forms a barrier to healthy relationships and motivates hurtful ways of meeting core needs.

Continuing with the case of sexual abuse in the Taylor family, the occurrence of incest was significantly related to shame. Mr. Taylor masked his sense of inner deficits through outer actions such as being a choir director and pastor-teacher to the adult Sunday school class, often preaching against the corruption of sin. He inwardly believed he had to be active and successful in ministry to "measure up" to church expectations. To appear spiritual, he even required his daughter to memorize certain sounds so that, at age seven, she would appear to be speaking in tongues. He chastised her because it didn't look good for Daddy to have a disobedient daughter who wasn't "filled with the Spirit." The church defined the "father" role as keeping children in subjection to demonstrate family leadership, and he made every effort to "subdue" his children. Mr. Taylor believed God expected a rigid discipline of daily devotions and Bible study; thus, he felt that any lack of discipline in these areas proved he was a failure.

Underneath the "Christian behavior" was a gnawing emptiness, a sense of being unloved, worthless, and alone—a shamed and shaming father. Unable to experience love and acceptance from God, he turned to his wife with unrealistic expectations, and when she proved too preoccupied to meet his needs, he demanded those needs be met by his daughter.

Mrs. Taylor was also wrestling with shame, investing a great deal of emotional energy in maintaining the family image. She believed that in order to measure up to expectations of others, the family must always look good on the outside, even if they were hurting on the inside. She sensed an unspoken neediness in her husband but inwardly scorned him for it. She had little time to meet his emotional or sexual needs because of her endless activities. Her source of core value was her "image," and when the effort for others' approval became too great, she took to her bed with a "spell" and expected to be taken care of.

She knew that even though everyone praised her for her many church activities, the praise was really about her "servant behavior" not her value as a person. From such inner bankruptcy, she had little to give. Transmitting shame was the only "gift" she knew how to give her family.

Issues related to shame of child victims, such as Melanie, are highlighted throughout this book.

Treatment Goals for Shame

Intervention in family incest will require families to learn the differences between shame and guilt. Facing shame will require tremendous effort on the part of all family members to work through feelings of anger, fear, and pain experienced within a shame-based family setting. Family members will need to eventually learn and practice different patterns of interacting with one another, modeling an increasing awareness of personal value and unconditional acceptance by God, which can then be reflected to one another.

Perfectionism is an outgrowth of shame in incest families. Families that are primarily concerned with looking "good," or of keeping the peace at all costs, tend to have "living arrangements" rather than real relationships. An inherent message of perfectionism is that worth is based on performance or behavior. In Melanie's experience, she learned early on that trying to be perfect and "good" was a way to keep families from falling apart, and that if sexual behavior was required as a sacrifice to maintain family harmony, then the price must be paid no matter the cost.

If there is to be hope for restoration of families after incest, family members will need a great deal of help to view themselves realistically, looking to God for strength and courage to undertake relationship skill-building education and to practice new behaviors. While Paul exhorts that God's grace is sufficient for all, and that power is made perfect in weakness (2 Corinthians 12:9), families in which incest has occurred will be greatly challenged in giving themselves permission to try new ways of relating, to make mistakes, to be imperfect and fallible. (See also chapter 10.)

ADDRESSING FAMILY ISSUES: INTERVENING IN ABUSES OF POWER

Child sexual abuse is always an abuse of power by offenders, even when there is no force or violence employed. (See also chapter 2.) Because offenders and other powerful family members can be expected to continue to abuse power until they are confronted, abuse of power becomes a primary family treatment need.[8]

Power can be exercised by physical force or intimidation or by dependent/passive/weak behavior. For example, "frail" Mrs. Taylor was, in reality, a powerful family member because her fragile health and subsequent "spells" essentially manipulated and controlled others.

Powerful family members may rigidly demand one kind of behavior one day and, without notice, abandon the first expectation and substitute another. Such misuses of power teach family members that powerful people can make their own rules and change them whenever they want.

Treatment Goals for Abuse of Power

Families will need to understand how misused power has been destructive to all family members. For hope of restoration, those abusing power must be willing to replace aggressiveness with assertiveness while those who have been victims of abuses of power must learn to become assertive rather than passive. (See also chapters 13 and 15 for communication skills and interaction patterns.)

In family counseling sessions, family members who have been abusing power are not going to give up those positions easily and may be manipulative, threatening, or aggressive in subtle ways. It is imperative that counselors confront these behaviors:

The therapist must convey by his or her own attitude and

behavior that he or she understands how power is exercised and is able to use power in a responsible fashion. This involves confronting clients whenever they abuse power, interpreting the abusive and inappropriate aspects of their actions and refusing to back down from a stance which insists that they stop their abusive behavior and acknowledge their responsibility for their actions. It requires the counselor always to behave with absolute consistency, to be unflinching in the face of hostility and threats from the client, to refuse to be manipulated, to demonstrate that he or she is willing to be held accountable and to insist that others do likewise, and unfailingly to be honest in all dealings with clients.[9]

Christ has role-modeled intervention into abuses of power. In Matthew 23:4, Christ confronts the Pharisees for loading the people with "impossible demands that they themselves don't even try to keep" (TLB). Incest offenders also place impossible demands on their child victims. Manipulative behaviors of offenders are similar to behaviors of the Pharisees who were "careful to polish the outside of the cup," leaving "the inside . . . foul with extortion and greed" (v. 25). An offender's denial is like "polishing the outside of the cup."

Family counselors call attention to the "inside of the cup," addressing abuses of power that have resulted in using children to meet sexual and emotional needs of adults. Christ straightforwardly identified blindness and hypocrisy within the Pharisees, held them accountable for their wrong behaviors, was unflinching in the face of their hostility, was not manipulated by them, and yet gave them hope: "First cleanse the inside of the cup, and then the whole cup will be clean" (v. 26). A therapeutic balance comes from confronting wrong behavior and holding persons accountable for abusing power while at the same time reinforcing that condemnation is not the issue but rather hope for restoration.

ADDRESSING FAMILY ISSUES: CORRECTING SKEWED COMMUNICATION

Families in which incest occurs display many types of skewed communication. Feelings are denied or disregarded. Certain feelings may be singled out as "wrong" or "silly," and victims sometimes feel "crazy" because they are told verbally or nonverbally that their feelings are invalid or "should not" exist.

Maintaining Silence: Keeping Secrets

Families maintaining the secret of incest usually impose non-verbal communication rules on family members. In counseling terminology, these powerful rules are often referred to as "no-talk rules," which means that certain topics or behaviors are not to be discussed or even recognized as real.

In many families, sex is never discussed, which communicates a nonverbal message that it is wrong/bad to talk about sex. One danger of such silence is that child victims may assume others "know" they are being abused. As well, children will not speak up because they sense the "no-talk" rules that exert powerful influence on them to remain silent.

Incest occurring in families has been likened to having an elephant in the family living room. When a family member speaks up about the incest, it becomes the equivalent of reporting to the rest of the family that there is a huge elephant in the living room. However, other members of the family are astonished and reply that there is most certainly *not* an elephant in the living room! Meanwhile, family members walk around the "elephant" to avoid running into it. This may take the form of denial such as "You misunderstood what happened" or "He would never do such a thing." The function of "no-talk" rules is to convince the questioning family member that the incest "elephant" is not the problem but rather that *he or she* is the problem for breaking the no-talk rule and "noticing" the problem.

In Melanie's case, when she was thirteen, three of her mother's sisters approached her asking if her father had "touched her wrong." The aunts were concerned about Melanie and came to warn her. Melanie's aunts broke the silence when they disclosed that Mr. Taylor had sexually abused them in earlier years. When Melanie told her aunts they were too late because her father had been abusing her for years, the aunts reported Mr. Taylor to the police. Due to Mrs. Taylor's "frail" health, her sisters accompanied her to her doctor's office and, in that setting, told her about the incest. Melanie was sitting outside the exam room and heard her mother screaming; she was terrified that her father's prediction would come true and that Melanie's "telling" would "kill" her mother. After the disclosure, the aunts reassured Melanie that her father would no longer be molesting her. However, Mrs. Taylor looked intently at her thirteen-year-old daughter and asked, "How could you do this to me? You took my husband away and you have ruined the family." From Mrs. Taylor's viewpoint, the incest wasn't the problem. Melanie had become the problem for speaking about the problem.

Walking on Eggshells/Appeasement

Family members tend to relate superficially and are "on guard" to say the right thing because everyone is preoccupied with fault and blame and therefore finds it almost impossible to admit mistakes. Because of underlying shame, anything that goes wrong must be someone else's fault because it is crucial to "look good" in order to protect the system from exposure. Family members often appease, or defer, because they cannot bear to have someone be angry or "upset" with them. They become convinced to go along with what others want and to avoid conflict by agreeing with others.

Blaming

Blaming is another outgrowth of underlying shame. A father committing incest might say, "If only my wife had met my needs, I wouldn't have turned to my daughter." In another case, an uncle insisted the incest was "not his fault" because his three-year-old niece ran around the house wearing only her underwear, trying to "seduce" him.

A mother may blame a child victim for "telling" about incest and "causing" family break up or may blame the child for not resisting sexual advances. When Jean told her mother that the mother's live-in boyfriend was abusing her, Jean's mother responded, "You got yourself into this; you get yourself out of it." Certainly some of the most devastating blaming occurs within children who blame themselves for the abuse.

Controlling

Communication in incest families may be transmitted through patterns of regimented control, in which persons appear very correct, unemotional, abstract, detached, or uncaring as a defense to avoid facing painful reality. Communication may resemble a computer, presenting data as intellectual and factual without emotional expression, and often in a very controlled tone of voice or monotone.

In her counselor's office, Sandy told of her father's abuse, which led to her running away, walking the streets, and ultimately engaging in prostitution. She related several beatings by her pimp that required hospitalization. Her voice was monotone and unemotional as she chronicled traumatic events of her life in a controlled, precise, and detached manner. She seemed to be speaking about someone else. The pain in her life, beginning with incest, had forced her to master the skill of controlled communication.

Scattered and Confused

The pain of reality can result in communication that is scattered, confused, and irrelevant to the current situation. Family members using scattered communication will be adept at changing the subject, will tend to talk in circles, and will make statements and responses that do not make sense. For example, Jane was abused by her stepfather for many years while receiving damaging double messages from him. He beat her and blamed her for everything that went wrong in the family, but he also told her she was a "good girl" because she met his sexual needs. When the abuse became known, both he and Jane's mother left town, abandoning Jane to an aunt. As a result of Jane's family patterning, she would flit from one thought to another, monopolizing conversations by talking incessantly about self-focused trivia.

Treatment Goals for Skewed Communication Patterns

A primary goal is to assist families to develop direct communication that is honest, free-flowing, and non-threatening to the self-esteem of other family members. Developing active listening skills is foundational to rebuilding interpersonal relationships. Active listening skills teach family members not only to hear the *content* of what someone is saying but to understand accompanying *feelings* as well. (See chapter 15.)

Addressing Family Issues: Precursors to Restoration

Several changes in family environment must be made to assure that families can be safely reunited after incest. Changes must be made not only in family functioning within the family but also in reducing isolation of the family unit from others in their churches and communities.

SOCIAL ISOLATION

Fearing that "outsiders" will find out about the incest is one of the primary characteristics of family incest. Protecting the family secret effectively prevents intervention and forces family members to depend solely on one another for meeting all their needs. This kind of closed family limits personal growth of individual family members and creates an overdependence between members of the family, which is sometimes termed *enmeshment*. The Taylor family isolated the secret of Melanie's abuse by multiple church activities with superficial participation that allowed an image of spirituality to be projected. The "spiritual image" functioned as a mask for the abuse.

Treatment Goals for Social Isolation

It will be extremely difficult for families to consider positive aspects of a more open family system, in which they begin to develop trusting relationships outside the family. In addition, the family experiencing incest will likely take a long time to establish trust with a counselor or be able to receive support and care from others outside the family. Over time, counselors can become trusted sources of continued support and encouragement to break through fears of involvement with others.

DENIAL

In families where incest is occurring, denial is a defense mechanism against the greater pain of knowing what is really happening. Therapist Susanne Sgroi observes, "Constant denial can be destructive to the individual who employs this defense mechanism because it diminishes one's capacity to empathize with others."[10] Denial robs adults of empathy for children.

Sexual abuse is so secret that those participating in it can even deny that it is happening. A father may consider incest to be "sex education," or child victims may refer to incest as "helping Dad." Mothers often exercise high degrees of denial. For example, one father ritualistically washed the sheets and put them away each time after abusing his daughter. His wife never asked where the clean sheets came from, who had washed them, or why.

The following poem captures a sense of denial regarding family incest:

Danger

Danger threatened!
I knew I had to get away,
but there was no place I could go.
A girl of six

can hardly leave
the yard alone.
I stayed.

Instead, I ran into my mind.
I dodged between the messages
of Mother's eyes
and Grandma's sighs—
messages which said:
don't tell the truth
we cannot bear to hear.
Cowering in the dark recesses
of an attic in my head,
I crept behind the broken furniture
of my unacceptable rage and fear.
Dust of decades,
my forbidden secret,
settled over me as I choked in guilt.
Abandoned and abused,
I sealed the doors
so that no one would know.[11]

Treatment Goals for Denial

Even though families must be willing to confront denial, the impact of the truth can be so overwhelming that it is difficult to face all at once. The scriptural principle of "the truth will set you free" (John 8:32) can be a reality for incest families. However, in order to be set free, layers of denial must be removed, one at a time, in the process of facing the painful truth, in asking and answering the question: *How did incest happen in our family?*

LACK OF INTIMACY

Family intimacy can be defined as the experience of closeness and familiarity between two or more family members in many different contexts of family life with the expectation that the relationship will continue to be close over time.[12] Healthy intimacy flows from a secure identity and from a position of equal respect for self and others. In cases of family incest, lack of trust, poor self-image, and limited ways to meet core needs may translate into intimacy needs being expressed through sexual means.

Treatment Goals for Intimacy

Trust is the foundation upon which intimacy is built. A counselor or pastor may be the first person with whom family members develop a trusting relationship. Over time, a therapeutic relationship with a trusted counselor may be a stepping-stone to begin, or renew, a trust relationship with God. (See chapter 11.)

BLURRED BOUNDARIES

Boundaries can be defined as "the invisible shield surrounding us, something like a capsule. This invisible line marks our limits—where we end and the rest of the world begins. When our boundaries are well defined, we can express and take responsibility for what we think, what we feel, and what we do."[13] In cases of family incest, children are not permitted to regulate their own boundaries. When violations occur it is as if someone outside of them is "unzipping" them against their will. Child victims come to believe that they are regulated by those in the outside world. Incest victims have a sense that anyone can approach them, "unzip" them, and "take their stuff."[14]

Where family incest occurs, family members are rarely permitted to set limits regarding their belongings, personal space, or their own bodies. People wander into bedrooms or bathrooms, opening closed doors, walking in on others while they are taking a bath, using the bathroom, or undressing. Parents show little respect for the privacy of children: their property, bodies, and feelings. Voicing a no is not allowed and refusing a request is not an option.

Boundary violations sometimes occur through situations created by "faulty sleeping arrangements," by requiring opposite-sex children to share the same room or bed, or the bed of the parents.

Treatment Goals for Blurred Boundaries

One's personal boundaries can be thought of like a zipper, of sorts, that can be zipped/unzipped from the inside—associated with self-identity and self-respect. One needs a sense of control of their own person in order to establish intimacy in mature relationships.[15] The family will need to learn appropriate family roles—parents in parenting skills, and children as to what is appropriate for their particular age. Children need to be taught to be children, not the caretakers of their parents. By clarifying boundaries and correcting reversed roles, the family can learn to meet needs in appropriate ways. (See also chapter 15, personal boundaries.)

DEPENDENCY/EMOTIONAL NEEDINESS

Everyone has emotional needs that must be met to ensure personal growth and development. From infancy, each person learns to depend on some "source" to meet those needs. When emotional needs are not met in childhood, children can become adults with a sense of emotional deprivation and unmet dependency needs. In some cases, adults with this background will use pathological and destructive means, such as incest, to meet core needs for love, value, and belonging.

In *The Road Less Traveled*, Scott Peck describes hurtful dependencies:

> Passive dependency has its genesis in lack of love. The inner feeling of emptiness from which passive dependent people suffer is the direct result of their parents' failure to fulfill their children's needs for affection, attention and care during their childhood.[16]

Adults whose needs from childhood remain unmet often develop a pattern of *taking* from others rather than giving. Even though they may appear physically mature, they remain emotionally immature. It is not uncommon for passive dependent people to be addicted not only to people but to drugs and alcohol as well. "They are addicted to people, sucking on them and gobbling them up, and when people are not available to be sucked and gobbled, they often turn to the bottle, or the needle, or the pill as a people substitute."[17] In family incest, dependent family members may desperately try to meet core needs from sources that can never fulfill—food, work, overspending, alcohol, drugs, or sexual contact with children.

Treatment Goals for Dependency

In families with incest, family members must learn new ways to adequately meet emotional needs of others in the family in healthy ways. They can learn to show care and concern for one another and to give appropriate physical affection. Family members will need to develop individuality and an awareness of themselves as unique and valuable, apart from other family members.

Ultimately, the counselor can direct them to depend on God as the source for meeting their deep emotional needs for love and value. (See also chapter 11.)

FORGIVENESS AND RESTORATION

The concept of forgiveness is usually met with considerable resistance by families with incest. For example, an incest victim will often angrily challenge the validity of forgiveness. In Sara's case, she had been a victim of physical and sexual abuse by her father for ten years and was consumed with rage toward him. With clenched fists and reddened face, she shouted at her counselor: "Are you trying to tell me that I have to forgive my father?" As she continued venting her rage, an underlying issue emerged: "If I forgive my father that means what he did to me was okay."

Sara's reaction illustrates a prevalent and hurtful misconception about forgiveness—that it means somehow excusing the offender's behavior. Too often victims are told to "forgive and forget" and that if they have not forgotten the abuse, they have not truly forgiven. The purpose of forgiving is not to forget (that is, deny) that the abuse happened. Forgiveness interrupts the process of internally replaying lingering pain, which, if not relieved, has the effect of keeping the victim "captive" to the offender.

Another misconception is that forgiveness means family members should excuse the sexual behavior because the molester was "sick" or drunk or because a spouse didn't meet sexual needs. In truth, forgiving does not make excuses for wrongdoing. Individuals must be held accountable for the full extent of their behavior.

Another misconception is that forgiveness means family members should be "peacemakers" and not cause conflict by talking about the abuse. Some have reinforced this concept by using Ephesians 5:12: "For it is shameful even to mention what the disobedient do in secret." However, verses 11 and 13 exhort families to "expose deeds of darkness" so that "exposed by the light," they become "visible." True forgiveness occurs in the light of truth, not in the suppression of it.

Many times families are re-victimized by another misconception about forgiveness: If they "truly" forgive, they will "trust" one another implicitly. However, forgiveness is a process, and trust must be rebuilt after betrayal. In cases where family members have taken full responsibility to change their behavior, trusting might be an appropriate response. But in our experience *forgiveness* can be just a word that is exchanged without any accompanying evidence of personal responsibility to change.

For example, Sam consented to meet with his pastor after his wife discovered he was sexually abusing their six-year-old daughter.

After meeting with the pastor, Sam came home, asked his daughter for forgiveness, and told his wife everything had been dealt with. Sam's wife called the pastor to request further counseling for her and her daughter. Her pastor told her that Sam had repented and asked forgiveness, and she should now forgive him and trust him. Trusting Sam at this point led to his re-abuse of his daughter within six months.

Treatment Goals Toward Forgiveness

Family members will be unable to forgive that which has not been completely identified. It will be critical to the forgiving process that the family members not be allowed to minimize their pain or rationalize their behavior. To begin the forgiveness process, each family member will need to evaluate the impact of the incest on him or her personally. In addition to attention to effects on abuse victims, counselors must also be attentive to effects on non-abused siblings of victims.

Counselors can assist family members to separate reality from denial, which may surface in statements such as "It's not that bad" or "This really didn't happen." It is also necessary to assess multiple areas that need forgiveness, such as broken trust, emotional and/or physical trauma, humiliation, and shattered self-image. Family members need the safety of a trusted counselor to facilitate the process of expressing feelings openly and honestly to one another, especially anger and shame. Ephesians 4:25 encourages this: "Therefore each of you must put off falsehood and speak truthfully . . . for we are all members of one body." Putting off falsehood is more than telling the truth. It involves lowering defenses and slowly removing "layers" of protection so that relationships can develop. This is a monumental task for families who have never experienced a safe way to be close in relationships with one another. It is not uncommon for family members to rush into asking forgiveness, or express forgiveness to one another, before they have processed underlying pain. Premature expressions of forgiveness may be motivated by a desire to do the "right" thing, to please the pastor or counselor, or to have everything "over with" because the situation is so intensely painful for the entire family.

David Augsburger writes:

> Forgiveness, which is a complex and demanding process,
> is often reduced to a single act of accepting another. In spite of
> the pain, hurt, loss, and wrongdoing that stand between us,
> we are encouraged to forgive in a single act of resolving all by

giving unconditional inclusion. Such a step becomes too large for any human to take in a single bound. Forgiveness is a journey of many steps, each of which can be extremely difficult, all of which are to be taken carefully, thoughtfully, and with deep reflection.[18]

To facilitate forgiveness, each family member will benefit by individual counseling sessions to help identify feelings, perhaps even writing out those feelings. Family members will need to express themselves first to the counselor and then to one another. Counselors must advise family members that strong emotional feelings will be aroused, and they may experience a great deal of painful intensity, anger, and sadness. Each individual family member must be reassured that she or he should not be ashamed for experiencing intense feelings nor try to hold them in.

Counselors play a critical role in discerning the right timing for the family to come together to express their feelings about incest. Sharing with family members should come only when all family members have been strengthened enough to stand up against powerful individuals in the family and when counselors can intervene to assure that stronger members will not inflict further pain on vulnerable members. A great deal of time may be needed to facilitate the expression of honest feelings as part of the restoration from incest. Final outcomes in the process are decisions about forgiveness.

Most families will experience significant barriers to forgiveness, such as fear of change, some members wanting others to feel sorry for them, or wanting to be taken care of. Other barriers to forgiveness may be desire for revenge or fearing being hurt again. Counselors may find some family members to have an ability to forgive others but unable to forgive themselves or accept God's forgiveness. Barriers such as these should be expected, because most of these have been necessary survival skills in families of incest. Counselors will need to model God's grace and unconditional acceptance to encourage each family member to "put off" the old, negative behavior patterns "and to put on the new self, created to be like God in true righteousness and holiness" (Ephesians 4:22–24). (See also chapter 15.)

Prerequisites to Family Restoration

If families are to experience restoration from incest, several prerequisites must be in place to warrant safe reunification. Some preconditions for reuniting families would be:[19]

Victim

- Able to acknowledge and discuss the sexual abuse
- Does not blame self for abuse
- Willing to be united with entire family
- Confident about ability to report further abuse
- Feels safe/protected in the home if perpetrator is to be reunited with family

(See also chapter 2, "Indicators for Termination of Therapy.")

Offender

- Accepts full responsibility for the sexual abuse
- Shows empathy for the victim
- Shows not only remorse but repentance for the offense
- Willing to talk with victim about the abuse, making appropriate apologies
- Demonstrates self-awareness/understanding about underlying *motivations* for the abuse
- Resolves residual issues from his/her family-of-origin (such as own past abuse)

(See also chapter 6.)

Spouse

- Able to put victim's need for protection first
- Able to confront offender and express anger
- Able to discuss abuse openly
- Holds offender responsible for abuse
- Does not blame the victim

Family members as a family unit

- Are able to answer: *How did this happen to us?*
- Desire to be reunited
- Have completed family treatment
- Have openly discussed the sexual abuse together
- Have identified potentially risky situations and formulated a protection plan
- Are connected to others in a network of family support and are not isolated from others
- Have demonstrated healthy ways of interacting with one another and have made concrete changes in family dynamics

Understanding Sexual Abuse Offenders

6

Sexual Abuse Offenders: Brethren, This Ought Not to Be

Brad Smyth, a dentist, faithfully attends his church and belongs to a nationally known Christian evangelism and discipleship ministry. He appears to be a loving father of a close-knit family.

Those who think they know him, however, have not seen what God has seen inside the family. Behind closed doors, Brad fondles eleven-year-old Karen's breasts and forces her to "practice" kissing him. She feels very uncomfortable and afraid of what her father is doing, but he ignores her attempts to stop him. This week Brad became so forceful in his advances that he pushed Karen down onto her bed while she cried and screamed and tried to push him away. Four-year-old Brian stood by Karen's bed, hitting his father with his Teddy bear and sobbing, "Daddy, stop! Daddy, stop!"

CAN CHRISTIANS BE SEX OFFENDERS?

It is a grievous fact that child sexual abuse can be perpetrated by professing Christians. Christians have been hesitant to believe this as a reality. Some have insisted that the issue of sexual abuse should not be discussed because it *should not* and, therefore, *does not* happen among Christians. They may further believe that even to speak of it is wrong. Current news headlines about clergy abuse and abuse within the church is making this denial more difficult to maintain.

Those who are willing to face the fact that Christians are sometimes sex offenders may differ on how to address that reality. Some consider sex offenders to have spiritual problems that can only be dealt with through Scripture reading and prayer. Others view sex offenders as having psychological problems that can only be addressed through psychiatric interventions outside of the church. In our experience, however, Christians sometimes *do* commit sex offenses, and the restoration process for them includes both spiritual and psychological components.

SPIRITUAL INFLUENCES:
The World, the Flesh, and the Devil

Although Christians are not to be conformed "to the pattern of this world" (Romans 12:2), Christian therapist David Peters notes that "the world affects both Christians and non-Christians in a number of different ways. Entertainment, advertising, peer pressures, educational systems, and prevailing philosophies are only a few of the influences affecting the beliefs and behaviors of people."[1] External influences are often complicating factors of sexual abuse. Societal exposure to sexual stimuli is ever increasing, with "sex" reported to be the number one topic searched for on the Internet. Americans spend ten billion dollars a year on pornography, which is as much as they spend on sporting events, movies, or music.[2]

When this book was first published in 1989, many within the church found it difficult to comprehend how a Christian brother or sister could struggle with worldly influences such as pornography. However, in 1996, a Promise Keepers survey at one of their stadium events revealed that more than 50 percent of the men in attendance were involved with pornography within one week of the event. In 2003, a Focus on the Family poll reported that 47 percent of families said pornography was a problem in their home.[3] As well, a recent poll of *Today's Christian Woman* reported that 34 percent of female readers admitted to intentionally accessing Internet pornography.[4] Christians are definitely being influenced by the world around them.

In addition to *external* influences, Peters also notes that there are "*internal* influences which the flesh and lust have on human moral choices."[5] Christians are exhorted to make choices that reflect their identity in Christ: "Don't let anyone under pressure to give in to evil say, 'God is trying to trip me up.' God is impervious to evil, and puts evil in no one's way. The temptation to give in to evil comes from us and only us" (James 1:13–14 THE MESSAGE). If weaknesses of the flesh, accompanied by lust, are allowed to gain control of Christians, sexual abuse can be one destructive outcome.

Satan is described in Scripture as "the god of this world" (2 Corinthians 4:4 RSV). In the contemporary language of THE MESSAGE, Christians are advised to "Keep a cool head. Stay alert. The Devil is poised to pounce, and would like nothing better than to catch you napping. Keep your guard up" (1 Peter 5:8). Devastating spiritual forces are poised for the destruction of children and families; spiritual battles for the mind, will, and emotions can be influential in those who sexually offend children.

Spiritual influences must be considered as part of the context that affects sex offenders. That which is of darkness must be brought into the Light.

PSYCHOLOGICAL INFLUENCES

Perpetrators sexually offend children from many contexts and from different motivations. However, there are also some common themes among offenders. A high number of sex offenders were physically and/or sexually abused as children. As a result, they experience low self-esteem, deep feelings of inadequacy, a sense of alienation and isolation from others. Adults who were abused as children may try to "regain" power by victimizing others. High levels of anxiety and limited impulse control may contribute to sex offenders' abusing others. Offenders often have little insight into their own behavior and may be totally unaware of the needs of others. Rigid defense systems of denial and rationalization can function to the point that offenders do not perceive that what they are doing is wrong or that they are inflicting damage on a child.

Kevin's story illustrates some of these factors in the sexual abuse of his five-year-old cousin. Kevin was raised in a large family of ten children, made up of a blended family with parents who married each other after each had been divorced. He felt lost in the crowd of sisters and brothers, finding it hard to make friends outside the family. He was physically abused by older cousins and stepbrothers who resented the marriage. Even though he was unable to protect himself from older siblings, his stepfather belittled and demeaned him, calling him a "wimp" for not fighting back. When Kevin's stepfather told him it was time for him to "grow up and be a man," he initiated Kevin into "manhood" by forcing Kevin into mutual masturbation with him.

The stepfather's sexual violation began a cycle of compulsive masturbation in Kevin's life. At age thirteen, he became immersed in pornography and obsessed with his sexual needs. He felt disrespected by family members. He felt powerless to escape from his brothers and powerless to control his compulsive masturbation. He hated himself for both situations.

In the midst of Kevin's inner anguish, he was asked to baby-sit for his five-year-old cousin, Rhonda. She considered Kevin her big brother and enjoyed his special attention. He felt accepted and loved by her, and for the first time, he felt in control of a relationship. Because Rhonda trusted him, he was able to gain power over her and to manipulate her into doing whatever he asked of her. He enjoyed her willingness to do special favors for him.

Kevin's neediness, desire for control, and his preoccupation with his sexual desires triggered by the traumatic sexual introduction from his stepfather intersected with the vulnerability of his cousin. The stage was set for sexual abuse. In the exhilaration of the initial sexual contact, Kevin felt fulfilled as never before. Increasingly, he turned to the little girl to meet his isolated inner emptiness. He was blinded to the damage that he was causing in Rhonda's life, unwilling to admit that it was wrong. Instead, he deluded himself into thinking that sexual contact with his five-year-old cousin was just part of their special relationship.

While the context of Kevin's sex offenses contains common themes of sexual abuse, the inner motivations of those who sexually abuse children are varied and complex.

ADOLESCENT OFFENDERS

Kevin represents a large percentage of sex offenders who are male adolescents. An adolescent sex offender may be the "boy next door" in appearance. He is typically nice, quiet, a loner who keeps to himself. He is an average or above average student, often appreciated by teachers because of pleasing behavior. Adolescent male offenders are often isolated from peers, have a low self-esteem, and have experienced a history of abuse, often including sexual abuse. Because of his quiet demeanor, he is often asked to baby-sit for young children. His small charges usually become very fond of him and will participate in sexual activities for long periods of time before they would ever tell anyone. And if the children do tell, they may not be believed because the adolescent appears to be such a "nice kid."

In the past, teenagers who committed acts of sexual abuse were thought to be awkward explorers of their emerging sexuality. Abusive acts were dismissed as misguided sexual experimentation or developmental anomalies—the "boys will be boys" rationalization—by professionals interested in protecting adolescents from social stigmatization.

However, research suggests that adolescent offenders represent a serious social problem. Sexual assaults committed by youth are a growing concern. Currently, it is estimated that adolescents (ages 13 to 17) account for up to one-fifth of all rapes and one-half of all cases of child molestation committed each year.[6] Not only do adolescents commit a relatively large number of sexual crimes, but these often represent the early stages of a developing sexual deviance that can carry over into adult life.[7]

A study was conducted that revealed the trends of adolescent sex offenders who continued to offend well into their adult life:

> After securing a federal guarantee of immunity from prosecution for respondents, researchers interviewed over 350 sex offenders, many of whom had never been prosecuted. Over half had committed their first sexual crimes before they were 18. Child molesters who were attracted primarily to young boys had the earliest onset: 53% reported deviant arousal patterns by age 15, and 74% by age 19. Sex offenders who were adolescents when they began victimizing children had committed an average of 380 sexual crimes by the time they were interviewed as adults.[8]

Adolescents display many different motivations behind abusive behavior. The following are some general categories with brief summaries of treatment processes.[9]

The "Experimenter"

Some adolescent sex offenders are naïvely experimenting with their newly developing sexuality and commit a few isolated events of sexual exploration with young children, usually between the ages of two and six.[10] Experimenting offenders need appropriate sex education and teaching about their own sexuality. He or she needs to acknowledge responsibility for the sexual abuse and recognize its implications for his/her child victims. Families of these offenders generally need to develop more open communication about sexuality.

The "Loner"

The loner adolescent offender feels isolated from family and peers. He or she is usually raised in a hurtful, emotionally needy family and functions in more of a parental role than as a child. These offenders do not use force or threats, but rather manipulate child victims with enticements. They use sexual contact to meet needs for intimacy and self-esteem. The loner offender can benefit from individual/group counseling to build self-esteem, explore issues of sexuality, and take responsibility for the abuse. His or her family generally benefits from family counseling that targets role reversal, dependency issues, and assertive communication skills as goals.

The "Boy Next Door"

Some adolescent offenders are often a bit older, have good social skills, and are high achievers, with little or no history of "acting out" behavior. The boy-next-door type of offender was probably a victim of early childhood abuse or neglect, becoming needy and self-centered. He can be narcissistic, using children entirely for his sexual pleasure without regard to the damaging impact on child victims. Because this type of offender usually abuses over a longer period of time and appears to have little remorse or guilt, he is very likely to develop a lifelong pattern of sexually abusing children—if there is no intervention He may be poorly motivated to change, requiring long-term treatment to break through denial and rationalization. These offenders must take responsibility to stop hurting *others* if they are to demonstrate true repentance, rather than displaying only remorse about sexually offending because it caused consequences for *them.*

The "Aggressor"

Another type of adolescent offender uses aggression and/or violence to accompany his abuse.

> Troy, age 15, was a victim of severe physical abuse at the hands of his stepfather, his mother's third husband. The mother was passive and often suffered from physical beatings from her husband as well. Troy had a history of fire-setting, theft, vandalism and truancy over several years.
>
> Very social and flamboyant, he took a 14-year-old girl out on a date and when she refused to 'go all the way,' Troy slapped her and forced her to perform oral sex by threatening her with a screwdriver.
>
> Sexual aggressors are typically products of disorganized and abusive families. They have good peer age social skills and are often charming and gregarious. Typically having a

long history of anti-social behaviors and poor impulse control problems, they often fight with family members and friends and are likely to abuse chemicals. The sexual abuse typically involves the use of forced threats or violence. The victims can be peers, adults or children. Psychological testing usually reveals an anti-social and character-disordered teenager. The offender's motivation for abuse is the use of sex to experience personal power through domination, express anger, or humiliate his victim. In more extreme cases, there may actually be a learned sexual arousal to violence itself so that violence alone becomes sexually arousing and the expression of violence enhances the pleasure of a sex act.[11]

Due to living in poorly functioning families, it will be difficult for aggressive offenders to make significant and lasting changes in their behavior. Such families are likely to sabotage treatment goals because of the impact family counseling will have on their family system. Character-disordered adolescents most often require residential long-term treatment to learn appropriate ways to express anger, to work through their own abuse issues, and to take responsibility for abusing others. These offenders will not change unless they are truly able to repent of destructive behavior.

The "Group" Offender

Another type of adolescent may not sexually abuse alone, but might become involved in abuse as a result of pressure in a group situation, especially if the leader of the group was one of the previously described types of sex offenders. In the case of a group sex offense, each of the offenders must be held individually accountable for their actions rather than allowed to blame others for their involvement. In counseling, individual offenders will need to look at areas causing vulnerability to peer pressure and at ways to reduce that vulnerability to outside influence. This offender will need to address issues of self-esteem, as well as issues of passivity with peers and aggressiveness toward others.

Adolescent Female Offenders

Just as child victims can be male or female, adolescent sex offenders can be male or female. For example, one mother observed her three-year-old son lying on top of her eighteen-month-old daughter. When she asked her son what he was doing, he replied, "I'm making honey like the baby-sitter does." The parents were able to piece together the events to realize that the thirteen-year-old female baby-sitter had been sexually abusing their son and calling it the "making honey" game.

While limited information is available about adolescent female sex offenders, the National Center on Sexual Behavior of Youth reports that the average age of the adolescent female offender is fourteen, with a typical child victim around the age of five. Child victims seem to be equally male and female and are most often relatives or close acquaintances.[12] The most common type of female sexual offenses are non-aggressive acts, such as mutual fondling, occurring during caregiving, although more aggressive acts are occasionally reported.[13] On average, adolescent female sex offenders have experienced more severe, long-term physical and sexual abuse than adolescent male sex offenders and are more likely to have been sexually victimized at young ages by multiple perpetrators.[14] Some female adolescents offend once or twice and then stop because they have a tendency to think more about how their victim feels or what others would think of them if the abuse was made known.

In the authors' experience, it is not an uncommon occurrence for adult survivors who are in a support group for victims of sexual abuse to disclose that they have sexually victimized a young child during their adolescence. On such occasions, when an adult survivor of abuse reveals that she herself has abused a child, she will most often need to work through issues in overcoming shame for committing a crime for which she feels there is no forgiveness either from God or from others. As part of the process of her recovery, she will also need to take full responsibility for the abuse and its effects on the child victim.

ADULT FIXATED OFFENDERS

Adult fixated offenders are defined as pedophiles. A pedophile is a man, or occasionally a woman, who receives emotional, psychological, and sexual gratification from children. "Almost half of fixated offenders were victims of child sexual abuse, usually victimized by a non-family member in a violent manner. And from this, the message begins: 'The world is a cruel and demanding place, void of love from adults.' "[15] Whether the offender was sexually abused as a child or not, his family system was poorly functioning, leaving him with feelings of sadness, loneliness, and emptiness, which he tries to fill with his involvement with children. He may even believe that by being a "special friend" to his victim, he is giving the child something he never had as a child.

To understand male pedophiles, it is necessary to look at the abuse from their perspective. This adult male is threatened by adult relationships, which he perceives to be very demanding. Thus, he chooses relationships with children—who make very few demands on him—in order to derive as much care and nurturing for himself as possible. From his perspective, the more the child is sexually involved with him, the more he feels the child is committed to the relationship and, therefore, the more the child "loves" him. From the distorted perspective of the pedophile, he sees the child as his equal or, perhaps even more often, as more powerful in the relationship. He intensely fears rejection and often will try to keep the child in the relationship by pleasing the child and giving the child anything he or she wants.

Many times a pedophile offender is emotionally immature and irresponsible to the point that he will do anything to coerce the child into remaining in the relationship. He even rationalizes that because of his "love" for the child, he is powerless to control his own behavior. For example, a thirty-one-year-old offender says: "I really loved this kid—not just for his body—but really just for him. He told me to get the money for the mini-bike, or he'd leave me. So I stole to get it. What else could I do?"[16]

"Sometimes he molests a child only once . . . as did an otherwise exemplary Boy Scout leader who molested one of his charges on an overnight camping trip. More often, however, the pedophile seeks a long-term, loving relationship with a child . . . as in the case of the single adult male who adopted a youngster and subsequently molested him over a period of years."[17]

Pedophiles may be single or in a marriage of convenience, as was Jim's stepfather in chapter 1. The majority of fixated offenders are over eighteen,[18] and almost all pedophiles tend to be passive, lonely men. "Only about 1% are sadists who cruelly assault their victims through rape and torture."[19] There is usually no history of addiction to alcohol or drugs; they are instead addicted to sexual behavior with children. "Some incestuous fathers engage in extrafamilial pedophilic acts. In these cases, the fathers are classified as pedophiles because their primary orientation appears to be toward children in general and not just toward their own offspring."[20] Fixated offenders usually have immature social skills, tending to avoid relationships with adults and, instead, seeking out children to meet social and sexual needs.

Almost half of all pedophiles use their occupation as an access route to child victims. Adult pedophiles who have an authority position in the lives of children are often able to survey a child's family history to assess that child's vulnerability to his advances. A pedophile may be in such authority positions as teacher, city health officer, school bus driver, Sunday school teacher, camp counselor, or scout leader.

Sometimes the pedophile's status in the neighborhood helps to legitimize his interaction with children and their parents and fosters unquestioned exchange of young people in and out of his home. Pedophiles are often well-liked by many of their neighbors. Pedophiles usually befriend and interact closely with only those neighbors who have children of a preferred sex and age. In some cases, a pedophile may be willing to develop a friendship for years while waiting for a neighbor's child to reach the age preference of the pedophile.

The fixated offender can show incredible patience in his premeditation of the crime as he waits to be accepted as "one of the guys." States a 28-year-old offender:

> I got busted for molesting these boys on my baseball team.
> But it wasn't like I was exploiting them; I'd worked with those
> kids for a full year on nothing but their batting and fielding
> before I ever molested them. It took me that long before they
> trusted me and stopped treating me like a tough adult coach.[21]

Pedophiles exploit children in various ways to persuade them to participate in sexual acts. A primary method of exploitation is through enticement, as offenders attempt to seduce children through persuasion, as Jim's father did when he took Jim on camping trips—doing special things with him to earn his favor. Other enticements might be bribes and rewards such as money, gifts, treats, good times, and/or affection. Receiving such rewards obligates children to the offender, setting children up for the next steps of exploitation. Offenders then entrap children by taking advantage of their feelings of manipulated obligation. Once children have been victimized, pedophile offenders may use threats or coercion to maintain control.

REGRESSED ADULT OFFENDERS

Regressed adult offenders tend to have sexual contact with children in circumstances of extreme stress in their lives. Prior to the specific stressor, sexual interest and social activities were focused on same-age relationships. Regressed offenders can be drawn to children in attempts to replace losses of adult relationships that were meaningful or to compensate for another significant loss in life. Losses might involve a deteriorating marriage, illness or death of a spouse, a spouse working odd hours or being away from home. Aging can be a stressor that precipitates sexual abuse. An elderly offender might be reacting to the loss of sexual function, retirement, or death of a spouse and/or friends.

A case of financial loss was a major stressor that occurred in the life of John Jones, an elder in his church. He began sexually abusing his adolescent male foster children in the context of a crushing business failure. A bankruptcy crisis occurred and he felt hopelessly inadequate—a failure as a provider for his family. Most of all, he harbored high levels of suppressed anger because he felt he had little control over the situation. When his wife expressed her frustration and anger at their situation, John's feelings of failure and inadequacy were compounded. He sexually abused his foster sons as an outlet for his anger and despair.

Regressed offenders are usually married or in a common-law, live-in situation. Female victims are primary targets, and sexual contact with a child coexists with sexual contact with adults. In some instances, sexual offenses occur when offenders are using alcohol. Alcohol use may increase the likelihood that someone already predisposed to sexually abuse a child will act on their impulses, but alcohol use is not the "cause" of the abuse.[22] A first episode of sexual contact is often an impulsive act. Unlike pedophiles, initial sexual acts by regressed offenders are not usually premeditated.

Most regressed offenders are involved in incest. In the *Handbook of Clinical Intervention in Child Sexual Abuse,* Susanne Sgroi reports that her clinical experience has revealed "that in fact the majority—an estimated 90%—of incest offenders fall into this category."[23] Sgroi notes that fathers committing incest often feel inadequate and unsure of themselves in handling adult stresses of marriage and parenthood, which can influence them to respond in one of two ways.

On the one hand, fathers may adopt a passive-dependent withdrawal from their roles in families and, like a child, expect others to take care of them and meet their needs. In this scenario, an incest relationship becomes a substitute for a marriage relationship. On the other hand, fathers may become over-controlling and rigid authoritarians to prove that they are "in charge." In this scenario, an incest relationship provides a means of exerting control and bolstering feelings of adequacy.

"For both types of offenders, the passive-dependent-submissive type and the aggressive-controlling-dominant type, the incest behavior is a precarious and unsuccessful attempt to compensate for or replace a feeling of loss or deprivation."[24] (See also chapter 5.)

TREATMENT GOALS FOR ADULT OFFENDERS

In considering treatment for adult sex offenders, discernment is crucial to determine which offenders are amenable to treatment and what type of treatment might be most effective. The following treatment goals provide but a brief summary of issues that must be addressed with sexual abuse offenders. These guidelines are meant to be used for evaluation and to assist churches and counselors in making appropriate referrals.

Clinical evaluation of offenders must address the risk of repeat offenses, whether offenders pose threats to victims, whether offenders are receptive to treatment, and whether in- or out-patient treatment is most appropriate. The counselor will need to assess the offender's personality functioning, communication skills, ability to think rationally, and ability to respond appropriately and adapt to stressors. Offenders must be willing to take full responsibility for offenses, admit wrongdoing, be concerned about damage the abuse has caused the victim, and be truly repentant for what has been done.

Poor prognosis for recovery is anticipated with offenders whose personalities are characterized by lifelong ingrained maladaptive behavior. Certain offenders seem to lack an ability to learn from past experiences or punishments/consequences. Although appearing outwardly charming, certain offenders are masterful at manipulating others and using them for sexual purposes. These offenders incorporate defense mechanisms of shifting blame to others, denying their own actions and how those actions have affected others, and rationalizing why they committed sexual offenses.

If an offender displays the following characteristics or behaviors, the most suitable treatment response may be in-patient programs that are found in psychiatric hospitals and prisons:

Psychological Patterns	*Behavioral Patterns*
1. Absence of guilt or remorse	1. Using violence

2. Low tolerance for frustration
3. Inability to tolerate criticism/confrontation
4. Chronic sexual fixation on children, especially young boys
5. Inability to be empathetic

2. Using sadistic brutality
3. Record of sexual offenses
4. Sexually addictive behavior, especially sexual deviancy beginning in adolescence

Offenders who are not exhibiting these characteristics may be appropriate for a community-based, outpatient program. Even though offenders may be appropriate for treatment, they may refuse to attend unless court-ordered to do so. An offender's sexual offense is not only a symptom of spiritual deficits and psychological dysfunction, his sexual offenses are also a crime and must be dealt with on multiple levels. Churches need to know how to work in conjunction with social service intervention as well as the criminal justice system.

Traditionally, churches have desired to handle problems within church families in the privacy of congregational settings rather than under civil authorities. However, in the circumstance of sexual abuse, sex offenders have broken civil law in addition to violating God's moral laws. Thus, Scripture advises that civil crimes be referred to civil authorities:

> Everyone must submit himself to the governing authorities, for there is no authority except that which God has established. The authorities that exist have been established by God. Consequently, he who rebels against the authority is rebelling against what God has instituted, and those who do so will bring judgment on themselves. . . . Therefore, it is necessary to submit to the authorities, not only because of possible punishment but also because of conscience. (Romans 13:1–2, 5)

It is a sad and difficult obligation to have to report Christians who have committed sex offenses to civil authorities. However, God is ultimately in control over those civil authorities because he has ordained them. To maintain a clear conscience before God, churches must trust that even though reporting seems to create greater difficulties for offenders, victims, and the families involved, the fact remains that, ultimately, reporting offenses provides significant opportunities for intervention and restoration. (See Suggested Resources for assistance.)

In the past, Christians did not want to report abuse because they wanted to "protect" those involved from facing shame through exposure within the church and community. However, as is apparent in contemporary society, sometimes a lack of reporting has been motivated to "protect" churches from exposure of wrongdoing by not confronting abuse of which the church was aware. Pastors and priests have been transferred from one church position to another while those in authority over them "ignored" or "overlooked" abuse allegations and did not investigate or report sex offenses. This has caused great anguish and pain in the lives of many children who have been abused by trusted persons in their churches.

Additionally, by not reporting abuse, Christians demonstrate a lack of trust in God's ability to work all things out "for the good of those who love Him" (Romans 8:28) and those who look to him for help.

For example, in the case of Mark and Mary Hanson, reporting the abuse of their three-year-old daughter proved to be a situation that resulted in positive outcomes. The Hansons' twelve-year-old neighbor boy, Jeff, had taken a particular interest in their daughter, Lisa.

One night, after Jeff had been baby-sitting, Mary found the guest room bed unmade and she questioned her children about it. Lisa told her mother that Jeff had told her older brothers to go watch TV while Jeff took Lisa into the guest bedroom to play "where babies come from." Further questioning revealed that Jeff had removed Lisa's clothes and fondled her, under the pretense of teaching her this new "game."

Mark was appalled when he first heard about the abuse. He had befriended Jeff and felt betrayed. Mark's pastor counseled him to report the abuse to child protection services, but Mark refused. He knew Jeff's father was physically abusive to Jeff. Mark feared further retribution for both himself and Jeff if he disclosed the abuse. The Hansons got into a family argument about whether or not to report the abuse. Mary wanted to call the authorities right away. Mark accused Mary of overreacting, arguing that Jeff was only twelve and was just going through some adolescent experimentation. Mark had been sharing his faith with Jeff and felt that if he reported the abuse, it would damage their relationship.

Mark's pastor reassured him that reporting the abuse and getting Jeff some help was the way to show real care for Jeff. Reluctantly, Mark called child protection and reported the abuse. After talking with Lisa, a protection worker confronted both Jeff and his parents about the seriousness of the abuse. The Hansons then took the opportunity to meet with Jeff and his parents at their home. The Hansons told Jeff he would no longer be allowed to baby-sit their daughter, that he needed to tell their daughter that he had been wrong to play that "game," that he was sorry about what he had done, and that it would not happen again.

Even though the Hansons felt tremendous anger and betrayal due to the incident, and they were appropriately protective of Jeff's further contact with their daughter, they still desired to show care to Jeff. Mr. Hanson took Jeff out fishing, as he had promised he would before he had learned about the abuse. Once the abuse was reported, Jeff's family was required to receive counseling. Mr. and Mrs. Hanson, along with Lisa, also sought out a counselor who specialized in abuse counseling.

Because of the pastor's faithfulness in educating his congregation about issues related to sexual abuse, the Hansons were equipped with some basic skills in handling this crisis. They were also aware of the distinction between confronting Jeff's wrong behavior and yet ministering to Jeff as a needy young boy. In this actual case, the outcomes were positive. However, while the Hanson case is shared as an encouragement to follow through in the reporting process, not every case will bear such favorable results.

Treatment Programs for Sex Offenders

Sometimes Christians are concerned about the advisability of utilizing sex offender treatment programs provided outside of the church. In spite of valid conflicts with some treatment philosophies, in the absence of a Christian alternative, offenders can benefit from a professional community program with the assistance of a knowledgeable and equipped support system within the church to supplement the treatment program where it lacks appropriate spiritual dimensions. One program in the Midwest[25] contains components in the treatment of adolescent sex offenders that are amenable to Christian principles. The program requires that the offender take full responsibility for the abuse by writing a letter to the victim stating:

1. I am sorry.
2. It was not your fault; it was mine.

3. It won't happen again.
4. I'm getting help now.
5. Thank you for telling.

This letter is not written until the offender is being truthful about taking responsibility for the abuse, and is often accompanied by the offender paying for counseling for the victim. This is a philosophy of confession and making restitution that is compatible with Christian faith.

Sex offender therapy needs to occur within a treatment program that is knowledgeable and specialized in dealing with sex offenders. Most often, an offender will not seek help voluntarily and will not often reveal the full extent of his secretive activities. Many will pretend to cooperate in order to enlist pastors or counselors as their protectors. Christian therapist David Peters has many years of experience in dealing with sexual abuse. He advises that "the average family counselor is not prepared to deal with child molesters."[26]

A case in point involved a father who was sexually abusing his four-year-old daughter. The mother found out and went to her pastor for counseling. The pastor called the family in for counseling, where the father asked the young child for her forgiveness while in the pastor's office. Even though the child's mother felt relieved that this was her husband's response, there remained many unresolved conflicts within her about the abuse. How had this ever happened? What did she do to cause it? Why did her daughter keep silent for so long? How could she trust her husband again? Had this damaged her daughter? What had changed to prevent reoccurrence if she were not at home?

She called the pastor once again for some follow-up counseling for herself and for a referral for her daughter. Her pastor informed her that it had been taken care of, that her husband had repented, and that her responsibility now was to forgive and forget because it was in the past. It was only a matter of months until the abuse resumed. This time, however, the child kept the secret.

Again, David Peters cautions pastors and Christian counselors:

> First of all, it is extremely important to the victim of sexual abuse that counselors be aware of the danger of re-molestation after sexual abuse is discovered. To accept the assurances of a molester or non-offending parent that sexual abuse will not continue is to place the victim in danger of further abuse. It should never be assumed that the molester is able to control

his sexual feelings toward the victim or the victim's siblings, no matter how socially or emotionally stable he may appear.[27]

It is essential that offenders initially be involved in individual counseling and group counseling with a peer group of sex offenders before they are permitted into family counseling situations. An offender must be ready to take full responsibility for the abuse as well as understand the fullness of its impact on the victim and the victim's family. (See also chapter 5.)

BARRIERS TO TREATMENT SUCCESS

Several treatment issues need to be addressed in individual therapy and group therapy. Offenders are likely to minimize their offenses, withhold inner feelings, experience shame and guilt, and misuse power. Brief summaries highlight some of the challenges of sex offender treatment.

Minimizing Offenses

Because offenders are fearful of legal and social ramifications if complete truth is disclosed, they will have a tendency to minimize or deny the offense. Offenders must not be allowed to blame others or minimize the seriousness of their behavior. From the case history at the beginning of the chapter, Brad Smyth was confronted by his wife about sexually abusing their daughter. He greatly minimized his responsibility for the abuse. He told his daughter that if she did "her part," and he did "his part," the abuse would not happen again. In other words, he placed much of the responsibility for preventing further abuse on his eleven-year-old daughter. He then told his wife that he had "taken care of things" and instructed her not to bring it up again. When the abuse recurred, Brad's daughter assumed she had failed to do "her part" to prevent it, and she took responsibility for it, while her father remained an unrepentant perpetrator.

Withholding Honest Feelings

Offenders need to learn basic communication skills so that they are able to share feelings related to the abuse. However, more than communication skills are needed. Unless there is a willingness to honestly identify feelings—anger, fear, loneliness, sadness, loss, inadequacy—there can be little progress in therapy. Most offenders are not going to be vulnerable enough to share feelings honestly with anyone, and will need a great deal of encouragement to see any benefit in doing so.

Experiencing Shame

An ability to overcome internalized shame is crucial to recovery. Offenders need to look in detail at family system interactions, identify shaming messages about personal value, consider sexual messages, resolve issues of physical and/or sexual abuse, and examine personal, emotional, and sexual development. Completing a sexual history will assist offenders in taking into account additional impact of parental sexual behavior, any inappropriate sexual acting-out of siblings, or possibly the previous sexual victimization of their spouse. (See also chapter 10 for dynamics of shame.)

Experiencing Guilt

Resolving some of the shame related to core issues may enable an offender to begin to deal with appropriate guilt resulting from abusing a child. Saying "I'm sorry" is not the same as asking forgiveness, just as remorse for being "caught" is not the same as repentance. True repentance for an offender involves viewing his actions through the eyes of his victim, and having some sense of the pain he has inflicted on a child victim. When an offender can begin to experience some degree of pain that he has inflicted on a vulnerable child, and can take full responsibility for causing it, he is ready to confess his sin to his victim. When asking forgiveness, the offender does not merely apologize, as if the offense was something trivial, nor does he simply admit that he did something wrong. True repentance invites an offender to tell his victim that he hurts with the pain he has caused her or him and that he realizes what he did was intolerable and inexcusable. In a context of brokenness and humility, an offender experiences true repentance and allows the victim the freedom to make an honest response to his request for forgiveness. Requesting forgiveness may be in the form of a letter if circumstances do not warrant a face-to-face encounter with the victim. (See also chapter 14.)

It may take a great deal of time before an abuse victim is enabled to forgive an offender. Regardless of a victim's response, an offender is held accountable before God for his actions. An offender must come before God with a broken spirit and a contrite heart and ask him to cleanse him from his sin, and create a clean heart and a right spirit within him, as David did in Psalm 51.

After Kevin's sexual abuse of his cousin, Rhonda, Kevin entered counseling in his mid-twenties for depression and issues related to shame. Kevin was able to resolve some of his personal shame from his own abuse and poorly functioning family system, and through experiencing God's grace modeled by his therapist, he began to be able to accept his worth in God's sight. In that context, he was enabled to respond to the guilt from his abuse of his cousin. He experienced a truly broken spirit and contrite heart over what he had done. After asking God to cleanse and forgive him, he went to Rhonda's mother and father and told them about the abuse, taking full responsibility for it. In brokenness, he asked them and Rhonda for forgiveness, and made restitution, in part, by paying for counseling for his cousin and her family. The scars from the deep pain Kevin experienced over what he had done are slowly healing, as his true repentance has borne the fruit of forgiveness from his cousin and her family.

Misusing Power

Offenders have been operating from a position of power over less-powerful child victims, and they will attempt to manipulate therapy sessions to remain in a position of power. This manipulative and controlling behavior needs to be confronted not only in individual therapy, but an offender must also be held accountable by a group of his peers in a therapy group for sex offenders, as well as by his victim, by his family, and by his church.

Sexual Addiction

Many are becoming aware of the idea that sex can be considered an "addiction." *Addiction* is a term used to describe any kind of self-destructive behavior that one is unable to stop in spite of predictable and known adverse consequences.[28] For some sex offenders, sexual abuse fits that description. Abuse of children can involve frequent high-risk activity that is not emotionally fulfilling, that one is ashamed of, and that one is not able to stop even though it may be causing repeated problems in a marriage, social relationships, or with the law.[29] Sexually addicted offenders use sexual contact as a quick fix or as a form of medication for stress, anxiety, pain, or loneliness. Most who struggle with addictive sexual behaviors have feelings of shame and unworthiness that interfere with a sense of true intimacy; they are certain they would be rejected if others knew what they are "really" like.

It is imperative for the offender who is involved in an addictive cycle of sexual behavior to learn ways to cope with the everyday stress of life situations. Because those involved in addictive cycles feel like "victims" themselves, and feel inadequate to meet the demands that life makes of them, they may turn to a mood-altering sexual experience as a dysfunctional coping skill. An addictive cycle, as defined by Dr. Patrick Carnes in his book *Out of the Shadows: Understanding Sexual Addiction,* progresses through a four-step cycle that intensifies with each repetition:

1. Preoccupation—the mood wherein the addicts' minds are completely engrossed with thoughts of sex. This mental state creates an obsessive search for sexual stimulation.
2. Ritualization—the addicts' own special routines that lead up to the sexual behavior. The ritual intensifies the preoccupation, adding arousal and excitement.
3. Compulsive sexual behavior—the actual sexual act, which is the end goal of the preoccupation and ritualization. Sexual addicts are unable to control or stop this behavior.
4. Despair—the feelings of utter hopelessness addicts have about their behavior and their powerlessness.[30]

The despairing hopelessness that a person feels after acting out sexually can be "medicated," masked, or numbed by beginning the preoccupation stage. As the first stage proceeds to the next, the cycle is activated once again. Dr. Carnes describes the despair of this cycle: "Sexual addicts are hostages of their own preoccupation."[31] This is especially true of the fixated type of offender who is snared in sexually addictive behaviors.

James 1:14–15 clearly addresses the addictive cycle:

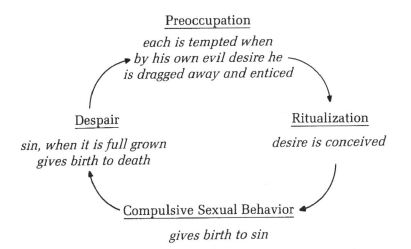

Preoccupation

*each is tempted when
by his own evil desire he
is dragged away and enticed*

Despair

*sin, when it is full grown
gives birth to death*

Ritualization

desire is conceived

Compulsive Sexual Behavior

gives birth to sin

Sexual addiction is a complex issue, beyond the scope of this book. See endnote for additional resources.[32]

FEMALE OFFENDERS

Although the majority of sex offenses are committed by men, women are also offenders. Statistics on female sex offenders are extremely difficult to compile, and estimates vary widely. The Center for Sex Offender Management reported in 2000, "Studies indicate that females commit approximately 20 percent of sexual offenses against children."[33] Whether any estimates can be truly accurate, female offenders are among the least reported cases, possibly because of their maternal caretaking roles. Their behaviors may not be perceived as sexual or abusive because female offenders may disguise the sexual acts as normal caretaking tasks. Also, females in maternal roles are not perceived by child victims as sexual persons. Therefore, children do not have information that relates in any way to a sexual experience with a mother or mother figure. If a child protests or questions behaviors, female offenders may accuse the child of having a "dirty mind." Since female offenders are often mothers or the only parent figure giving love and care to a child, the child may continue to maintain the secret to keep the love of the parent.

A female offender often has extreme dependency needs, may be a single parent or have an emotionally or physically absent husband, and tends to be extremely possessive and overprotective toward a child victim. Some adult female offenders with deep dependency needs may also use alcohol, which tends to break down the barriers that would normally inhibit them from being sexual with children.

In *Betrayal of Innocence: Incest and Its Devastation*, therapist Susan Forward quotes a letter from a fifty-eight-year-old adult survivor of sexual abuse by her mother:

> My mother was a teacher and a steady churchgoer. She did the fooling around when she bathed me. I never knew there was anything unusual about her behavior until my father walked in on us and made a terrific scene. (I was twelve years old at the time—much too old to be bathed by my mother.)
>
> She never touched me after that, but the damage she had done was considerable. When I married I had a hard time enjoying sex—and still do. I was afraid to bathe my four daughters and had to force myself to do it. Even now I have trouble diapering my granddaughter.
>
> There must be others like me—grown women who still bear the marks of early abuse and have never told a soul. What a relief it has been to write this letter.[34]

Mother-Daughter Incest Offender

The mother-daughter incest offender is not primarily looking for sexual gratification, but rather emotional nurture from physical closeness and a sense of being loved. A common history of this type of offender often reveals a childhood of physical or sexual abuse or emotional neglect and isolation. Never having received affection, she is unable to express appropriate care. A child victim often remains in the abuse situation for long periods of time, sensing the extreme neediness of the mother and feeling responsible to meet those deep needs. Intense conflict usually occurs as child victims mature and try to disengage from the mother, while at the same time, the developing child feels guilty for wanting to separate.

Andrea was four years old when her father died, leaving her mother and the three children destitute. The family moved to a small two-bedroom house where Andrea was designated to sleep with her mother. Not long after these sleeping arrangements were in place, the mother began to fondle Andrea during the night.

Andrea was frozen with confusion and shame and pretended to be asleep, even though her mother sometimes took Andrea's hand and forced her to fondle her mother. No words were ever spoken at night before or after the abuse. Being extremely emotionally needy and unable to give nurture to her daughter, Andrea's mother was cold and distant during the daytime. Once, when Andrea reached up to her mother for a hug during the afternoon, her mother whirled around and slapped her face. From her warped perspective of parental discipline, the mother would lock the children in a coal bin for punishment, often for hours at a time. Because of the isolation of the family and intensely conflicting feelings that kept the children from telling, there was no intervention in the mother's abuse, and all three of her children grew up to be deeply scarred from her disturbed behavior.

Mother-Son Incest Offender

In cases of mother-son incest, a female offender places a male victim in an adult male role where he feels responsible to meet her emotional and sexual needs. A male victim "is torn between guilt, desire, love and hate. He loves his mother, yet he hates her for the guilt she has created in him by allowing the role transformation to take place."[35] Male victims can feel responsible for the abuse, especially if there is no element of force used. Often the sexual abuse takes place in a pseudo-nurturing circumstance. The great travesty of this type of sexual abuse is the premature arousal and exploitation of male victims that cause extreme guilt and shame over participation in sexual acts. Even when sexual actions are covert, the damage is often the same. One middle-aged man, struggling with sexually addictive behavior, shared about tremendous conflicts arising from being a sixteen-year-old boy required to sleep with his mother. His mother said she couldn't "sleep comfortably" since her husband had left her unless her son slept in her bed, with his back toward her, allowing her to press her body against him.

Treatment Goals for Female Offenders

The limited amount of research on female offenders indicates that mother-child offenders can be extremely disturbed or even psychotic. In that case, the only appropriate treatment would be inpatient psychiatric hospital programs.

If female offenders are amenable to treatment, in addition to the issues listed above for male offenders, they need to look specifically at dependency issues and learn how to appropriately meet emotional needs. Female offenders will also need to learn appropriate nurturing and parenting roles with children, such as not allowing children to sleep with them and not bathing preadolescent children. Learning appropriate boundaries and correcting the role reversals in the family will be crucial in helping to develop healthy relationships with their children.

A Christian Treatment Program for Male Offenders

A Christian sex offender treatment program has been developed since the first edition of this book, and is highlighted here by Dr. Jeanette Vought:

A program called RESTORATION PROJECT is a highly successful, long-term, outpatient treatment program for men who have sexually offended children.[36] It was started at the Christian Recovery Center, Brooklyn Center, Minnesota, in 1994 as a pilot program, was restructured, and has been in full operation since September 1995. The name RESTORATION PROJECT conveys the dynamic nature of this program, being a major project of considerable time and energy that is deeply involved and invested in restoring the lives of men and families shattered by the sin of sexual abuse. We believe that the spiritual work of Christ is essential to completely restore a person or family and that God blesses restorative justice. The prophet Joel (2:25) gives this word from the Lord: "I will restore to you the years that the locust hath eaten" (KJV).

The program is designed to allow the client to follow two "tracks" throughout the treatment process. Track One outlines the psycho-therapeutic elements of the program and contains therapeutic goals and methods. Track One highlights psycho-sexual development and explores the evolution of personal factors leading up to and including the choice to sexually offend. Track Two contains twelve psycho-social sexual educational components, which are designed to further educate and explore psycho-sexual development and teach pro-social life skills. The client learns to recognize the addictive cycle of sexual abuse, inappropriate and appropriate methods of coping with stress, true intimacy versus sex, how to identify and get needs met, and how to develop trusting coequal relationships.

A Christ-centered philosophy is woven throughout both tracks. Those who profess a relationship with God are challenged and encouraged to apply their faith in God to receive the strength and courage needed to face their social and moral deficits that contributed to their choice to sexually offend. Members are encouraged to pray for each other and to request help through prayer when facing difficult issues or life situations. Verbalized prayer appears to break down barriers, reduce isolation and secrecy, and help members develop trusting coequal relationships with others in the group. (See also chapter 17.)

Helping Adult Survivors of Sexual Abuse

7

BECOMERS: An Introduction

This section is designed to equip others to facilitate a healing process for adult survivors of childhood sexual abuse. The following chapters include the history of the development of the BECOMERS sexual abuse support group and the nine steps used in the BECOMERS recovery program. Specific material and homework that are included are meant to be modified as needed to be useful for others who work with groups of adult survivors.

BECOMERS HISTORY

Lynn Heitritter relates the following account of how the vision for a recovery program for adult abuse survivors was planted in her heart and has grown into a ministry spanning over twenty years:

> A few years prior to founding the BECOMERS program, my husband and I were called to care for our first sexually abused foster daughter. Out of this personal experience came a next step—writing a prevention education workbook for parents to use in protecting their children from sexual abuse. The workbook led to speaking and lecturing to groups of parents that put me in contexts where adults who had been victimized would approach me with stories of their sexual abuse—sometimes speaking about their abuse for the first time. In the light of great need, and in the absence of any ministry to abused adults, the vision for BECOMERS was birthed in my heart.
>
> During 1983–84, I felt personally called to the task of

creating the BECOMERS sexual abuse support group program.
Many were extremely influential in the early days of the ministry, in particular my coauthor, Jeanette Vought, and the first
BECOMERS co-facilitator, Julie Woodley. Over the years, both
of these dedicated women have gone on to found their own
ministries and have also followed their personal calling to
minister to those who are hurting. At this revision of *Helping
Victims of Sexual Abuse*, further reflections on ministry to
adult survivors of sexual abuse are found in "Second
Thoughts," chapter 17.

Jeanette Vought is the founder and executive director of the
Christian Recovery Center. Jeanette says:

> Because of some trauma in my own childhood experiences,
> I had a deep desire to help children and families. At first, this
> desire was realized in helping adolescents within the church.
> As I furthered my education, I became interested in working
> with female adolescents in residential treatment programs;
> many adolescents in treatment programs have been sexual
> abuse victims. Out of concern for those victims, another thera-
> pist and I began conducting sexual abuse groups.
>
> I continued working with female sexual abuse victims for
> eight years. In 1981, I began working with New Life Family
> Services. My experiences in working with children and ado-
> lescents through foster care, in a group home, and with
> women in crisis pregnancies again revealed many victims of
> sexual abuse. When Lynn contacted me for consultation and
> shared her ideas with me, I told her that I had the same per-
> spective. God had given both of us a vision for ministry to vic-
> tims of sexual abuse, and he had brought us together. My role
> was to give consultation to Lynn as she created, implemented,
> and directed the BECOMERS program.
>
> In 1993, God gave me a ministry vision to dedicate my
> time and energy solely to founding a center specializing in the
> areas of emotional, physical, and sexual abuse recovery. This
> ministry vision has resulted in establishing the Christian
> Recovery Center. The focus of the center is on recovery issues
> for men, women, and children in both individual and group
> settings. In addition to local ministry, the Christian Recovery
> Center is committed to providing consultation services, train-
> ing workshops and resources, and to the development of
> abuse recovery groups across the country.

THE BECOMERS PHILOSOPHY

BECOMERS is a support group designed to promote emotional and spiritual restoration from the experience of childhood sexual abuse. BECOMERS takes its name from 1 John 3:2: "Here and now we are God's children. We don't know what we shall *become* in the future. We only know that, if reality were to break through, we should reflect His likeness, for we should see Him as He really is" (PHILLIPS TRANSLATION, italics added).

This verse offers hope of restoration after the destruction of sexual abuse. Many adult survivors of abuse are unable to experience God in their recovery journey because their image of God has been damaged by abuse. This verse reassures abused adults that experiencing God's grace will reflect God to them "as he really is." And further, that they may be enabled to reflect "his likeness" in grace to others because the reality of God's love has broken through.

THE OBJECTIVES OF BECOMERS

One of the most important objectives of sexual abuse support groups is to *provide a safe and accepting atmosphere* in which group members can reduce their sense of isolation and share feelings related to their childhood sexual abuse. BECOMERS groups maintain strict confidentiality. BECOMERS sessions are closed to the public, allowing only group members who have completed the intake process to participate. No information about group members is shared within the group, or outside the group, unless written permission is given by the individual group member for a specific purpose.

A second objective is to *provide support group interaction* that models healthy interpersonal relationships to enhance group members' experience of God's grace through the support and encouragement of others. BECOMERS teaching, personal application homework, and interaction between group facilitators/participants are all intended to affirm the worth of each person in a non-shaming setting through perspectives that reflect God's unconditional acceptance.

A third objective is to *empower group members to actively participate with God* in healing the damage of sexually abusive experiences. To this end, BECOMERS offers teachings, homework, other materials, and group process as tools to assist group members in their recovery journey. Group members are encouraged to keep a journal and complete weekly personal application homework. Group members make a commitment to attend group sessions regularly, and have the option to continue or terminate at the end of each session.

A fourth objective is to *help group members recognize negative thoughts and beliefs and explore biblical alternatives* to untruths they have believed about themselves. It is foundational to healing to identify and understand sources of destructive thoughts and beliefs, many of which originated from the abuse itself. Group members come together each week with a shared background of sexually abusive experiences, and group members are encouraged to share with one another from that common ground. In BECOMERS support groups, personal sharing focuses on thoughts and feelings resulting from sexual abuse rather than on disclosure of explicit events of abuse. Detailed descriptions of graphic sexual acts can be appropriate in individual therapy or in therapy groups but can inhibit support group processing. A focus on specific and graphic individual experience may cause some in the group to withdraw and minimize their experience or may harm some who experience re-victimization through visualizing graphic descriptions.

BECOMERS also serves to *provide ongoing support and help* for group members. BECOMERS offers a nine-step recovery program in which a recovery step is highlighted each week for nine weeks. Several groups have modified this original structure by providing a first-week introductory session, spending two weeks on each step, and having a closure session resulting in sessions of twenty weeks in length. Each recovery step focuses on different aspects of the healing process, and each nine- or twenty-week session focuses on different issues related to sexual abuse. Group members have the opportunity to continue in the BECOMERS program for whatever length of time it takes them to make significant progress in their healing journey. Members are often active in the group process for one to three years.

Finally, the BECOMERS program is intended to *provide support that is an adjunct to, not a replacement for, professional individual counseling.* The BECOMERS group structure requires each group member to be in individual therapy/counseling concurrent with their participation in the BECOMERS program. A professional referral is requested to begin the group entry process, which is followed by an intake interview with a BECOMERS staff member. Group members are also requested to give written permission to allow consultation, as needed, between the BECOMERS staff and their individual counselor.

BECOMERS GROUP STRUCTURE

The BECOMERS support groups meet for two hours once each week. The first segment of group time is dedicated as a teaching time where a psychologist, other professional, or BECOMERS staff person presents a topic relevant to sexual abuse. The week prior to that topic presentation, group members will have corresponding personal application homework to relate their life experience to that topic. If there are two or more BECOMERS groups meeting at the same location, the teaching is presented to combined groups.

At the conclusion of the short presentation, the larger group breaks into pre-assigned small groups of no more than eight group members. The purpose of the small groups is for support, application, and discussion of homework. These small groups are in session for an hour and a half and involve the same group members and group facilitator each week throughout the nine- or twenty-week session.

At the end of the nine- or twenty-week commitment, group members may choose to continue or terminate their participation in BECOMERS. Groups may have changes in group members at the end of each session, but it is important to keep previous group members together, even as new members are added, in order to enhance levels of trust. Occasionally, some group members may prefer to be situated in another group. The group facilitators will need to discern when it is appropriate for a particular group member to stay in his/her group and work through difficulties in relationships with other group members or the group facilitator, or if it might be more productive for that group member to be in a different group setting.

BECOMERS NINE-STEP RECOVERY PROGRAM

Listed below are nine steps that are used as guidelines in the BECOMERS recovery process.[1] However, the healing journey does not occur in an orderly progression. Each group member is encouraged to follow an individual timeline to work through specific aspects of her or his abuse. Some aspects of the healing process may be cyclic, and personal growth and restoration in these areas may occur over many years. In the chapters immediately following, each step will be expanded to offer a model for applying these principles in the healing journey.

Steps to Recovery

- Step One: I recognize that I am powerless to heal the damage resulting from my sexual abuse, and I look to God for the power to make me whole.
- Step Two: I acknowledge that God's plan for my life includes victory over the experience of sexual abuse.
- Step Three: The person who abused me is responsible for the sexual acts committed against me. I will not accept the guilt and shame resulting from those sexual acts.
- Step Four: I am looking to God and his Word to affirm my identity as a worthwhile and loved human being.
- Step Five: I am honestly sharing my feelings with God and with trustworthy others to help me identify those areas needing cleansing and healing.
- Step Six: I am taking responsibility for my responses to being sexually abused.
- Step Seven: I am willing to accept God's help in the decision and the process of forgiving those who have offended me and those I have harmed.
- Step Eight: I am willing to mature in my relationship with God and others.
- Step Nine: I am willing to be available to God in the healing and restoration of others.

8

Step One: Recognizing Powerlessness

Step One: I recognize that I am powerless to heal the damage resulting from my sexual abuse, and I look to God for the power to make me whole.

Recognizing powerlessness: a process of realizing one's inability to achieve wholeness through self-reliance and self-effort.

This understanding of powerlessness is foundational to restoration from sexual abuse. In the past, adult survivors have associated powerlessness with victimization. From this vantage point, it would seem that feeling powerful would be the antidote and that self-reliance would promote a sense of personal power. However, recovery through self-effort is perpetuated by the myth that all a person needs to recover from trauma is self-discipline and will-power.

In the Christian community, self-effort to heal damage from sexual abuse is often disguised as perfectionism, rationalization that the abuse did not have any effect, or through "good works," such as extensive church activities or compulsive Scripture reading and prayer. While these spiritual disciplines are vital tools in the healing process, they can actually become barriers to spiritual growth because the underlying premise is self-defeating—trying to "earn" approval from God instead of recognizing one's powerlessness to gain what has already been freely given.

One outcome for abused adults who are relying on Christian good works as the measure of their personal value is that they often look so "good" on the outside that their inner pain remains hidden. External behaviors can mask internal core beliefs that God has failed them, or that they have failed God in some way. There may come a point where this incongruence between the inner and the outer worlds causes abuse survivors to lose their faith in God and leave the church, or perhaps remain in the church, denying the pain within.

Accepting one's powerlessness lays a foundation for restorative dependence on God, and movement toward healing begins with restoration of personal worth. The basic issue in restoration of personal worth is one of *source*. Every person relies on some kind of "source" for being loved and accepted, feeling worthwhile, and a sense of belonging. Because messages from sexual abuse have been such a destructive "source," a new and trustworthy source must be found.

God is the only source with the legitimate power to confer infinite value on each human being. One way this truth can become tangible to abused adults is through experiencing God's grace reflected to them by those who are "Jesus with skin on" in their lives, such as those in their BECOMERS support group.

Abuse survivors can be encouraged to think about powerlessness in light of the dynamics of power and control as defined earlier. (See introduction to chapter 2.) In the BECOMERS program, God is considered to be the primary power of influence in the recovery process. While abuse survivors are powerless to influence God's love toward them, they may still exercise personal control by limiting his influence on them. Resisting God is likely to be a common experience at the beginning of the recovery process due to fears and distortions about who God is. At the same time, people and circumstances in the lives of abused adults will likely have significant power to influence them. BECOMERS groups can encourage abuse survivors to begin to exercise their personal control to limit the influences on them of other people and circumstances. Realizing powerlessness, then, is the gradual transfer of reliance to God as the foundational source for one's personal worth instead of any other "source."

It is often helpful to examine ways that an understanding of powerlessness can be redirected to actually *empower* adults in their healing process. As children, abuse victims felt powerless to stop the abuse from happening and had no recourse other than to yield to abusive power. According to Proverbs 22:6, a child "trained up" to have no control over wrongful power exerted by others may have difficulty "departing from" such training. For example, adult survivors may perceive themselves to lack physical control over their bodies and may be re-victimized as a result. Part of the healing process will include being empowered to see where choices can be made to protect one's physical person. In adult relationships, abuse survivors may continue to find themselves feeling like "victims" or, alternatively, may try to overcome feelings of "being a victim" by exerting power over others. Perhaps most often, survivors swing back and forth between passive and aggressive emotional responses in relationships. With God's unconditional love as the stabilizing foundation, abused adults can instead learn to be emotionally assertive, respecting both themselves and others.

Intellectual power can be regained by adult survivors who have been convinced that they are stupid or intellectually inadequate. God has endowed adult survivors with abilities to educate themselves about abuse, its effects, and the recovery journey itself. Cognitive restructuring, or positive self-talk, is a helpful tool to use to facilitate intellectual healing from destructive messages of abuse. Scripture reading and memorization provide a basis for replacing harmful messages with true messages about personal worth and purpose in life and can encourage thinking patterns that promote a healthy lifestyle. Reading other supportive resources about abuse recovery can supplement scriptural truths and provide additional help in restructuring thoughts to regain control over destructive beliefs.

In 2 Corinthians 12:9, Jesus tells us, "My grace is sufficient for you, for my power is made perfect in weakness." Unfortunately, this verse is frequently quoted "at" abused adults as a "quick fix" kind of approach to a difficult and challenging restoration process. Thus, we need to take a fresh look at what Jesus is saying. The power for healing lies in the *experience* of *grace*. A limitless flow of grace is poured out from God's fullness and sufficiency, based on God's mercy and not dependent on perceptions about whether one feels worthy to receive it. While this fact may be true, the actual experience of God's grace is usually appropriated over a period of time. A sense of spiritual strengthening comes from repeatedly turning to Christ as "source" and, paradoxically, being empowered by him through the recognition of being powerless to heal oneself.

The amount of effort required to incorporate this truth into actual life experience should not be underestimated. First Timothy 6:12 encourages believers to "fight the good fight of the faith." Most abuse survivors are fighting the wrong fight—that is, either fighting to obtain grace by self-effort or striving to earn self-worth from others. Most may not even be consciously aware of the emotional cost of these misplaced efforts. But God understands our frailties and weaknesses and speaks of his being "tender and sympathetic to those who reverence him" (Psalm 103:13–14 TLB). In this passage, God tells us he knows we are but dust. As dust, we cannot win the fight to heal ourselves, but the good news is that Christ has fought the fight *for* each of us, and it is finished.

The opportunity to accept the validity and sufficiency of God's provision is always available. Because his "power is made perfect in weakness," we can encourage adult survivors to ask God to enable them to see the "weakness" of relying on others or their circumstances to meet core needs. We can support adult survivors to "fight the good fight of the faith" wherever they are in their ability to ask God for the strength to resist powerful influences from the wrong sources and to have faith to rely on the True Source. Restoration involves a daily process of renewal to maintain forward movement in the healing journey. Recognizing powerlessness is a beginning step.

Suggested Personal Application Questions to Accompany Step One

- What is "power"? What does it mean to be a powerful person? What might be some different kinds of power?
- In what ways or in what areas of your life do you feel powerful?
- What is "powerlessness" according to the dictionary? What is your personal definition of "powerlessness"?
- What are some ways you have experienced powerlessness?
- What might be some differences between the powerlessness of being a victim of sexual abuse and being powerless apart from God?

The following art therapy technique is often helpful in thinking about different areas in life that might illustrate different forms of "power."

Complete your own personal "Coat of Arms" by drawing a picture or a symbol that represents the answer to each of the following questions. In space #1, draw a picture or symbol or word that corresponds to question #1 below. Complete all six questions in the same way. Bring your "Coat of Arms" to the group. Feel free to change the size or shape of your "Coat of Arms" or vary it from the design below. Just be sure to include all six questions in your design.

1. What do you regard as your greatest personal achievement in life so far?
2. What do you regard as your family's greatest achievement?
3. What is the one thing people can do to make you happy?
4. What do you regard as your greatest personal failure in life so far?
5. What would you do if you had one year to live and were guaranteed success in whatever you attempted?
6. What *one thing* would you most like to be said of you?

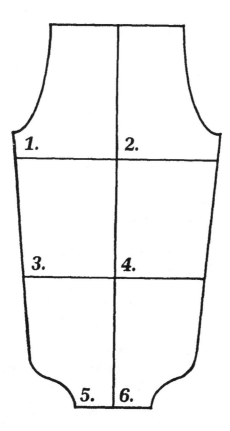

9

Step Two: Acknowledging Victory in Christ

Step Two: I acknowledge that God's plan for my life includes victory over the experience of sexual abuse, and I look to God for the power to make me whole.

Victory in Christ: a lifelong process of matching outer behaviors with inner realities of God's grace.

Many Christians define *victory* from an all-or-nothing perspective. When *victory* is defined as "always choosing correct behavior," then anything less than perfection is *defeat*.

At its very core, victory lies in experiencing our identity in Christ and behaving on the outside consistently with who we are on the inside. Victory is a process of claiming and reclaiming our worth based on God's love and grace toward us rather than trying to achieve perfect behavior—which is impossible. Viewed in this way, victory involves many learning experiences rather than a once-and-for-all event, although pivotal events sometimes occur as turning points.

The diagram on the next page shows a common view of victory in Christ. While there is truth in this diagram, it is only a partial reflection of truth. If this diagram is the only definition of *victory* known to abuse survivors (or anyone else), then defeat is guaranteed. And often with feelings of defeat comes hopelessness.

Sherry was a twenty-four-year-old abuse survivor with a history of three suicide attempts. She visited church after church looking for the right combination of things she might *do* to earn God's favor so that God would heal her. After some intensive individual counseling, Sherry began to shift her focus from trying to come up with a self-effort "guarantee for success" in her life to a beginning awareness of God's acceptance of her just as she was. This restoration of hope replaced her view of "victory as perfection" that almost resulted in taking her life.

If abuse survivors believe that God defines victorious Christians as those who always make right choices, then victory will prove impossible. In our experience, this unrealistic expectation is the most common view most abused adults have of God's expectations of them for victory over the effects of abuse.

When BECOMERS participants are asked to define *victory,* many offer pat answers, describing all-or-nothing, success/failure struggles in which they inevitably come out as failures. They compare their struggles with lingering effects of sexual abuse against a common definition of victory that characterizes victorious Christians as never experiencing struggles or defeats.

As an adult survivor, Jan declared, "I *should* be able to have victory. I wouldn't struggle if I just had enough faith." Mark was asked to define *victory* in a BECOMERS homework assignment. He wrote that there are no victorious Christians because God always has to keep punishing them for wrong things they do. Mark uncovered a core belief about God: He felt he would never be able to experience victory in his life because he could not live up to God's standards. This exercise often provides a measure of an abuse survivor's sense of hope for restoration.

BECOMERS offers a definition of victory that gives a more

comprehensive view of God's grace. The diagram on the next page illustrates that in following a wrong choice, a person sins, and that he or she may experience many consequences from that sinful choice. A sense of defeat can be very heavy. However, it is at this very point that there is great potential to experience the process of victory. Acknowledging that the behavior is not consistent with an identity rooted and grounded in Christ, a person has an opportunity to turn to Christ to meet the need that the sinful behavior was insufficient to meet.

Nancy was a thirty-five-year-old career woman who was sexually abused by her uncle during her junior high years. She was brought up in a Christian home and wanted to live her life for the Lord. However, she had been cohabiting with a forty-year-old man for four years. She felt trapped by her feelings of love for him, which conflicted with her belief that living with him was wrong. Many times she left him with a sincere resolve to end the relationship, but found herself returning to the same situation again and again. She felt defeated and convinced that there was no victory possible for her. She felt she had disappointed God so many times that there was no hope.

Through her BECOMERS group sessions, Nancy began to realize that God could, and did, accept her for the person she was. Her inner conflict and discomfort were caused by the choices she was making, which were not consistent with who God saw her to be in Christ. She began to view feelings of guilt as a positive signal indicating that the source she was turning to for love and acceptance was not sufficient to meet those needs. She could see the deeper issue of her struggle as not merely an outward behavior of living with her lover, but an inner issue of dependency on an insufficient source for unconditional love.

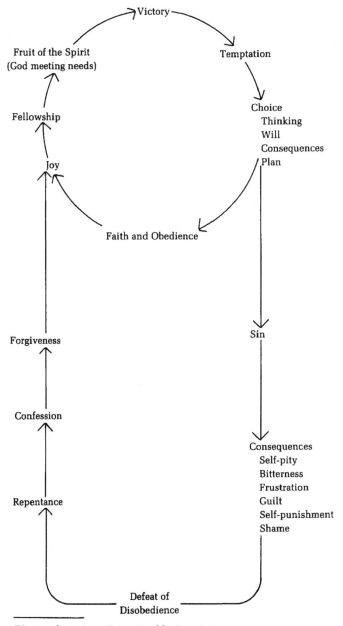

Diagram from Anna Gates. Used by Permission.

Survivors of sexual abuse may have developed deeply entrenched destructive behaviors. Many find themselves going through outward actions of repentance, confession, and forgiveness, but when they do not experience inner fellowship with God or experience fruits of the Spirit, they lose hope and give up. The process of *experiencing* victory involves many aspects: changing thinking processes, ongoing encounters with God's love and forgiveness, and receiving help and Christian support to maintain hope that God's plan includes restoration from pervasive effects of sexual abuse.

Matthew 5:48 reads: "Be perfect, therefore, as your heavenly Father is perfect." Verses such as these seem to place a crushing burden on those struggling with effects of abuse as it relates to meanings of *perfection* and *victory in Christ*. However, be encouraged! The Greek root *telei*, translated into English as *perfect*, does not mean "sinless," or "incapable of sinning," but more along the lines of *growing into* completeness. That is, experiencing maturity and spiritual growth throughout the healing journey.

Paul tells us he was not perfect and encourages us to pursue an ongoing sanctification process. He tells us in Romans 7:18–19 how he wrestles with victory himself: "For I have the desire to do what is good, but I cannot carry it out. For what I do is not the good I want to do; no, the evil I do not want to do—this I keep on doing." Paul also felt hopelessness and despair at times, but he kept reminding himself (and us), "Thanks be to God, who gives us the victory through our Lord Jesus Christ" (1 Corinthians 15:57 RSV).

Suggested Personal Application Questions to Accompany Step Two

Think about any religious training you have had.

- Were you raised in a Christian home? If so, what did *Christian* mean in your family?
- Was the person who abused you Christian/religious? Describe the abuser's "Christian" behavior and attitudes.
- What behaviors and attitudes did your family teach about God? (Include verbal and nonverbal teaching.)
- Describe a "victorious" Christian. Do you consider yourself to be a victorious Christian?

The following is an art therapy exercise that might help group members to discern views of God and relate those views to their experience of victory in their Christian journey.

Write down thoughts as if you were writing in a diary or journal. Feel free to use any form of written expression with which you feel comfortable, e.g., poetry, prose, symbols, literal description, etc. The questions are designed to stimulate your thoughts and feelings but are not intended to limit you to one answer per question.

Think about your images of God from the very earliest impressions/thoughts/feelings/"facts" that you can remember up to the present time.

* What was God like?
* How did God feel about you?
* Where was God?
* Where is God in this process of healing in which you are involved?
* How do you sense God's presence?
* Draw a picture of God.

With permission, we include the following pictures of God drawn by men and women involved in the BECOMERS program. These illustrations will assist readers to "see" God through the eyes of abused adults. Drawing pictures of God can reveal a great deal. If the exercise is repeated over time, these drawings may provide an illustration of changes in the way God is "seen" along the healing journey, as illustrated by the last two sequences of drawings.

etc. etc. etc.

There are no "successful" Christians. God always has to punish us for being bad. He thinks I am a loser.

mE

God

I feel distant and unimportant.

3a)

Good things
Do Do Do
Work Work Work

Bad behavior, negative
emotions, conflicts, stress,
sin.

3b)

3c)

Do Do Do
Repent Repent Repent
Try Try Try

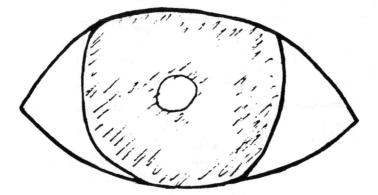

God is disgusted with me;
He wishes I'd never been
born. He doesn't "see" me—
He just looks through me.
I'm angry at God and afraid
of Him. I feel abandoned
and think He is cruel.

The following series of drawings illustrate changes in images of God over time as abuse survivors continue to discover God in their healing process.

Initial image of God:

God loves me and He sent His Son to die for me and I'd better be grateful. He is a stern, arms-crossed judge and a cold authoritarian. I never "measure up."

Change in image of God eight months later:

Is He
Smiling or
frowning?

I am beginning to believe
that God really does love
me, but I am afraid to let go
of my anger because I don't
know what will happen to
me if I do. Do I have to
please God continually? I
fail so much. . . . I still feel
intimidated like I did as a
child.

Initial image of God:

I am a failure; I never do things good enough. Deep down inside, I think I hate God.

Change in image of God eighteen months later:

Right now I feel that He is pretty uncaring, that He's turned His back on me, decided to leave me alone. . . . I feel hurt when I think of God because of how I think He feels about me. I feel angry at Him for not coming through for me. But I don't hate Him . . . usually I just feel an empty apathy about Him.

(Note: The following five pictures illustrate a three-year healing process.)

This is what God was doing
while I was being abused as
a child.

This is me as an adult when
I became a Christian.

I was sexually abused by an elder in the church who was supposed to be "counseling" me. This is how I saw God—He mocked people who came to Him for help and threw lightning bolts at them.

He's gotten kind of blurry
recently, but at least He's
not throwing lightning bolts
at me anymore.

He's become my source of
protection, shelter, and
safety. He nourishes me, as
He does this tree, with sun
and rain, and is helping me
grow in Him.

10

Step Three: Experiencing Freedom From Shame and Guilt

Step Three: The person who abused me is responsible for the sexual acts committed against me. I will not accept the guilt and shame resulting from those sexual acts.

Recognizing responsibility: Discerning the difference between the prescription for guilt resolution and the restorative process for shame.

Offenders are responsible for sexually abusive acts. They *are* guilty. Adult survivors feel responsible for abusive acts but they are not. Survivors *feel* guilty, but, in truth, they are heavy-laden with shame.

Guilt and shame are very different. Guilt can be a status or an emotion. By contrast, shame is experienced as a sense of defectiveness related to self-image and a view of others in relationship to self.

GUILTY STATUS: ACQUIRED

God had explained to Adam and Eve that on the day they ate of the forbidden fruit, they would surely die. After their choice to do so, they not only anticipated the advent of future physical death, they also experienced spiritual death. The Bible highlights what it was that Adam and Eve lost—their spiritual connection to God. This is comparable to flipping off a light switch. The resulting darkness is not the *opposite* of light, but the actual *absence* of light. The light inside our first parents went out in the garden.

After they breached their relationship with God, Adam and Eve experienced a piercing awareness of spiritual death and a sense of defectiveness and inner emptiness. However, they did not take responsibility for their transgression. Instead, their subsequent response resembles two dimensions of shame: protection and performance. They tried to *protect themselves by hiding* from God, thinking this might prevent their being exposed. And they tried to "perform" to cover up their defectiveness by sewing fig leaves together to hide their sense of being naked. Our first parents started a chain reaction of distorted relationships with God and resultant spiritual death that persists to this day.

The inheritance of spiritual death constitutes one's guilty status before God: "Yes, all have sinned; all fall short of God's glorious ideal" (Romans 3:23 TLB). The basis of a guilty status before God is not dependent on whether one *feels* guilty or not but rather on the fallen state of humanity. We are separated from God based on this deficiency, and yet he made provision through Christ to remedy that very condition.

GUILTY STATUS: REMOVED

God outlined an extensive moral code of rules and laws to make it abundantly clear that no one could manage such a "to do" list. Trying to measure up to such impossible standards on our own efforts would not only be exhausting but also pointless. However, due to an amazing gift called *grace,* we did not even have to try. God's grace to us was, and is, a free gift—offered by Christ. No strings attached. Because of Christ's gift to us from the cross, and based on our personal and grateful acknowledgement of receiving that gift, our guilty status is removed!

> But God is so rich in mercy; He loved us so much that even though we were spiritually dead and doomed by our sins, He gave us back our lives again . . . all because of what Christ Jesus did. Because of His kindness, you have been saved through trusting Christ. And even trusting is not of yourselves; it too is a gift from God. Salvation is not a reward for the good we have done, so none of us can take any credit for it. It is God Himself who has made us what we are and given us new lives from Christ Jesus. (Ephesians 2:4–6, 8–10 TLB)

We are in relationship *with* God . . . and *without* condemnation.

"Therefore, there is now no condemnation for those who are in Christ Jesus, because through Christ Jesus the law of the spirit of life set me free from the law of sin and death" (Romans 8:1).

The chart below shows some differences between guilt and shame.

	GUILT	SHAME
SOURCE	*Conviction of Holy Spirit*	*Condemnation of the enemy, others, and self*
AREA CONFRONTED	*Behavior, wrong choices*	*Identity; bad person*
MOTIVATION	*To confess*	*To internalize, keep inside*
GOAL	*Experience forgiveness*	*Experience pain*
RESULT	*Freedom, growth*	*Bondage*
OWNERSHIP	*Given to God*	*Shame "owns"/ controls me*

Guilty Feelings: Taking Note, Taking Action—A Prescription for Relief

Feelings of guilt differ from the *status* of guilt. Feeling guilty comes as the Holy Spirit encourages us to take note of behavior and wrong choices (sin). The feeling of guilt can be positive because it is a signal from God that our behavior on the outside is not matching who we are on the inside. Although guilt can be a painful emotion, it is not negative unless it is ignored.

Just as physical pain is a signal that something is wrong in our bodies, guilt is a signal that something is wrong in our spirits. Guilt motivates us to take action by taking responsibility. Scripture gives us the "prescription" for repairing a violation of our values: confess our sin to God—and to others, if appropriate. Make restitution, if warranted. Take responsibility for wrong behavior. The result of taking action is experiencing forgiveness and a deeper experience of God's exceedingly abundant grace. We develop personally and grow from being accountable to our values, developing increased empathy, and repairing the wrong. We are freed from the burden of guilt: "As far as the east is from the west, so far has he removed our transgressions from us" (Psalm 103:12).

SHAME: A PROCESS OF CONDEMNATION AT THE CORE

Shame differs from guilt in that it is not so much an emotion as it is a mindset or a perception about being a defective person. A person's identity becomes associated with feelings of inferiority, worthlessness, and self-contempt.[1] Shame is feeling "bad," stupid, inadequate, incapable, a failure, worthless, empty.

A person's self-concept is a deeply private experience. Shame gives the perception of being completely exposed and aware of being looked at ("naked"—like Adam), of being visible but not ready to be visible. In his book *Why Am I Afraid to Tell You Who I Am?*, John Powell says, "I'm afraid to tell you who I am because if I tell you who I am, you may not like who I am, and it is all that I have."[2]

Shame usually originates from specific beliefs we are taught about ourselves by family members or other significant people. Shame is perpetuated by treating ourselves the way we were treated by others and giving ourselves the same "messages" we were given by others. Sandra Wilson, author of *Released From Shame*, writes that shaming parental "You are" statements are often internalized into personal identities as "I am" statements, such that if a parent said to you as a child, "You are so stupid!" when you made a mistake, then as an adult when you make a mistake you will likely tell yourself, "I am so stupid!"[3]

Sometimes the enemy launches attacks of condemnation upon us in an attempt to convince us that our shame messages are truthful. Sometimes condemnation comes from others and sometimes from within. Sometimes Christians feel unforgiven long after they have repented in response to an appropriate conviction of guilt. In such instances, persons are no longer struggling with guilt, but with a sense of shame.

In *Shame and Grace*, Lewis Smedes notes that sometimes the difference between shame and guilt might be clearer in theory than in practice. It is true that the two can overlap at times when we feel "bad" for "doing" something bad, such as the husband who feels guilty for telling a lie to his wife and bad for being the kind of person who would do such a thing.[4] However, most adult survivors of abuse have found distinctions between shame and guilt to bring a breath of fresh air to their souls. They have carried such heavy loads of "something" for which they had no name other than "feeling guilty," but found no relief from multiple confessions or asking forgiveness. Naming shame with its rightful name is a first step in the process of recovery from its condemnation of the soul.

Shame attacks the identity; guilt involves a confrontation of wrongful behaviors. The message of guilt is: "I made a bad choice." The message of shame is: "I am a bad person." Shame motivates adult survivors to internalize an incredible sense of defectiveness, which results in painful efforts to hide who they are or to cover up their shame. The end result is a process of increasing bondage to shame, not the freedom of resolving guilt.

Guilt is confessed to God and removed. The tragedy of shame is that the shame actually "owns" people and holds them in bondage. The bondage of shame reminds us of the figure of Lazarus as he was called forth from the tomb by Christ. He was very much alive, and yet bound up with heavy graveclothes. Christ's instructions to Lazarus' friends were to "unbind him" (John 11:44 NRSV). Such is the work of the Holy Spirit today, who uses God's truth and the supportive care of friends alongside to help "unbind" the heavy layers of shame that so often immobilize adult survivors of sexual abuse.

One of the primary purposes of BECOMERS is to facilitate a process where the "graveclothes" of shame can be gently released from abuse survivors through the *experience* of unconditional acceptance and eventually removed by an ongoing *experience* of the fullness of grace.

Signs and Signals of Shame

Unlike Lazarus, whose bondage was quite visible, identifying a person in bondage to shame is not always easy. The following signals may help in understanding when someone is experiencing shame.

- Wanting to hide or disappear from the presence of others
- Inflicting physical punishments: cutting one's flesh, burning self with cigarettes, being accident prone
- Inflicting emotional punishments: setting self up to be hurt or rejected by others, indulging in negative or destructive self-talk
- Feeling "defensive" when criticized, whether the criticism is constructive or destructive
- Drooping body posture—slouching shoulders, hanging of the head, avoiding eye contact
- "Acting out" behaviors: drugs, alcohol, arson, cruelty to others or to animals, stealing, prostitution, suicide attempts, eating disorders, compulsive behaviors.

Sources of Shame

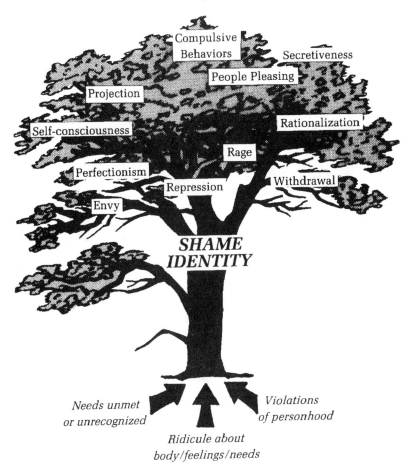

THE FACES OF SHAME

I feel
like a tree who has been defoliated,
a slender birch
who has been stripped
of her bark.
My trunk has become a dart board
for the archer.
Inscribed on my spine
is the word SHAME.
My limbs have been twisted,
they hang by my side.
The sap has been drained
from my punctured veins.
My larynx is ruined.
I cannot scream.
The birds of the air
are awed by their vision.
The deer cannot watch.
The squirrels bury their heads.
Even the rodents run from the sight.
The sun looks away
and my blackness remains.

—Jane Ault[5]

Many faces can hide an inner sense of shame. Adult survivors . . .

- . . . are tired—physically, emotionally, spiritually exhausted. They are tired of trying to please others, trying to please God, and often just tired of living.
- . . . have a shame-based identity, nearly always feeling that something is wrong with them or that they are "less than" others. This identity produces a "shame filter" that colors every aspect of life. This "shame filter" hears shame messages, even when they are not intended. This "shame filter" governs their responses to life circumstances, such as finding it very difficult to admit mistakes, needing to "prove" themselves, or always having to be "right."
- . . . feel that their value comes from what they do or don't do, what they have or don't have. This faulty perception makes it very difficult to believe they can be loved and accepted

without strings attached. They tend to think they must earn or repay any acceptance they receive from God or others. They find it very hard to accept gifts, whether it is the free gift of salvation from God or material gifts, compliments, or rewards from others.

• . . . are unaware of personal needs or how to get those needs met. Not knowing what "normal" needs are or how they can be appropriately met, the "norm" is often feeling that they should not even *have* needs or, conversely, that *others* are totally responsible for meeting their needs.

• . . . usually feel over-responsible for things that happen. They develop "radar" that looks for signals in situations around them to see what they did to "cause" the circumstance to happen. Their "radar" also tunes in to find out what they need to "do" to be accepted. Their "radar" is often extremely accurate in picking up hurting family problems; but because of their shame "filter," they do not trust their "radar" and usually end up feeling that *they* are the problem, instead of the *problem* being the problem.

• . . . tend to feel helpless and incapable, perpetuating a "victim" identity, and are often victimized by others.

• . . . do not often speak directly or straightforwardly, especially about their feelings.

• . . . feel as if they don't "belong," desperately wanting intimacy but being afraid of others and pushing them away.

• . . . cannot have guilt-free fun, because they feel they don't deserve to take time for themselves; if they are not producing something, they have no value.

• . . . often have "idols" as their core sense of worth—pleasing others, children, spouse, money, sex, ministry, food. When seeking to meet core needs from such "idols" continues even in the face of negative consequences, an addiction occurs.

• . . . are "survivors" of their sexual abuse, but they tend to stay in relationships where they can use those same "survival skills" rather than taking risks necessary to learn new skills to get out of negative situations.

• . . . have a very hard time trusting God or people.[6]

RECOVERY FROM SHAME

Breaking the silence and revealing the "secret" of sexual abuse is the first step of recovery from shame. The cost of breaking this silence should not be underestimated. In *Released From Shame,* Sandra Wilson writes that the truth may set you free, but it first makes you miserable.[7] Sharing about sexual abuse must take place in a safe and caring setting with those who are trustworthy. Sharing will help adult survivors to identify shaming messages they have internalized from their abuse and other sources. The process of growth and freedom from shame will take place *over time* as adult survivors face the pain of saying out loud the "truth" of their abusive experiences.

Getting support from others is crucial to breaking the bondage of shame. It is often very difficult for abuse survivors to ask for support because of feelings of unworthiness to receive help. However, a concrete way to confront shame is to receive new feedback from trustworthy sources such as a therapist or support group. Feedback that reflects truth and reality about sexual abuse and hurtful family systems helps abuse survivors confront the original sources of shame messages. In BECOMERS, abuse survivors are often reminded of their value and worth to those in their support group and also their value to God—a practical application of Romans 12:2, which encourages transformation by renewal of the mind with truth to replace lies.

New feedback, new ways of thinking, and expression of authentic feelings contribute to the rebuilding of self-esteem over time. An ongoing rebuilding process will hopefully enable abuse survivors to feel compassion for the abused children they once were and help them not to treat themselves in the same abusive ways that they were treated by others.

Becoming aware of self-protective defense mechanisms is a key component of recovery from shame. (See also chapter 13.) Defense mechanisms are a result of trying to cope with the effects of abuse, and in that regard served a useful purpose. In the process of recovery from shame, the need for defense mechanisms can be reduced as adult survivors experience support and unconditional acceptance that encourages them to let go of some of the self-protection provided by rigid defenses. At the same time, survivors need to acquire appropriate defenses for protecting personal boundaries and for developing discernment to realize when they are in unsafe environments.

Evaluating current relationships as healthy or shame-producing is another significant part of restoration from sexual abuse. Abuse survivors may discover that some of their present relationships feel like childhood abuse experiences, reenacted in adult situations.

Developing healthy adult relationships helps abused adults to experience freedom, support, affirmation, and open communication with those who will support their healing process.

RELIGIOUS SOLUTIONS TO SHAME VS. GOD'S SOLUTION TO SHAME

Religious solutions to shame often put people under the "law" by requiring rigid adherence to certain Christian behaviors. Religious systems tend to define "victory" as perfect external behavior, where God is presented as a critical and demanding Shepherd who drives his flock rather than a gentle Shepherd who tends and leads his flock.[8] Religious systems emphasize performance, focus on sin, and rebuke sinners rather than calling God's children to worship, offering restoration and refreshment in the journey of faith. A performance mentality tends to push people into a cycle of trying hard to self-improve and then subsequently giving up. Trying harder is not the solution to shame; it can actually generate greater shame when acceptance is never achieved.

God's solution to shame involves an ongoing process of reliance on inner resources provided by daily dependence on him. For survivors of sexual abuse, this process is best accomplished in settings with others who reflect God's grace, confirm their competence, and communicate a sense of belonging. The fight against shame is a fight to hold fast to an identity rooted in unconditional acceptance; a fight to appropriate value and peace from God on the inside, not just to exhibit "good" behavior on the outside. Change in external behavior will likely come, but will come from the inside out.

God's commitment to the restoration process in recovering from shame is this: "Come to me, all you who are weary and burdened, and I will give you rest. Take my yoke upon you and learn from me, for I am gentle and humble in heart, and you will find rest for your souls. For my yoke is easy and my burden is light" (Matthew 11:28–30). In this verse, "weary and burdened" refers to striving and carrying a load that grinds one to powder. Adult survivors of sexual abuse have been ground to powder under a heavy load of shame. They can *experience* God's provision of rest through support and grace in settings such as restorative church families and supportive groups of adult survivors.

Suggested Personal Application Questions to Accompany Step Three

The following BECOMERS homework projects can be used over a period of several weeks. The process of addressing shame is costly. Encourage abuse survivors to be gentle with themselves as they continue along their healing journey.

Shame Recovery Project One

It is essential to identify sources of "messages" that have convinced us that we are "shameful" and "bad." Once those "messages" are exposed and brought into the light of what is true about us as individuals, we have the risky but freeing opportunity to make different choices about how we view ourselves.

Read through the following situations in families experiencing shame. Which ones were (or are) present in the family in which you were raised? This exercise can relate to your birth home, an adoptive home, a foster home, or any combination of living situations that have left "messages" with you.

- Were you shamed in front of others for your behavior? If so, note a specific time.
- Were you belittled/ridiculed? About what?
- Were you constantly compared to another child? Who?
- Were you humiliated in front of others? Who did that to you?
- Did you somehow feel that you were a "disappointment" to your parents? In what way?
- Were you expected to be "perfect"? Did you ever feel as if you were "good enough"?
- Did it seem like it was your responsibility to make sure no one's feelings were hurt and that there was no conflict?
- Did your parents communicate to you (with words or by their attitude) that they were "helpless" to do anything about any problems in the family? Have you sometimes found yourself feeling "trapped" by your circumstances, feeling as if things might never change?
- Was there physical violence in your family? If so, note a specific incident.
- Was there an attitude of seduction with sexual comments that were made to you by someone in your family? Was anyone in your family involved in any form of pornography—on the Internet, viewing magazines (either "soft" or "hard core" pornography), movies, photographing others? Was anyone in your family involved in same-sex relationships?
- Were there addictions in your family, such as drugs, alcohol, sexual addictions, overeating, compulsive gambling, compulsive overspending, workaholism?

- What were relationships like within your family?

    a. Enmeshed: all mixed up, no boundaries, everyone over-involved with one another, no privacy.

    b. Isolated: everyone keeping to themselves, stuffing feelings, no communication; little or no physical affection.

    c. Over-Controlled: rigid rules, "legalistic."

    d. Chaotic: no one seeming to be in control, unsupervised freedom, lack of concern about you, neglect (lacking either physical or emotional nurture, or both).

    e. Perfectionistic: an "all-or-nothing" atmosphere in the family; that is, any situation not considered perfect was considered terrible.

- Did you feel that you always had to "look good" or "do the right thing" so that it would look good to others?
- In your family, was someone always to blame whenever anything didn't go as planned? Were you punished for making mistakes?
- How does your family define success? Are you a success?
- When there was trouble in your family or some kind of conflict, did your family deny it by ignoring it?

After you have considered these questions, reflect on what you've written for a day or two. Summing up your thoughts above, write out several "messages" you have believed about yourself that have come from what others have communicated to you about you.

Shame Recovery Project Two

It is difficult for adult survivors to acknowledge shame experienced in childhood, especially if feelings have been repressed for a long time. Beginning a journey through shame can be intensely painful. Exercises like this one can be significant in helping to release feelings associated with shame by allowing those feelings to be experienced in a somewhat detached way using a childhood photo as a focus. Later on, insights gained from this exercise can be applied to current adult life.

Bring a photo of yourself as a child to your group as part of your homework.

Attach photo here:

Looking at the child in the photo, complete the following statements:

This child was sexually abused by . . .

This child was sexually abused because . . .

This child needed . . .

This child felt . . .

This child believed that . . .

This child decided to . . .

If I were to adopt this child, I would . . . because . . .

Consider some of the negative "messages" this child received. Think about some differences between shame messages and guilt messages.

In your current understanding, where does guilt come from; and where does shame come from?

How would the child in this photo know the difference?

How has shame affected this child's response to self? To others?

How has shame affected this child's ability to resist abusive power?

Contrast these thoughts about yourself as a child with the thoughts and responses you now have as an adult.

How does shame affect your responses to yourself and to others in your adult life?

How does shame affect your ability to use power/control in your adult life? As an adult, do you have a sense that others exercise power over you or "use" you?

This exercise can be a very powerful tool in helping abuse survivors identify deep inner shame. With permission, we include some responses from BECOMERS participants, reflecting some of their anguish and depth of pain revealed through the use of a childhood photo:

"This child was sexually abused because
   . . . she was born.
   . . . she had sick parents who took out their misery on her and got away with it because no one cared.
   . . . of his need to be nurtured from a father figure.
   . . . because she developed too soon.
   . . . because she didn't say no.
   . . . because she was there, and she was small."

"This child needed . . .
   . . . to be stillborn.
   . . . to be born to other parents.
   . . . to be taken out of the home.
   . . . someone to listen to her.
   . . . to have someone care about him and help him.
   . . . love and attention from her dad.
   . . . her mom."

"This child felt . . .
   . . . powerless.
   . . . momentary satisfaction and acceptance from someone he thought really cared.
   . . . feelings of guilt for allowing the abuse to happen.
   . . . that she deserved her treatment because she wasn't worthy of anything better.
   . . . that life will never change.
   . . . confused, abandoned, rejected, alone."

"This child believed . . .
   . . . that something was wrong with her, that she was bad.

. . . that sexual feelings were bad and were to be kept secret.
. . . it was okay to be abused as long as it made Dad happy.
. . . that it was an acceptable way to show love.
. . . that she was unloved, despised, worthy of ugly, abusive treatment.
. . . that if she told anyone, she would get in a lot of trouble."

"This child decided . . .
. . . to withdraw, put up a front to be whatever those around her wanted her to be.
. . . to play along and hide what she was really feeling.
. . . that no one could be trusted and everyone was out to hurt her.
. . . to just be quiet and forget about it."

"If I were to adopt this child, I would . . .
. . . show the child more love in a nurturing, nonsexual way, because otherwise the child will look for acceptance in a sexual way.
. . . help him to feel loved and safe about talking about his feelings because he is a special person and very gifted.
. . . not do it because she has wounds and scars that are too deep to heal. The best I could do is leave her alone and not hurt her anymore.
. . . hold her as long as she wanted to be held and give her lots of hugs."

Shame Recovery Project Three

Progressing from understanding the differences between guilt and shame to identifying sources of shame messages, abuse survivors must further address the issue of responsibility for the occurrence of sexual abuse. The following homework is designed to help abused adults uncover levels of responsibility they continue to bear for their abuse.

- What have you told yourself that you are responsible for concerning your sexual abuse? That is, who is "to blame" for the abuse?
- What do you think are the responsibilities of the offender/s concerning your abuse?
- In God's sight, what do you think you are responsible for?
- What do you think God holds the offender/s responsible for?

- How have you assumed responsibility (blamed yourself) for the abuse, or parts of the abuse?
- What do you think might hinder you from "releasing" feelings of being responsible for the abuse?

The issue of who is responsible for the abuse is critical to restoration. The offender is responsible. However, holding offenders fully responsible for the abuse is not often the response of survivors to these questions. Some abuse survivors discovered they felt responsible for the abuse because they were quiet and didn't resist; because there were some "good feelings" associated with the abuse; because they were *told* they were responsible for it; or because they believed God had "predestined" them to be abused. Hindrances to releasing themselves from responsibility for the abuse are often embedded within abused adults' beliefs that they are "garbage," that something is "wrong" with them, that others must be right or more important, that nothing can change, or a feeling that God does not care.

A Note on Sexual Shame

Sexual shame is a residual effect of sexual abuse and shaming sexual messages from hurtful families. These difficult issues must be faced in the light of God's truth and in an atmosphere of unconditional acceptance. Questions may arise about exposing abuse survivors to this kind of introspection. However, buried areas of sexual shame are actually "buried alive." If not exposed to the Light as part of the restoration from sexual abuse, they will continue to exert control from the inside and may become an instrument of abuse to self or others.

The purpose of this exercise is to increase awareness of shaming messages relating specifically to sexuality. BECOMERS participants who are part of a couple are encouraged to answer the homework questions personally and to invite their spouses or significant others to answer the same questions. It is recommended that this exercise be discussed in depth in individual counseling or in marital counseling with professionals who have expertise in dealing comfortably with issues related to sexuality and sexual shame.

Shame Recovery Project Four

Identifying Sexual Shame
Note messages you received about sexuality. Messages may

have been spoken or unspoken; sometimes they may be identified as "instinctive feelings," such as, "Sex is dirty," "Be sure to save it for the one you love," "*Nice* girls don't enjoy sex," or "Real men take sex any way they can get it."

Identifying Childhood Messages About Sexuality

What were early "messages" in your family about your body? What were your parents' attitudes about nudity/modesty?

What did you learn in your family about: pregnancy, birth, sexual intercourse, masturbation, homosexuality, sexually transmitted diseases, HIV/AIDS? Who told you about these things, and how did you feel?

Identifying Sexual Shame From Adolescent/Adult Experiences

Did you experience sexual activity with an older person/persons? If so, how old were you, and how old was the other person/persons? What kind of sexual activity was involved: looking, genital touching, vaginal penetration, oral/genital contact, anal contact, other kinds of contact . . .

Did you observe (hear or see) parents or others having intercourse? Note feelings.

Regarding masturbation, note age when it began; were you punished; frequency; method (self/others); accompanying fantasies; marriage partner's knowledge about . . .

Regarding sexual intercourse, note frequency, number of partners, sex of partner (opposite/same), kinds of partners (spouse/fiancé/lover/friend/prostitute/hooking up . . .)

Regarding use of pornography, note frequency, type (Internet/X-rated movies/adult bookstore/other)

Identifying Sexual Shame in Feelings About Femininity/Masculinity

Note: Couples are encouraged to note their individual perceptions about themselves as feminine/masculine, and then invite their spouses to do the same to process together in a safe and supportive setting.

For Women:

Do you feel feminine? Note your sense of being popular, accepted by peers, feeling sexually adequate . . .

What are your feelings about your body size, appearance, breast size, hips, genitals . . .

For Men:

Do you feel masculine? Note your sense of being popular,

accepted by peers, feeling sexually adequate . . .

What are your feelings about your body size, appearance, voice, hair distribution, genitals . . .

Identifying Sexual Shame Messages in Intimate Relationships

Regarding dating/engagement, note feelings related to sexual activity, kissing, French kissing, making out, intercourse, number of partners, feelings about sexual involvement . . .

Regarding marriage, note feelings related to premarital sex, sex in marriage, levels of sexual satisfaction, concerns about sexual dysfunction . . .

When dealing with sexual issues in support group settings, a respectful balance needs to be maintained. It is important for abuse survivors to have permission to tell "secrets" that have kept them in bondage to shame. It is equally important for others not to be victimized by the telling of explicit details of sexual acts related to those "secrets." Group members are encouraged to share their thoughts and feelings about the process of completing this exercise relating to sexual shame. Group members are encouraged to process explicit details of this exercise in individual, marital, or therapy group settings.

11

Step Four: Discovering Self-Identity

Step Four: I am looking to God and his Word to affirm my identity as a worthwhile and loved human being.

Identity formation: a process of developing a sense of "self" and recognizing that the self has boundaries and value. The ultimate source of identity is founded upon God's grace.

How is an identity formed? The process of developing a sense of "self" is formed through interactions with other people and by making decisions regarding who and what one will be.[1] In addition, significant impact on a child's potential for developing faith in God is formed through childhood experiences of intimate relationships in which families provide the setting for spiritual growth.[2]

IDENTITY FORMATION: "BUILDING BLOCKS"

Identity formation begins in infancy.[3] The first two years are foundational to a child's developing sense of who they are. Throughout infancy, children develop a "template" about how their basic needs will be met. This process of attachment is repeated thousands of times in the earliest years of childhood: A child becomes aware of a basic need, such as hunger or discomfort; "arousal" builds as the child uses distressed behaviors to "signal" there is a need. When the need is met, the child is soothed. Consistent meeting of needs fosters the building of trust because children trust that their caregivers can and will care for them.

If there is delay in a child's need being met, the child's distress increases. At this point, significant "learning" takes place: A child might learn that needs will consistently be met, needs will inconsistently be met, needs will be met with violence, needs will be neglected or ignored, and/or needs will be sexualized.

When children are physically abused (such as being slapped for crying), they experience abuse instead of nurture at times of high arousal—at times when they are already distressed. From within their cognitive reasoning, children conclude that they must have the "power" to cause others to act out anger and abuse toward them. They may eventually lose fear and learn to numb pain. Such early formative experiences influence children not to trust but instead to believe that abuses of power are ways in which needs are met.[4]

When children's needs are neglected, other lessons are learned. Children experience distressed arousal but to the point of exhaustion because needs are not met. Eventually, neglected children develop fewer needs and learn to develop ways to gratify needs themselves, such as head banging or rocking back and forth. Children who are consistently neglected tend to develop a self-reliance that interferes with a desire or capacity to depend on others.[5]

When very young children are sexually abused, sexual stimulation may bring gratification to a child simply because certain kinds of stimulation are pleasurable to the human body. However, adults who sexually abuse a child often both hurt and please the child, creating pain, fear, confusion and distrust. Children can learn to both desire and fear sexual contact.[6]

Thus in the first two years the first stage of a child's identity formation has settled into place as a "template," primarily reflecting *trust* or *mistrust*.

From that foundation, a child negotiates through the next stage in identity formation: *autonomy* or *shame*. Autonomy is expressed through a natural curiosity and exploration of new things. The famous "no" of toddlers is the beginning development of boundaries, of having a "me" that is distinguished from "you." Alternatively, a sense of inadequacy can be incorporated into a child's identity at this stage through early shame messages, such as being repeatedly told they are "bad" for normative toddler behaviors.

From a sense of autonomy or shame, children encounter the next stage of development: discovering a sense of self as *capable* or as *inferior*. During elementary school years, children learn from responses of others around them. From responses of encouragement and affirmation, children incorporate a sense of feeling capable. Alternatively, doubt and inferiority will shape a child's identity through patterns of coercion or abuse. The gift of imagination blossoms at this developmental stage, and images about God can be very powerful in positive ways, such as "Jesus loves me. I am his little lamb." In stark contrast, spiritual images of terror can be transmitted through sexual abuse, such as a father sexually abusing a four-year-old and telling her "I'm cleansing you for Jesus. If you tell, God will kill you."

In adolescence, children are capable of more complex ways of thinking about themselves. Previous stages of development have set the stage. Adolescents integrate messages from earlier development along with their feelings about themselves, and begin to integrate them into a sense of identity as they look toward their future. Over time, this process results in a greater sense of *identity* in "who I am" or, alternatively, less clarity and more *confusion*.

In her book *Secret Shame: I Am a Victim of Incest,* Martha Janssen shares her struggle with identity development as a young adolescent:

Thirteen

Textbooks say that thirteen
is the age when one
wrestles with identity.
Am I weak or strong
    loved or rejected
    female or male
    capable or inept?
Who am I? the child-adult wonders.
I wondered too.
I stood before the screen door
looking at the countryside
from Grandpa's house in summer.
I was blank inside
    lonely
    bored
    wondering.
I was struggling
    wrestling
not just with identity
    but with what you said about me
    by what you did.
I was weak—
    you always won.
I was rejected—
    you went away angry.

I was female—
and hated it.
I was not capable
because I could not change my life.
Young, tender, frightened
I was a textbook case of the struggle
and doomed to lose.
A blank empty life
looking out the screen door.[7]

From adolescence, young adults move toward ways of developing *intimacy* in relationships or, alternatively, experiencing an increased sense of *isolation*. Intimacy involves a capacity to commit to significant relationships, which may call for sacrifice and compromise but does not result in a loss of a sense of self. Avoidance because of fearing a loss of self pushes some toward isolation—the counterpoint to intimacy.[8]

Middle-age adults can move into a developmental stage of *generativity*, that is, investing in those in the generations coming along behind them. Or, alternatively, middle-age adults can experience *stagnation* by failing to find ways to contribute to the nurture of younger generations and fall into complacency or cynicism.

Older adults can come to a crossroads in development, experiencing a sense of *integrity* with life, that is, sensing that one's life has been lived purposefully and with meaning. Alternatively, elders can develop into a stage of *despair* that life is near its end, has not gone as they had hoped, and it is too late to go back and do things differently.

These "developmental building blocks," along with other complex influences, come together to shape one's identity across the lifespan.

IDENTITY FORMATION: FROM THE OUTSIDE IN

It is clear that the destructive experience of sexual abuse can cause great damage to a developing self-identity. Healthy development is disrupted through violations of physical, emotional, intellectual, and spiritual boundaries. Instead of developing a sense of "self" who has boundaries and value, adult survivors are more likely to be shaped into a "victim" identity from the outside in.

A damaged identity can be recognized by many hurtful outcomes. Instead of trust, adult survivors may have had no foundation of trust from their earliest experiences of caregiving, or perhaps any trust that had been formed has crumbled under the weight of sexual abuse. While hope often corresponds to trust, a sense of hopelessness corresponds to mistrust. Hopelessness contributes to perceptions of being "frozen" in the pain of present life circumstances, that things will never get any better, that pain is unending and irreversible.

Pervasive effects of *shame* on identity formation were outlined in chapter 10. Building blocks of *inadequacy* and *inferiority* often contribute to a sense of helplessness. Resulting beliefs might be that one's fate depends on other people's evaluations, or luck, or capricious factors outside one's control. Even God isn't there—or, if he is present, he is perceived as having no power. Re-victimization can be a tragic outcome of an identity significantly shaped by inadequacy, inferiority, and helplessness. Another outcome of inferiority may be an underlying fear of being discovered as a failure, with subsequent rejection and pain that may make trying to change seem too risky.

A sense of identity *confusion* about "who I am" can contribute to an identity of self-condemnation and a view of self as "nothing." Adult survivors are often unable to have any positive regard for themselves, let alone love themselves in ways warranted by Scripture. Perfectionism compounds self-defeat when goals and standards are seen as personal values that are unattainable rather than viewed as unrealistic. Feeling motivated by internal "shoulds" and "oughts" can lead to frustration and discouragement, reinforcing an identity of worthlessness. Efforts required to make changes seem too great and rewards not worth struggling for; thus, self-condemnation plays a role in feelings of defeat.

Instead of an identity building block toward healthy intimacy, an identity building block of *isolation* can contribute to a fear of intimacy and connection to others. Adult survivors with this perception will tend to avoid commitment or involvement, which increases their isolation.

Taking into consideration these building blocks of a damaged identity, it becomes apparent that making a transition from a "victim" identity to an identity in Christ and from a self-condemning identity to one that values self requires a process of re-formation from the inside out.

IDENTITY FORMATION: FROM THE INSIDE OUT

In our experience with BECOMERS, churches sometimes raise concerns when we discuss the importance of abuse survivors learning to value themselves and "love themselves." The critique is raised related to vanity or pride or humanistic self-centeredness because these types of self-love are inconsistent with Scripture. A point well taken. At the same time, learning to love oneself is part of the fruit of an identity based on the love of God through Christ. When a scribe came to Jesus and asked him which commandment was most important, Jesus replied, "Love the Lord your God with all your heart and with all your soul and with all your mind and with all your strength. The second is this: Love your neighbor *as yourself.* There is no commandment greater than these" (Mark 12:30–31, emphasis added). In *Christian Child-Rearing and Personality Development,* Paul Meier writes that persons "who don't love themselves in a healthy way will find it impossible to develop genuine love relationships with others. Two of the most important concepts I learned from my psychiatric training, both of which agree totally with scripture, are: (1) you cannot truly love others until you learn to love yourself in a healthy way; (2) lack of self-worth is the basis of most psychological problems."[9]

In *Do You Sometimes Feel Like a Nobody?* Tim Stafford writes about resistance to the exhortation to love oneself:

> I will refer to people who believe this as the "Nothings" because they say, repeatedly, "I am nothing; Christ is everything." . . . They emphasize that all pride is bad. I think all Christians would agree that there is a kind of pride that is deadly—the pride that says to God, "I am self-sufficient. I don't need you. I'll make it on my own." But Nothings believe in extinguishing all pride—pride in a good job, pride in an act of kindness, pride in an attractive, healthy body. They think it detracts from loving God. They quote Paul: "If I am going to boast, let me boast in the Lord."
>
> Also, Nothings believe that all our problems were destroyed when Jesus died on the cross, and that we are meant to have the full results of that immediately. Thus all problems are religious problems; a person is depressed or discouraged or sick only because he hasn't "yielded" to God, or "put God on the throne of his life. . . ."
>
> A Nothing philosophy can work, especially for people blessed with a strong ego and a stable personality. Since these people already tend to think highly of themselves, the Nothing philosophy keeps their feet on the ground. Others are damaged by such a philosophy.[10]

Adult survivors of sexual abuse are working from damaged

identities that must be rebuilt upon foundations other than shame and self-loathing. To learn to love themselves as God does involves a process that highlights scriptural truths and directly confronts lies from childhood abuse.

IDENTITY IN CHRIST: PUTTING AWAY CHILDISH THINGS

The process of developing a sense of "self" identified with Christ is just that—a process. It is easy to lose sight of the ongoing nature of identity formation when speaking about "identity in Christ" because the term sounds like a static condition—frozen in time. The Word of God calls on us to rework concepts of ourselves through the principle in Proverbs 23:7 (NKJV) that reminds us that as one thinks in the heart, so one is. One's identity exists primarily in mental images and in specific ways that thought patterns have come to be associated with those images.

Adult survivors of abuse can be encouraged to undertake a joint venture with God, asking for divine intervention in deconstructing hurtful identities from childhood, and reconstructing identities grounded in his unconditional love and acceptance. Adult survivors of sexual abuse know the painful truth of feeling and thinking as a child as expressed in 1 Corinthians 13:11. We personalize this verse specifically for survivors as it relates to the development of a "victim" identity:

> When I was [abused as] a child, I spoke and thought and reasoned as a [victimized] child does. But when I became [an adult] my thoughts grew far beyond those of my childhood, and now I have put away the childish things. (TLB)

BECOMERS is intended to be a place where adult survivors can be empowered in the process of "putting away" a victim identity from childhood through the power of God's grace and with tangible ongoing support from the body of Christ.

Suggested Personal Application Questions to Accompany Step Four:

Identity Restoration Project One
How might this new identity begin to be experienced?[11]

• Define your current identity.

Who are you? How do you think of yourself? Select ten words

that you frequently use to define yourself.

How do others define you?

- Identify changes in identity you would like to experience.

What part/s of your self-identity do you dislike?
What would you like to change?

- Identify a new identity you desire.

Who would you like to become?

Knowing (or trying to believe) that you are created in the image of God and that you are accepted and loved unconditionally, what would your new identity in Christ look like? What would it feel like? What would it sound like?

Visualize this new self so that it reflects the ten words you used earlier to describe yourself. Change the words above to fit your newly visualized self if they don't fit who you would like to be.

Visualize your identity in Christ and "hear" Jesus say, "That looks just right!"

Imagine yourself living the life of that person, "hear" others in your life talking to the new person Jesus has made of you.

Do you "hear" inner objections coming to mind as to why this new identity cannot belong to you? Pay attention to these objections so that they can be addressed in prayer, in sharing with others in your group, and with feedback from trustworthy sources.

- Experiencing your identity in Christ.

Commit yourself to the person you desire to become. What one thing could you do today to move in that direction? Who are the safe persons in your life who will support you in becoming this kind of person? Tell them about your goals.

Identity Restoration Project Two

- Select a passage from Scripture or some other reading that speaks to your identity in Christ. In response to that reading, who does God say that you are? Who do you say that you are?

Identity Restoration Project Three

- Select a photo of yourself between the ages of three and seven. Choose a special frame for the photo, and put it in a place where you will see it often. Use the photo to remind you of yourself as a precious child; notice how your carefully chosen frame confers specialness to the child within the frame. Talk to your group members about how you came to choose the photo and what it was like for you to select a frame. When it seems appropriate to you, bring your framed photo to share with your group. It may take some time for you to accomplish this exercise. Over time, you will come to accept and love the child in the photo as you come to accept and love yourself as a child of God.

12

Step Five: Sharing Feelings

Step Five: I am honestly sharing my feelings with God and with trustworthy others to help me identify those areas that need cleansing and healing.

Honestly sharing feelings: a process of giving voice to a full range of emotions in accordance with authenticity as portrayed by Christ and for the purpose of being set free.

God created human beings with the capacity to *experience* a full range of emotions, and he has given guidelines to deal responsibly with *expressing* emotions. Diane Langberg draws parallels between God's expression of himself and human self-expression: "God's word makes Him accessible; our word makes us accessible. . . . God's essence is found in the Word; our essence is expressed in our voice. To be created in the image of God is to have a voice and speak that voice out into the world."[1] Anything that silences someone's voice destroys God's image within that person; forced silence essentially destroys personhood.

In the context of empowering God-given "voice," adult survivors are encouraged to break the silence about their abuse and reclaim a sense of personhood. As for the process of emotional sharing, Jesus portrays the model of authenticity in response to emotions as he is seen responding appropriately to the full breadth of emotions within human experience.[2] Recovery from sexual abuse involves learning to recognize, experience, and share emotions rather than suppressing them. Safe places, such as therapists and support groups, allow intense emotions to be discharged without harm to self or others. Moving through a process of sharing deep inner pain most often reduces depression and anxiety and helps survivors regain a sense of control in their lives.

STUMBLING BLOCKS TO EXPRESSING EMOTIONS

Barriers to expressing feelings may be fears about hurting or offending someone; being disliked, rejected by, or losing relationships with significant people; beliefs that feelings such as anger or grief are not "Christian" feelings; and significant fears that feelings will be so powerful that survivors cannot cope with the intensity.

Other challenges are not related to *expressing* feelings but rather the *manner* in which feelings are expressed. For example, anger can become an obstacle when used to overpower others with rage. Anger may actually conceal shame, fears of abandonment, or feelings of helplessness. Out-of-control anger can indicate an underlying lack of communication skills or be a way of acting out learned behavior from childhood.

Addictions block emotional expression. Survivors may have been raised in families where family members had little confidence that they could hold up in the presence of strong emotion or challenging life situations. Thus, in a world that seemed chaotic and out of control, family members learned to count on what could be most easily controlled. Families with addictions often have problems with at least one of the "big three" quick-fix solutions to avoid pain of honest feelings: alcohol and drugs, food, and overspending.[3] Abuse survivors who are medicating their inner pain with some addictive substance or behavior must be supported to confront addictions that impair their progress of restoration.

Not knowing *how* to identify feelings or share feelings can feel intimidating for survivors. Early on in a group process, modeling ways to share feelings can be framed as learning skills that were not taught in families. It can be helpful for survivors to notice their use of the word *that* when trying to express their feelings. For example, when forty-year-old Martha was asked how she felt about a phone call from her mother, Martha replied, "I was wishing that she wouldn't call me all the time." When her group leader reflected back to Martha that her comment expressed what she was *thinking* but did not express how she was *feeling*, Martha replied, "I felt that . . . no, I felt angry. Really furious."[4]

Christians are often ambivalent about sharing feelings and may have been taught that experiencing or sharing certain feelings, such as anger, is sinful. Thus, it can be helpful to address these concerns by distinguishing between bitterness and anger.

Bitterness has different shades of meaning in the New Testament. It contains both the elements of "seized" and "pressed down" anger that becomes rooted within.[5] When anger is suppressed, it is pushed down into one's "memory bank." Attempts to "fence in" anger often occur when Christians believe that by suppressing anger, it will not cause hurt or loss of control.

Anger is an emotion of intense displeasure, usually antagonistic, often triggered by a sense of being wronged. For abuse survivors, anger can evoke fears of being out of control and vulnerability. Because anger is often a "cover" for hurt, sadness, or fear, it is a powerful emotional force. Locked inside, it can cause damage to self; out of control, anger can injure others emotionally, physically, or spiritually. However, anger can also be a positive force that provides motivation for change and healing.

Scripture does not instruct Christians to suppress anger. Rather, it assumes that we will experience anger and urges us to learn how to express anger appropriately. Unless new patterns are learned, suppressed anger will often cause a return to old patterns that remain from childhood: throwing things, withdrawing, yelling, transferring anger to others, blaming others, being hostile toward the body (being over/underweight, over-exercising, turning off sexually), being pessimistic, rebellious, having judgmental attitudes, being sarcastic, or escaping to fantasy. Often, expressing anger will disarm intense emotions so that pain will decrease and survivors will have emotional energy to invest in other ways.

Some struggle with whether Christians "should" express angry feelings, especially if directed toward God. Consider Job's response to his devastating circumstances, written in the contemporary language of *The Message*: "And so I'm not keeping one bit of this quiet, I'm laying it all out on the table; my complaining to high heaven is bitter, but honest." God did not shame or curse Job for expressing his anguish, but rather walked with Job through his trials. In the end, God praised Job "for being honest with me." He accepted Job's prayer, and "blessed Job's later life even more than his earlier life" (Job 42:7–17 THE MESSAGE).

God's guidelines for dealing with anger are found in Ephesians 4:26: "Go ahead and be angry. You do well to be angry—but don't use your anger as fuel for revenge. And don't stay angry. Don't go to bed angry" (THE MESSAGE.) In *Wuest's Word Studies in the Greek New Testament*, anger is unpacked from its original meaning in Greek. "When guided by reason, anger is a right affection, so the Scripture permits it, and not only permits, but on fit occasion, demands it. . . . The words 'Be ye angry' are a present imperative in the Greek text, commanding a continuous action. This *orgē*, this abiding, settled attitude of righteous indignation against sin and sinful things, is commanded, together with the appropriate actions when conditions make them necessary."[6]

Sexual abuse against children is most certainly sin that *demands* a response of anger. However, very few abused children are allowed to express any anger until years later. Adult survivors end up suffering even greater damage due to suppressed and repressed anger that manifests itself in depression, fears, anxiety, physical ailments, or symptoms of post-traumatic stress.

THE GRIEVING PROCESS: A TIME TO MOURN

Grieving is a pivotal part of restoration for adult survivors of sexual abuse. It involves an extensive and painful process through the incredible emotional investment of identifying and experiencing multiple losses. Moving through a grief process empowers survivors to make subsequent healthy life changes because they have renewed emotional energy to reinvest in other parts of life.

Helen Fitzgerald pioneered the nation's first grief program in a community mental health center and has outlined a process of grief and loss often experienced by adult survivors of sexual abuse.[7] Each abuse survivor will have a unique path through grief and loss. At the same time, there are general phases involved in a process of resolving grief. Survivors may cycle back and forth in this process many times as they face the multiple losses they have suffered.

Identifying Losses

An initial phase of the grief process occurs when memories of sexual abuse begin to surface and be acknowledged. Survivors often expend great amounts of energy trying to convince themselves that the abuse did not happen, even though they may be experiencing immense sadness "for no reason." Denial serves as a buffer or safety zone to shield survivors from the reality of the pain of the abuse. "We need denial—but we must not linger in it," writes Joyce Landorf. "We must recognize it as one of God's unique tools and use it. . . . We do not need to feel guilty or judge our level of Christianity. . . . However, we need not be dependent on it."[8] The tragedy for adult survivors is that they have often been in denial for years out of necessity for survival.

As survivors begin to break through denial, they may even find themselves returning to the places where they were abused to see if the abuse was "real." An adult survivor found herself going over documents from the court proceedings where her father had been convicted of sexually abusing her as a child. It took reading the court documents over and over to break through the denial that the abuse had occurred. A surfacing of emotions of the grief process often moves survivors into a next phase.

Experiencing the Pain

Surfacing emotions can be intense, making this the most difficult and frightening part of the process. Grief may fluctuate from being manageable to feeling explosive and out of control, coming in slow progression or erupting all at once. Emotions associated with the grieving process vary across a spectrum from anger, rage, resentment, and feeling "guilty" to despair, loneliness, worthlessness, and helplessness. Support from trustworthy persons is critical during these times.

Tremendous loss is experienced by adult survivors: loss of control over one's own body; a loss of innocence and, in many cases, a loss of an entire childhood; the loss of not having had a protective or nurturing family or appropriate role models. When survivors come to realize how different things could have been, they come face-to-face with the realization that their situation really was as painful and deprived as they had inwardly felt. Survivors may be so consumed with rage that they truly fear the expression of their anger—at the perpetrator and/or at themselves.

In the intensity of emotions, survivors may understandably want to short-circuit the healing process, or desperately want the pain to be over, and may attempt some sort of "bargaining" with God. Often the bargaining issue revolves around forgiveness: "God, I will forgive this person if you will take away my anger." Survivors may "forgive" their offender/s, but find no relief after doing so. Not realizing that the forgiveness process was prematurely short-circuited by a desire to avoid pain or to comply with someone else's demand on them to forgive, survivors may end up begging, threatening, trying harder to please God, or, alternatively, walking away from God because it seems to them that God did not keep his end of the "bargain."

Sometimes, after reality has pushed through denial, and the intensity of mixed emotions of grieving has depleted emotional resources, and "bargaining" has seemed to fail, depression may set in. Survivors may notice physical symptoms of depression, such as low energy level, changes in sleeping and eating habits, loss of sexual interest, or an unkempt physical appearance. Some psychological signs might include hopelessness, anxiety, loss of perspective, low self-esteem, emotional extremes in areas of dependency, avoiding others, or overreacting in uncharacteristic ways.

Readjusting to the Loss

As some of the emotional intensity subsides, survivors may experience a lighter load. They have been able to set aside old feelings and behavioral strategies that hindered their adult life and relationships. Some survivors may find themselves dissociating less frequently and be able to stay more focused on tasks of daily life. Some survivors have been able to share their grief and loss with family and friends and experience support. Others, however, may find themselves needing to distance themselves from family members and friends who are critical or judgmental about the healing process. As one adult survivor put it, "There is nothing wrong with us as survivors—something wrong was *done* to us!"[9] Survivors may experience a new wave of grieving if they have to step back from significant people in their lives.

Reinvesting Emotional Energy

As the grieving process provides a degree of restoration, survivors may carry less emotional weight and come to some level of acceptance with what has happened to them. Trust is being rebuilt. Their souls may feel revived, releasing energy to spend on rewarding and pleasurable relationships instead of being consumed by the painful grieving process.

Reconciling the Loss

This may be a time when an adult survivor will want to be involved in some type of ministry to others who have been abused. (See also chapter 16.)

Continuing the Journey: A Time to Heal

Abuse survivors may encounter other challenges along their healing journey in the form of fears, patterns of anxiety, or obsessive-compulsive behaviors. Each can be addressed both in individual counseling and support group experiences.

FEAR AND ANXIETY

The word *fear* comes from a root word meaning *peril*. Fearing that danger or evil is near underlies many responses of abuse survivors. Many fears are not experienced on a conscious level. Sometimes fears are expressed through nightmares or sleep disturbances. A thirty-five-year-old survivor had persistent terrifying nightmares involving two geometric figures—a circle and a square. In recovery, she was able to connect those nightmares with her sexual abuse experience. The circles and squares were patterns in the carpeting in her father's bedroom. He had forced her facedown into the carpeting when he abused her. She suffered the same recurrent nightmares until she was released from those fears in therapy.

Fears may manifest themselves during life transitions. For example, pregnancy is a life-changing event that involves an intense focus on the female body.[10] The transitions of pregnancy and childbirth can evoke many kinds of fears. A general fear of losing control during pregnancy and childbirth is shared by many survivors. Prenatal exams, labor, and delivery can be perceived by some survivors as invasive procedures that activate feelings that trigger "fight for survival" responses. A birthing mother disclosed, "When the contractions came I lost it and just pushed and screamed that it hurt, I cried for my mommy . . . I just went someplace else, someplace safe in my mind. I know it sounds strange, but I just could not handle it, and I was so tired of being touched."[11] Survivors of past sexual abuse are 25 percent more likely to experience postpartum depression.[12] Alternatively, for some survivors, pregnancy offers them new ways to relate to their bodies in creating new life. A survivor writes, "What a thrill to produce a precious new life out of my body. This body of mine could be of good use."[13]

Patterns of Panic

Survivors who experience a generalized anxiety disorder have a persistent "free floating" sense of tension or dread, and are constantly "on edge" waiting for something dreadful to happen to them or to someone they care about. Anxiety is distressing both for survivors who have panic as a constant companion and for those who experience panic descending on them "out of nowhere."

When anxiety is a constant companion, survivors have trouble making decisions, difficulty concentrating, and find it hard to follow through on commitments. They often experience physical symptoms as well: muscle aches, headaches, nervous twitches, difficulty breathing, racing heart rate, clammy hands, or insomnia.

When panic seems to descend "out of nowhere" in the form of a panic attack, survivors experience an acute sense of impending doom with a very real fear that they are about to die, that they are going crazy, or about to commit a terrible act. In addition to the physical symptoms previously mentioned, the individual can experience dizziness, sweating, gasping for breath, shivering, and a pounding heart. Because these panic attacks are unpredictable, survivors may be afraid to leave their home, fearing another attack.

Patterns of Obsession and Compulsion

Survivors may struggle with obsessive thoughts or images that keep recurring in their minds, even though they may feel the thoughts are senseless or unpleasant. Mild obsessions are experienced by everyone, such as a recurrent song or thought or feeling about something. Such obsessions pass. Of concern, however, is the involuntary dwelling on an unwelcome thought. A young mother, who was a survivor of childhood abuse, experienced obsessive thoughts about sexually abusing her own child. Because these thoughts were extremely distressing to her, she sought professional help and was able to break the cycle of the thoughts and find relief.

In contrast, a compulsion is an action that a survivor feels compelled to repeat over and over to relieve anxiety. For example, a compulsion of excessive bathing or hand washing may develop in a survivor who feels "dirty" because of sexual abuse.

Christian survivors often harbor a great deal of shame about experiencing fears or anxieties and will often feel like a "bad" Christian for even having fears.

A critical element for abuse survivors in overcoming tremendous challenges is not just being told or reminded that God's character can be trusted, but experiencing ways that God works through other Christians in reflecting God's grace to them.

SHARING EMOTIONS: A TIME TO SPEAK

A primary goal of both individual counseling and group support is to provide safe settings in which survivors can verbalize suppressed or "stuffed" feelings. Sharing honestly about abuse may seem insurmountable for survivors who have been unaware of their personal emotions for years.

Even though sharing emotions is central to the healing process, survivors will need encouragement and support to begin that process. A common fear of most abuse survivors is that when intense emotions begin to surface, they will lose control of themselves, "go off the deep end," or have a "nervous breakdown." In *A Door of Hope,* Jan Frank, herself a survivor of incest, suggests that while "going off the deep end" rarely happens, it is nevertheless essential to have the expertise of a trained therapist when dealing with deep emotions, and she advises survivors not to try to walk through their feelings alone.[14] Sherry Russell, a grief management specialist, puts it this way: "Trying to find a way to safely release the pressure valve without professional help is like trying to clean up a large oil slick with a straw."[15]

TOOLS TO FACILITATE EMOTIONAL EXPRESSION

Therapeutic tools presented in the following section are best implemented by trained group facilitators or professionals with expertise in the field of sexual abuse recovery.

Expressing Feelings Through Art

A variety of art techniques can be used to elicit expressions of internalized areas of conflict. Sharing artistic creations facilitates support through positive feedback as group members identify painful feelings through their art exercises and are able to express them to others.

A basic art tool might look like this:[16]

Group members use different colors of crayons to represent different feelings. They indicate where feelings, such as anger, sadness, fear, or happiness, might be felt in their physical body. Sometimes individuals who are unable to "feel" certain emotions, such as anger, might be able to discover that a tight jaw, clenched fist, or a knot in the stomach is actually a physical signal of anger. This may help survivors to more readily identify feelings of which they had been unaware.

Drawings created from experiences or scenes from past abuse can help survivors identify some of their past anguish. Stick figure drawings can be a powerful tool to help release feelings surrounding the abuse. Group members are asked to draw out a scene related to their abuse experience.

This drawing depicts a traumatic scene recalled by a fifty-year-old survivor. In her drawing, she is a six-year-old child lying undressed on the couch. Her nineteen-year-old uncle is actively abusing her, when her grandfather comes into the room. The grandfather sees the abuse occurring; he does nothing and walks nonchalantly out of the room.

The stick figure drawing helped this survivor uncover and eventually release the rage and betrayal toward both her uncle and her grandfather, which had been deeply imbedded in her memory. The verbal expression of these powerful feelings was a catalyst that helped her move into her healing process. Not only did she benefit from expressing her intense feelings but also from the validation of other group members who identified with her, empathized with her, and grieved with her. By her sharing, other group members were empowered to express themselves and know they would be supported as well.

A variation of this technique is suggested by Jan Frank in *A Door of Hope*. She suggests that survivors locate childhood pictures and draw floor plans of the location in which the molestation occurred as a tool to facilitate emotional expression.

Word association is another artistic exercise. Group members are asked to draw symbols that represent specific words, such as father, mother, home, family, sex, love, etc. One survivor drew a circle in response to the word *mother*. To her, "mother" was a closed person who kept everyone out. This woman always felt excluded from her mother's love and acceptance. A male survivor drew a snow-capped mountain representing "father." He was able to express how this mountain represented his father—cold, distant, and terrifying.

Writing poetry can be a vehicle for survivors to use to express themselves literally or symbolically. Personal prose can evoke deep images of intense rage and shame. The following poem is printed by permission of the author.

Inscription

> Your words, jagged as broken glass, sharp as icicles,
> Tore through the fine, white veil of my innocence
>   —my childhood.
> Your arms, your hands, plush, warmly stroking,
> Hypnotic . . .
> Have torn me limb from limb,
> Razor-like, slashing beauty and virginity and
>   femininity alike.
> I am like an ugly circumcision
> Done from pubis to lips.
> A surreal Picasso nude—
> chopped apart, re-formed in disarray.
> I have been dipped in the sludge of
>   your depravity,
> I am foul with your stench,
> I carry a granite load—your guilt—
>   upon my back.
> Chained, it will not shake off.

—Elizabeth Moore McGonigle[17]

Family Sculpturing

Another tool used to facilitate awareness is *family sculpturing*. An individual "sculptor" selects other group members to represent family members. The "sculptor" arranges group members in relation to each other for the purpose of depicting emotional closeness/distance, and roles, such as power, control, passivity, or helplessness. The "sculptor" explains who is representing each family member and how those family members interact with one another and with the "sculptor." Often, survivors are unaware of perceptions about their family system until they participate in this tangible representation of family members.

One twenty-five-year-old woman "sculptor" seated the first group member on a chair in the middle of the room. After asking permission to seat a second group member on the first group member's lap, the second group member was placed. A third group member was positioned on top of a table, with her back to the rest of the "family members." A fourth group member, representing the "sculptor," was positioned in the corner of the room facing the wall.

After placing her family members in "relationship" to one another, the "sculptor" realized how isolated she felt from the rest of her family as "she" stood in the far corner facing the wall. Her father was the most "powerful" person in the family, represented by a group member standing "high up" on the table, positioned with "his" back to the family—depicting the "sculptor's" perception of his coldness and lack of involvement with the family. The extreme closeness of the mother and her younger daughter was depicted by the placement of the "mother" sitting in the chair with her adult "daughter" sitting on her lap. The "sculptor" became aware of feelings of intense rejection that she had never measured up to what she felt her mom wanted in a daughter.

Both the "sculptor" and group members representing family members need therapeutic, emotional support in what can be a very intense experiential exercise.

Role-Play

In another type of role-play, a group member interacts with a "substitute" person who symbolically represents someone else, with whom the group member has unresolved feelings. One option for this role-play exercise involves the group member expressing feelings directly toward the "substitute" person sitting in a chair. The "substitute" person may or may not respond to the individual's feelings. Due to the vulnerability of most survivors in a support group setting, this exercise should be used in therapy or with a trained support group facilitator playing the role rather than a group member.

Another variation more suitable for support groups involves the use of an empty chair to represent an "other" person with whom there are unresolved issues. The survivor envisions that the "other" is present in the chair. This is particularly useful in cases where the "other" person is deceased, unapproachable, or unavailable. Role-play is a way for survivors to express powerful emotions in a safe setting while experiencing support, validation, and positive feedback.

Written Expression

Writing can provide a powerful vehicle for sharing emotions. Some survivors find it easier to process their feelings in writing rather than to verbalize them. Many group members keep a journal that allows them to express feelings, document experiences, and note changes in their recovery journey.

Writing can also be used for specific purposes. Group members can be encouraged to write letters to their offenders and to others who have harmed them. The letters are not meant to be sent, but rather used as tools to help group members express what they are feeling from the depths of their pain. Letters are often brought to a group session and read as part of group process. An example of one such letter to an offender is presented in chapter 14.

Many have found it insightful to write a letter to themselves as children, as if the letter were written to them by God. Such an exercise may help reveal to them their beliefs about God's presence during their abuse and in their present lives. Survivors often write letters to God expressing a wide range of emotions, and for many, it is the first time they have been honest about inner feelings toward God.

Survivors are also encouraged to write a letter to the child they once were. The adult survivor tells the small child how, as an adult, she or he feels about that small child. This tool often elicits feelings repressed from childhood, as the adult survivor stands back from the "child" and tries to look at the abusive experiences from an adult perspective. Over time, adult survivors may be able to integrate those childhood experiences into their adult experience, which is part of the restorative process of experiencing themselves as "whole" persons. An adult survivor wrote the following letter to herself as a child:

Dear Neener (my childhood nickname),
    I know this letter is very late in time frame, but I also know

that for your sake and mine I need to write it. There are so many things I want to say to you and that I want you to understand.

I guess I really want you to know that all the forms of abuse that happened to you were not your fault. You never asked to be hit, or screamed at, sworn at, cut down, or expected to be and do more than you were capable. Most of all I want you to know that it was not your fault that you were abused in sexual ways.

You were just a little girl. I know that it felt as if you were never a little girl. You always felt responsible for everyone. You wanted to protect your mom from your dad, and that was loving of you to want to do. But, Neener, you lost yourself. . . . All the blame that you got for the abuse and for all the times your dad left—it was not your fault. You could not have done anything more. It would not have helped if you were a better girl, and the sexual abuse still would have gone on even if you had physically fought harder. . . .

You were caught in a trap and there was no way out. You needed to keep all the secrets in order to survive and that was OK. You do not need to feel bad for that. You never could understand or figure out if it was OK to feel the way you did. You used to try to get your anger out on your dolls. You would talk, yell, and hit them just as mom and dad did to you.

You didn't understand what was going on with your body. All of the burning and discharges. You did not understand what they meant; all you thought was that you were bad and that somehow you were to blame. You were too scared to tell anyone because it was shameful. It's OK that you never told. At that point, you couldn't have emotionally handled it if everyone turned on you, just as you feared. And you always hoped and prayed that you would wake up the next morning and everything would be different. The sad truth and reality is that it never really got better.

I also want you to believe me when I tell you that it was in no way your fault that Jeff ran away. You felt responsible for him leaving because it was right after he raped you; but, Neener, it wasn't your fault. There was nothing you did to cause him to leave. It was his decision. You feel that if only you could have done something, then mom would have been happy, but that is not the truth.

Neener, you were very confused and you missed out on a lot. You lost your childhood, and you have a right to be angry and you need to grieve that loss so you can deal with the present and the future.

Please let yourself go and try to have less expectations of yourself. You do not need to put on all of your masks and act as if you have it all together when you really don't. Inside, you are emotionally just a frightened and hurt little girl. That little girl needs to be given permission to play, to cry, and to be angry. I want to give you that—something you never had. You can never have your innocence back, and that you can be angry at. But you have so much growing and learning to do. You need to start reaching out and asking for what you need. Start asking for help, hugs and support. You need to take risks and steps by letting everything out. You feel as if you are breaking, and it's scaring you, but it's OK.

You are just beginning to be really open and honest and look at all the traumatic secrets that you have held inside for so long. It is not easy but you can do it. Jesus is by your side.

I'm not trying to overwhelm you with things that you need to do, but I know that you need a direction and maybe this will help. Neener, one day you will be strong and healthy. Meanwhile, be patient with yourself; it will be a long process. You were abused for many years and you have a great deal of pain and anger to deal with. You need to believe in yourself and start to really love yourself. I know it is hard, but please remember that the abuse was not your fault. You were not and are not responsible. Take your time, please be patient, and remember you will get through this. Your past is only *a part* of you . . . it is *not all of you.*

13

Step Six: Taking Responsibility for Change

Step Six: I am taking responsibility for my responses to being sexually abused.

Taking responsibility: a process of decision-making involving the ability to make desired changes based on new information.
Considering the incredible shame that survivors feel for making any perceived "mistakes," the issue of "taking responsibility" must be approached in a nonjudgmental and non-shaming manner. Survivors often respond more positively to the idea that taking responsibility is an act of decision-making, and as such, it is a learned skill that can be "practiced" in safe settings in their healing journey.

Adult survivors have often acquired an all-or-nothing worldview as part of the legacy of shame. Life decisions are seen in terms of black and white, with right and wrong responses to every situation. Survivors have rarely viewed new possibilities as opportunities for successful change, but rather have thought about making changes as opportunities to make mistakes.

Adults who have been victimized as children have been conditioned to meet others' needs rather than their own. In addition, they have tended to live their adult lives defeated by what they *should* have done differently in the past or how they *should* be conducting their current lives. From this perspective, "shoulds" block growth because options for change are obscured behind fears about making mistakes. One therapist tells adult survivors that "should" really means "I don't want to but *they* want me to."[1]

In well-functioning families, children are given increasing responsibility for making their own decisions as they grow older, without fear of being considered "mistakes" for making mistakes. While such children may experience both success and failure as consequences for decisions they made, they do not experience condemnation from others or from within themselves. This concept is nearly impossible for shamed survivors to understand. Taking risks and making mistakes is not only difficult but requires tremendous leaps of faith. Survivors can be encouraged to take risks for change after experiencing some measure of trust within their support group setting and after shame has been reduced through support they have received for risking to disclose themselves to others.

There are any number of issues that survivors might want to work on as they continue their recovery journey. Most of those issues will be better addressed by developing communication skills to more clearly express feelings, needs, and define personal boundaries. Thus, this next step focuses on taking responsibility to practice more direct communication by gaining an awareness of defense mechanisms and protective "shields" that block straightforward communication.

IDENTIFYING DEFENSE MECHANISMS

Defense mechanisms protect us from awareness of thoughts and feelings we can't tolerate. Because of the intensely painful and shaming experience of sexual abuse, self-protection through defense mechanisms is not only understandable but was necessary for survival.

While everyone uses defense mechanisms at one time or another, excessive use can block progress in personal growth because defenses only allow hidden thoughts or feelings to come out "sideways" in a disguised form.[2] To illustrate, let's say you are angry with your BECOMERS group leader because you think she is very critical of you. This is how some common defenses might hide and/or disguise that anger:

- *Rationalization*—coming up with various explanations to justify the situation (while denying your feelings).

"My group leader is so shaming because she wants me to heal faster."

- *Suppression*—being vaguely aware of a thought or feeling but trying to hide it.

"I'm going to try to be nicer to my group leader."

- *Denial*—completely rejecting the thought or feeling.

"I'm not angry with my group leader!"

- *Displacement*—redirecting your feelings from one person to another.

"I hate the BECOMERS secretary over at the office."

- *Reaction Formation*—turning the feeling into its opposite.

"I think she's really a great group leader!"

- *Projection*—thinking that someone else has your thought or feeling.

"My group leader is angry with me," or "That group member over there really dislikes my group leader."

- *Undoing*—trying to reverse or undo your feeling by doing something that indicates the opposite feeling. It may be an "apology" of sorts for the feeling you find unacceptable within yourself.

"I think I will bake some cookies to surprise my group leader."

Becoming aware of defense mechanisms may help survivors to decide to "practice" using fewer defenses in their communication with others. In addition to defenses, a related inhibitor to direct communication is the use of "protective shields."

PROTECTIVE SHIELDS THAT HINDER DIRECT COMMUNICATION

Protective shields are "survival skills" of "sideways" communication that were taught to child victims by role-modeling and are the result of children's creative attempts to survive in hurtful families. These indirect communication skills, while providing protection in earlier stages, interfere with progress in the healing process. Part of taking responsibility for recovery involves awareness of defense mechanisms and indirect communication and beginning to notice situations in which they are most often used. That awareness, along with group support, can empower survivors to set goals and practice changes toward developing more direct communication.

To better understand the use of "protective shields" of indirect communication and their possible links to underlying self-beliefs, forty-two female adult survivors in the BECOMERS program completed a forty-question survey. The survey contained yes/no statements to describe beliefs that survivors held about themselves. The results of the survey are integrated into descriptions of "protective shields."

The Peace-Keeper

Peace-at-any-price is a high cost of seeking constant approval from others. Adult survivors who use "peace-keeping" communication are often praised for their willingness to "get along with" others. However, by continually conforming to others' wishes and opinions, survivors can become almost anonymous, lacking clear personal boundaries and having an unclear sense of personal identity. Of the forty-two respondents taking the BECOMERS survey, nearly three-fourths felt an acute need for others' approval to the point that they could not be successful or happy without it. Beliefs that criticism is "upsetting" (71 percent) and that one "must" be loved by others to be secure or happy (83 percent) contribute to indirect communication to avoid conflict or the risk of disapproval.

The Debater

Some people attempt to prove their worth by creating "win-lose" competitions with others. This pattern of communication is usually an attempt to cover shame, insecurity, lack of recognition, or a sense of failure. The Debater often succeeds in pushing others away. Because many survivors do not experience themselves to have personal value apart from their achievement, having to be "right" yields a hollow victory through intimidation, only reinforcing low self-image. Of the respondents in our study, 71 percent reported a need to excel/be right in order to feel valuable.

A variation of this communication pattern is intellectualizing. This "shield" is usually used to protect oneself from feeling or expressing true emotions out of a fear of displaying weakness or vulnerability. Over one-third (38 percent) of the respondents agreed that they should not reveal or share feelings or display vulnerability. Survivors can keep others at a distance by using detached, intellectual conversation that intimidates others into keeping their distance.

The Dominator

Some use this pattern to attempt to control the behavior, thoughts, and/or feelings of others. The same dominating pattern is also commonly used in self-talk to try to "control" one's own self. The most common belief shared by the female respondents was the inner domination of self-talk in which 85 percent felt they *should* be able to control their feelings. Harsh self-judgment is often projected out onto others and is destructive to close relationships. Over two-thirds of the respondents (69 percent) felt it was their responsibility to bring about changes whenever or wherever *they perceived* change was necessary. This belief contributes to over-responsibility in relationships and is linked to attempts to control or coerce others into "right" behavior.

A variation of the Dominator is observed in a self-focused pattern of communication. In his book *Why Am I Afraid to Tell You Who I Am?* John Powell states: "It is almost a universal law that the extent of egocentrism in any person is proportionate to the amount of pain in him. . . . One cannot fashion himself to be the center of the universe and be content that others do not accept him as such."[3] This indirect pattern dominates others by constant reference to themselves in conversation, and such an intense desire to be "known" actually pushes others away.

The "Eternally" Helpless

Persons who "always" appear to be victimized by others tend to have twofold distortions of reality. They are not clear about their own motives or the motives of others. They distrust others while at the same time communicate blame to others for their unhappiness. This essentially sabotages the very relationships that could potentially be restorative.

This is a self-destructive way of relating to others in which "helpless" persons may turn their relationships into battlefields, as people who love them are turned into "bad" people who are perceived to hurt the "helpless" ones. As this happens, the helpless ones will view themselves as only doing "good," and they overlook the hurtful behavior they, themselves, do. They will often say things that hurt, such as "Nothing I do is ever good enough for you."

Maria struggled with victimizing herself and was unaware of the martyr-type behavior pattern she had carried into her adult relationships from the wounding of her past abuse. Her distorted perception of those who were trying to help her was revealed by irrational responses when others expected appropriate give-and-take in their relationship with her. Maria had a caring and empathetic therapist who encouraged her to "practice" some new interaction patterns in the safe setting of therapy. The therapist suggested that Maria try to limit the number of counseling sessions per week to help Maria begin to reduce her dependency on the therapist. Maria jumped up from her chair, burst into tears, and accused her therapist of "never caring" for her and wanting to "dump" her.

Another interaction pattern that often coexists with a pattern of perceived helplessness is passive dependency. Passivity is characterized by believing one is unable to exercise any control over one's life. Of the survivors surveyed, nearly half (45 percent) responded that their moods were primarily created by factors that were largely beyond their control, such as the past, body chemistry, hormone cycles, biorhythms, chance, or fate. For over half (52 percent) of the respondents, their happiness was dependent on what happened *to* them, which also reflected a sense of powerlessness to change. Beliefs such as these, linked with "helpless" interaction patterns, may contribute to destructive relationships of further abuse.

The Fixer

The protective pattern of The Fixer tends to cover inferiority, insecurity, and a lack of self-identity. Fixers derive self-worth from needing to be needed. Fixers rarely admit needing help, and in almost all relationships tend to view themselves as "fixers" and others as "needing-to-be-fixed." Relationships are damaged, however, because Fixers attempt to "fix" others rather than encouraging others to take personal responsibility where it is warranted. In addition, Fixers are usually over-responsible for how others they care about feel and behave. Fully half of the survey respondents felt they were responsible to "fix" others. Many survivors inadvertently use this interaction pattern to avoid dealing with their own issues or to avoid relating to others as equals.

In Christian communities, those with needs are attracted to Fixers. Fixers can be perceived to be more spiritual because of extensive "ministry" involvements, which sometimes mask their own needs. A characteristic of Fixers is that their primary relationships include very few healthy peer friendships.

Our informal BECOMERS survey revealed belief patterns that contributed to the use of defense mechanisms and indirect interaction patterns. Nearly half of this group of female abuse survivors felt inferior to others; two-thirds felt that rejection by someone close to them confirmed their defectiveness and "proved" they were unlovable, and nearly three-fourths struggled with issues of shame, having a sense that something was "wrong" with them. It is true that such beliefs and self-protections inhibit abuse survivors from making decisions about changes in communication patterns. But that is not the end of the story.

Over time, in the framework of God's unconditional acceptance and love, and with the encouragement and support of trustworthy relationships, these very same survivors from this survey have taken courageous risks to change throughout their healing journey. The list below highlights some of the areas in which changes have been made:

- Deciding to make healthy choices for self—changing abusive relationships
- Believing new "messages" about self to replace old messages—practicing positive self-talk
- Actively seeking God for strength in the recovery process—beginning to be able to appropriate Christ more often as their source of identity to replace shame-identity
- Deciding to "let go" of blaming self for the abuse
- Working through conflict instead of avoiding it—attending individual and group therapy
- Being honest about feelings and "owning" them, even though they may be painful
- "Practicing" new thinking and new behaviors and continuing to keep trying
- Asking for forgiveness and/or making restitution for wrong choices in life that have harmed others
- Taking responsibility to move toward more healthy relationships—letting go of over-responsibility for those who tend to be "fixers"; assuming areas of responsibility for those who tend to feel "helpless"
- Willing to consider the possibility of forgiveness for offenses against them

RESISTANCE TO CHANGE: A WORD TO GROUP FACILITATORS

A prerequisite for change is a group member's need to identify his/her own areas needing change, and to make personal decisions about a recovery pathway, both in individual counseling and in a group process. When group members are encouraged to make changes, it may seem to them as if they are being confronted. If so, resistance is likely.

One signal of resistance is insincere agreement by a group member in response to a group facilitator or another group member's encouragement to move ahead. Another signal may be an uncharacteristically excessive emotional outburst when a sensitive area is confronted. Group members may also try to engage a group facilitator in irrelevant arguments by trying to avoid painful subjects or following a suggestion with "yes, but . . ." A sullen, quiet response to a group facilitator's suggestion, direct antagonism, or a refusal to discuss the merit of the suggestion could signal more active resistance.

Resistance is reasonable when a group member is open to considering what a group facilitator is saying but genuinely cannot understand it. The solution to reasonable resistance is reasonable thinking. Trust in the relationship with group facilitators and skills in honest communication in the group process are essential.

Unreasonable resistance arises when a group member is unwilling to consider seriously or try biblical solutions offered by the group facilitator or counselor. Unreasonable resistance cannot be overcome by rational persuasion and is often a source of power struggles in counseling. Leaders and group members can take the following steps to work through a time of resistance:[4]

1. *Identify what underlies resistance.* For example, a group facilitator might encourage a group member to look at the choices she is making in being sexually active for which she needs to take responsibility and be protective of her personal boundaries. The facilitator might confront her by saying, "Maybe it's time for you to start saying no when your boyfriend wants sex. . . ." If she were to reject that idea, it would be necessary to identify her resistance: "You seem resistant to considering breaking off the sexual relationship you are having with your boyfriend. . . ." It is important to express genuine appreciation for how difficult it must be for the group member to face the risks of taking responsibility in this area. The facilitator might continue with, "It must be intensely fearful for you to consider this, especially if you think he will leave you. . . ."

2. *Help the individual reexamine her personal goals concerning areas she wants to change.* The facilitator might suggest, "Let's look at the goals you set up for yourself. You want to develop healthy boundaries, true intimacy with others and with God, and you want to recover from the shame of your past abuse. How does your choice to continue in a sexual relationship with your boyfriend move you toward or away from your personal goals?"

This process may take time, as the group member vacillates from wanting to make changes and the fear of making those changes. Group members can be an invaluable support to one another by encouraging responsible changes. At times, a group member continues to make poor choices and is unwilling to change. If such resistance continues, however, a time may come when it may be necessary to terminate the group process. While these situations would be rare, in such a case, a group facilitator might communicate acceptance of the individual as a person while confronting the lack of responsible behavior in a statement such as, "I am committed to you as a person, and I care deeply for you. But I cannot enable you to continue in hurtful choices that are in conflict with your goals for yourself. Remember that you can return to the group process with a new agenda at any time."

3. *Encourage the individual to "move on," to let go of suppressed feelings, to take responsibility for hurtful choices or unhealthy relationships.* After the previous steps have built a foundation for trust and support, such encouragement can stimulate growth and change for a group member.

Many factors in a trustworthy support group can encourage individual group members to participate and to grow through group process: bonding within the group, receiving and giving support, validation of one's feelings, affirmations for being a person of worth, relief of some pain and shame, personal growth through risk-taking, gaining skills in identifying feelings and needs, increased capacity to listen to others, and a place to "practice" new skills of direct communication.

It is part of the learning process for group members to experience costs of not sharing or for not taking responsibility for change. Deciding not to share in group is a choice to miss out on significant relationships with other group members. A choice to refuse group support may find group members holding on to a painful past. The "safety" provided by little or no risk-taking has consequences of hindering personal growth toward restoration.

Suggested Personal Application Questions to Accompany Step Six

Discerning Responsibility Project One

- How do you define responsibility?
- What personal growth areas in your life do you think are your responsibility?

- In what areas do you consider yourself to be
  (a) over-responsible
  (b) under-responsible?
- Consider the following responses many have experienced from being sexually abused: shame, fear, rage, anger, bitterness, self-hatred, distrustfulness of others, depression, manipulation of others, dishonesty, denial, chemical use, indiscriminate sexual involvement, avoidance of men/women, bulimia/anorexia/overeating, suicidal thoughts/attempts, behaving abusively to others.

Which responses have you experienced in your life? Are there other responses you have experienced?

- Are you currently experiencing some of these responses in your life? Are there any that you would like to change? Which of your responses are you comfortable with as they are now?
- For those areas you would like to change, what might get in the way of your decision to make changes? What would encourage you to make those changes?
- What is God's responsibility in your personal journey at this time?

Clarifying Responsibility

- Who is responsible for the sexual abuse committed against you? Clearly define the offender's/s' responsibility and to whom they are responsible.
- In what ways have you taken responsibility for the abuse in the past? At present?

Discerning Responsibility Project Two
Note to group facilitators: Prior to completing this homework, the group members will need copies of the material presented in this chapter, defining defense mechanisms and protective shields, pages 187–192.

Worksheet to be handed out to group members:

Part of the hardest "work" involved in the healing process is taking responsibility for things that can be changed and "letting go" of things that cannot be changed. In order to take responsible care of ourselves, it is important to be aware of and identify some of the defense mechanisms and protective "shields" that have previously been survival skills but are now hindering recovery. Read the attached materials. After your reading, think about defenses and "shields" that you have learned from your experience of sexual abuse, from your family system, and from ways you feel about yourself. Then answer the following questions as they relate to your insights from your reading.

- Which defenses and/or "shields" do you find yourself using?
- What do these defenses and "shields" reveal to you about your self-image?
- How do these defenses and "shields" affect your relationships with others who are important to you? How might they affect your relationship with God?
- Identify one area in a personal relationship that you would like to change. What is one step you could take toward a change in this area?
- What could hinder you from taking that step?
- For your reflection, consider your personal definitions of *victim* and *survivor*.
- In your life right now, in what ways do you consider yourself a victim? In what ways do you consider yourself a survivor?
- What factors in your life contribute to each of those views?

14

Step Seven: Forgiving

Step Seven: I am willing to accept God's help in the decision and the process of forgiving myself and those who have offended me.

Forgiveness: a restorative process enabled by God's grace.

FORGIVENESS: A CRUCIAL STEP

Forgiveness is one of the most crucial, and often most misunderstood, steps in the healing process. Within the Christian community there is often a lack of understanding of the process of forgiveness. Misunderstandings result in offering simplistic solutions to very painful circumstances. Nothing about forgiveness is simple! Even though theologically forgiveness is not a feeling and does involve an act of the will, making the choice to forgive is much more complex than might appear.

Why Forgive?

Adult survivors of sexual abuse need to recognize that forgiveness is only possible as God accomplishes it through them rather than thinking they have to accomplish forgiveness on their own. The following poem by Martha Janssen helps to express the feelings of an adult survivor who is struggling with the decision-making process involved in forgiveness. She experiences feelings of anguish over forgiving, which she likens to "jagged rocks." These "rocks" may be intense feelings, such as hostility, rage, terror or fear. By expressing her feelings about being "rushed" into a forgiveness that would not reflect a heart change enabled by God, she begins a process of "knowledge and understanding" that leads her to believe that one day she will not only desire but actually be able to faithfully forgive. At that point, she understands that God's command to forgive will not be an impossibility for her.

Forgiveness

There are those who expect me to forgive
to let charitable kindness and reason
wash over me
    like a rushing stream
    over jagged rocks—
to forgive
now.
Seventy times seven—
the command may mean more
than first appears.
Not that one says "I forgive"
over and over and over,
nor that to will it
    makes it so,
but that one forgives
    as one loves—
gradually.
Forgiveness is a process
that begins with knowledge
    understanding
    believing in change.
I feel little charity now.
I can hope
    it may happen
    as I come to understand
    myself and you.
Seventy experiences and understandings
    times seven or seventy more.
I can believe I will forgive
    someday—then.[1]

In Matthew 18:21, Peter asks, "Lord, how many times shall I forgive my brother when he sins against me? Up to seven times?" The reply of Jesus gives insight to both counselors and adult survivors who are addressing the issue of forgiveness. When Jesus tells Peter that he was not to forgive seven times, but rather seventy times seven (KJV), he was confronting Peter's superficial approach to forgiveness. Jesus is teaching Peter that forgiveness is not about "numbers" but is a matter of the heart.[2]

People have many impressions of what "seventy times seven" means. Legalists might count the number of times they have said the words "I forgive you" and feel a self-righteous satisfaction at reaching the 490 mark. Offenders might use these verses to "preach" to their victims—after a quick "I'm sorry"—demanding that survivors of abuse are now responsible before God to forgive. This results in survivors being re-victimized by both the offense and the offender. Survivors of sexual abuse hear the words "forgive seventy times seven" and weep, thinking that this means they are not to hold the offender accountable or that they should return and continue to be victimized by an abusive relationship.

The question of forgiving "seventy times seven" makes it evident that such holiness is beyond the reach of human ability. Peter's "generous" offer to forgive up to seven times is answered by Jesus' reply that it is not seven but 490 times that is required. In this way, Jesus was confronting Peter's self-righteousness based on his human ability to forgive seven times and giving Peter a number so large that he would see his dependence on God for the ability to forgive from the heart.[3] This framework will help both counselors and adult survivors as they consider God's command to forgive.

MOVING TOWARD TRUE FORGIVENESS

Dave Johnson is senior pastor of Church of the Open Door, in Minneapolis, Minnesota (*www.thedoor.org*). In teaching his congregation about "false" forgiveness, he shared the following insights. False forgiveness is defined as speaking the words "I forgive you" to deny, minimize, or spiritualize the pain of abuse—a forgiveness void of the release that restores broken relationships. False forgiveness often leaves survivors feeling that they have not forgiven properly or that something is wrong with them or with God. Incomplete forgiveness can also be unsettling to survivors when the hoped-for reconciliation does not occur. Pastor Johnson illustrates three distinctions that contribute to both false and incomplete forgiveness.

Extended Forgiveness vs. Completed Forgiveness

Both counselors and survivors of abuse need to distinguish between *extended* forgiveness and *completed* forgiveness. Completed forgiveness involves forgiveness from the heart of a survivor, extended to an offender, which is then received *with repentance* by the offender for the fullness of the transaction that God intends forgiveness to accomplish. However, this does not always happen. Survivors of abuse will need to understand this transaction in order to recognize what might happen if there is genuine forgiveness from a survivor that is not met with repentance from the heart of an offender.

Jesus, from the cross, asked his Father to "forgive them; for they know not what they do" (Luke 23:34 KJV). Jesus extended forgiveness to all, but that forgiveness was not received by all. The fullness of that forgiveness transaction did not occur in all to whom the forgiveness was extended. The thief on the cross responded to Jesus' extended forgiveness by receiving it with repentance, and the transaction was completed to its fullness.

When an abuse survivor extends that kind of forgiveness to an offender, however, and when it is not met with repentance and acknowledgment of the grievous wound that has been inflicted, forgiveness doesn't feel "full" or complete. While it may be the desire of Christians to extend forgiveness from the heart as Jesus did, it is also important to realize that, like Jesus, we may not enjoy the fullness of a restored relationship. We may experience pain such as Jesus felt as he looked out over Jerusalem and said, "O Jerusalem, Jerusalem. . . . How often would I have gathered your children together as a hen gathers her brood under her wings, and you would not!" (Luke 13:34 RSV). And he wept and grieved that he did not have a relationship with the ones he loved.

And then Jesus released them . . . "Behold your house is forsaken. And I tell you, you will not see me until you say, 'Blessed is he who comes in the name of the Lord!'" (Luke 13:35 RSV). A similar outcome may be the end result of an abuse survivor's forgiveness of an offender—it may be a "letting go" that falls short of restoration for which the survivor no longer bears responsibility.

I'm Sorry vs. I'm Sorry

Many responses might meet a survivor who is extending a heart of forgiveness toward an offender. "I'm sorry" from an offender can mean "I don't want to talk about this anymore," or "Drop it!" or "I don't want to look at your wound," or "I don't want to grieve over what I did." A survivor of abuse who approaches an offender may hear words like, "I'm sorry you feel that way," or "Well, I said I was sorry! What more do you want? You're the one that is supposed to forgive me, so do it!" or "Why are you bringing this up now?"

These are indicators of lack of repentance. They leave abuse survivors with a sense that promised release and restoration of relationship did not occur, but not knowing why. David Augsburger is professor of pastoral care at Fuller Seminary. In an interview about forgiveness, he offers a biblical perspective that relates to an attitude of authentic repentance. Augsburger points out that the focus on asking for forgiveness is rightly placed on making amends rather than on asking a wounded person to "give" something back, such as changing the way they feel toward the offender. Augsburger emphasizes that if someone is wronged, "the focus is not on asking for something but on demonstrating repentance. I can go to the one I have injured and say, 'I have wronged you. I recognize that. I deeply regret what I have done. I will now live in a different way. And I hope that someday forgiveness will be possible between us.' This takes the injury seriously and allows the injured person however long they need for the process of forgiveness to move to completion."[4]

Counselors need to encourage survivors to differentiate between an insincere "I'm sorry" and godly sorrow coming from repentance that communicates messages such as "I didn't know this had affected you so deeply," or "I am willing to hear your pain." The offender who will listen without interrupting, defending, or correcting a survivor's feelings will communicate a spirit of repentance. Before offenders can truthfully say they are sorry, they need to know what they are sorry for. After having shared the wound, when repentance comes, when there is a groaning from the spirit that says, "I am so sorry . . . ," there can flow the fullness of extended and completed forgiveness from the heart that has potential to restore and heal a relationship.

Intent vs. Impact

A third significant distinction necessary for both counselors and abuse survivors is to be familiar with differences between *intent* and *impact*. Offenders may not have *intended* to inflict immeasurable damage on their victims, but in order for the fullness of forgiveness to heal the relationship, offenders must look at the *impact* of their actions. Abuse survivors must be able to express the full *impact* of what happened to them, from their perspective, in the process of forgiveness without being "shut down" by an offender who says that he or she did not *intend* to do such damage. Again, as Jesus forgave from the cross those who knew not the impact of what they were doing, survivors forgive the fullness of the crime of which offenders "knew not" the extent of the damage.[5]

WHY FORGIVE AN OFFENDER?

Why forgive? Particularly, why should someone who has been cruelly victimized forgive? It is understandable that anyone who has survived sexual abuse will find it extremely difficult to even consider forgiveness. Not forgiving may give abuse survivors a sense of being in "control" over the one who hurt them. It can be used as a means of self-protection from further injury or to "punish" the offender.

At several stages along the healing journey, abuse survivors may encounter unproductive motivations for forgiving their offender. For example, one unproductive reason to forgive in the early stages of recovery is to "get it over with," in order to be done with the pain of the abuse. However, forgiveness cannot be authentic or restorative if the pain has not been defined or declared. Another unproductive act of forgiving is used as an attempt to "manipulate" God into making the pain go away. Demanding action from God—"I did my part, now you better come through for me"—sets up a survivor for frustration and anger if desired results do not follow. Another fruitless motive is forgiving in order to please someone else. It is counterproductive to personal growth to state something outwardly that is not the outcome of inner heart change.

Because God Asks It of Us

Ultimately, the basic reason for forgiving one's offender is because God asks it of us. However, it is important to present a balanced view of Scripture when counseling survivors of abuse. Using the parable in Matthew 18:23–35, some counselors have drawn a parallel between abuse survivors and the servant who was forgiven much and who then refused to forgive a fellow servant. Ultimately, the king asks, "I forgave you all that tremendous debt, just because you asked me to—shouldn't you have mercy on others, just as I had mercy on you?" (TLB).

Seeking Balance

From a balanced view of Scripture, abuse survivors need to define what this "tremendous debt" was and who the king was who paid the debt that otherwise could not be paid. Scripture tells us that Christ was that king—"acquainted with bitterest grief. . . . Yet it was our grief he bore, our sorrows that weighed him down. And we thought his troubles were a punishment from God, for his own sins! But he was wounded and bruised for our sins. He was beaten that we might have peace; he was lashed—and we were healed!" (Isaiah 53:3–5 TLB).

"God sacrificed Jesus on the altar of the world to clear that world of sin. Having faith in Him sets us in the clear. God decided on this course of action in full view of the public—to set the world in the clear with himself through the sacrifice of Jesus, finally taking care of the sins He had so patiently endured" (Romans 3:25 THE MESSAGE).

The "tremendous debt"—the sin owed by the servant—does not denote any sin on the part of a victimized child. This "debt" refers to global sin as spoken of in Romans 3:23–24: "Yes, all have sinned; all fall short of God's glorious ideal; yet now God declares us 'not guilty' of offending him if we trust in Jesus Christ, who in his kindness freely takes away our sins" (TLB). This verse calls a survivor's attention to the "debt" forgiven by Christ's substitutionary death on the cross. Accordingly, a penitent heart that has experienced God's grace will be in a better position to consider an extension of that forgiveness to another. Even to an offender.

However, much damage can be done if counselors press the analogy further, comparing an abuse survivor with the king's servant who was forgiven much but who would not forgive a fellow servant, i.e., the offender. It must be acknowledged that the unforgiving servant would not forgive his fellow servant a "small debt." Who of us could describe the violation of sexual abuse as a "small" debt? While the magnitude of the debt is not the issue, it remains that the deeper the wound and the greater the pain, the more difficult and lengthy the process of forgiveness. Once again, it remains a matter of the heart.

Is Forgiveness "Fair"?

Another point of balance is to recognize that it will be difficult for abuse survivors to see any "fairness" in needing to look at their unforgiveness, because the sin of the abuse seems so much greater. Survivors need to be assured of the balance between the holy and just God who calls unforgiveness a sin and the merciful and grieving Father who laments, "My eyes pour out tears. Day and night, the tears never quit. My dear, dear people are battered and bruised, hopelessly and cruelly wounded" (Jeremiah 14:17 THE MESSAGE).

We stand before God in total dependence on him to resolve the paradox of his holiness and his mercy within the hearts of survivors of sexual abuse. It is not our work but his. Counselors must remember that they are responsible to present the truth and to model God's graciousness. It is God's responsibility to invite abuse survivors to forgive and enable them to move toward that decision.

MAKING THE DECISION

At some point an abuse survivor will be faced with the decision to forgive. This decision, then, is a choice of the will and is not dependent upon feelings. Jan Frank, herself a survivor of incest, offers this: There is a fine line "between hypocrisy and following a scriptural prescription in the absence of emotion. It all has to do with motive."[6] Because God is concerned that survivors forgive "from your heart" (Matthew 18:35b), abuse survivors may first need to approach God and ask for the gift of a forgiving heart. Regarding such a request, Christ promises to be "close to all who call on him sincerely. He fulfills the desires of those who reverence and trust him; he hears their cries for help and rescues them" (Psalm 145:18–19 TLB). Within the mystery of a human heart enabled by God's grace, survivors of sexual abuse can decide to forgive offenders even in the face of continuing emotional struggles.

PROCESSING THE DECISION

Feelings of anger and bitterness may return after a decision to forgive an offender. Ambivalent feelings are entirely natural and do not invalidate the forgiveness a survivor has extended to an offender. When these feelings recur, abuse survivors can share them with God and other trustworthy persons and ask for support in validating the feelings and in "letting go" of them. This process of emotional rest-recurrence-release may need to be repeated many times.

Liz was sexually abused by her grandfather between the ages of two and fourteen, and she was verbally abused and neglected by her parents in a family system that was full of violence and anger. Liz had to ask God for a heart to forgive her many offenders, and now, after a process over three years, she writes:

I've been able to forgive those who abused me. It was not a

simple step of saying the words "I forgive you," but a process I worked through, first expressing my anger in the privacy of a counseling session toward those who had hurt me, and then realizing the abusers are victims as I once was. They are still suffering from their own lusts. They have offended not only me but also God. God has forgiven me, so I have forgiven them. . . . I still have scars. When they are touched, I hurt. But now I have tools to deal with the pain. Now I know God's love.[7]

Liz's story is an encouraging testimony of the power of God's Spirit to change a person's heart. But Liz, like many abuse victims, did not begin the process of forgiveness with knowing God's love, but rather with a distorted view of God.

WHEN FORGIVENESS FEELS IMPOSSIBLE

It can be intensely challenging for survivors to obey scriptural directives related to forgiveness due to distorted images of God portrayed to them by Christian offenders, and their own residual anger at God. Early in recovery, nearly all survivors will consider forgiveness to be impossible. We must acknowledge this reality. Forgiveness does seem impossible. At the same time, Christ has demonstrated for us that forgiveness is more powerful than hate. Just as he cried from the cross, "Father, forgive them . . ." so survivors may eventually be able to cry out in forgiveness of offenders who "know not" the impact of sexual abuse on their victims. In Christ's identification with victims of abuse, he demonstrates that forgiveness is more powerful than hate.

RESTORATIVE RESULTS

In addition to obedience, there are several other practical reasons to support survivors in their struggle with forgiveness. One restorative result of forgiveness is personal freedom. Not only was the abuse unjust, but it is equally unjust for survivors to remain in emotional bondage to their offenders. Forgiveness can help loose the bond of hate and bitterness between survivor and offender and, ironically, set the survivor free. Once silence is broken about the abuse, and the pressure valve of emotions of devastation has been named and experienced and expressed, continued cultivation of intense rage and anger can weigh survivors down. Forgiveness has the potential to free up emotional energy for other steps on the path of healing.

Because sexual violence is an abuse of power, a restorative result of forgiveness is regaining a sense of control over one's own life. Forgiveness has the potential to empower survivors to experience what God means when declaring he "does not want you to be afraid of people, but to be wise and strong" nor to have "a spirit of timidity but a spirit of power and love and self-control" (2 Timothy 1:7 TLB/RSV).

Forgiveness brings freedom—freedom from being controlled by past abuse events, freedom from emotional ties to the offender, freedom from continual internal conflicts of bitterness and hate, freedom to move toward wholeness and enjoy fullness of life. Maintaining these freedoms will be a struggle. The Galatians were instructed that it was "for freedom Christ has set us free." They were encouraged to "stand fast" and not "submit again to a yoke of slavery," which was, for them, living under the "law" rather than God's grace (5:1 RSV). The "yoke of slavery" for abuse survivors might include returning to an abusive relationship, trying to earn God's approval by religious performance, or shaming themselves if or when feelings of bitterness or hate recur. The survivor is to stand firm in newfound freedom, and the body of Christ is to be Jesus-with-skin-on to them, standing alongside.

THE PROCESS OF FORGIVENESS

The following letter, shared by permission of the author, was written by a survivor in the course of the BECOMERS group program by a woman who was both physically and sexually abused as a child. Her letter was the outcome of an art therapy exercise and was not sent to her father. Its purpose was to facilitate an initial step in the forgiveness process, and it expresses some of her personal pain with great intensity.

> Dad,
>   I want you to know that I've told. I've told the secret. Somewhere in the hazy part of my mind I remembered you telling me never to tell "or" . . . something horrible would happen—you'd kill me? I would die? "They" would take me away from you and mother, and then what would I do? Where would I live? These memories are hazy, but this I know without a doubt—you hurt me and you did it with malice and intention—it wasn't a mistake. "Hurt"—what a nondescriptive

word to use for such influential circumstances. Tortured, ruined, tormented, destroyed, betrayed, hated—these words are better, but still not totally descriptive.

Maybe if I used words to describe how I came to feel about myself, about other people, about life, you would hear. But I know that is not possible—you hear nothing because you're deaf and see nothing because you're blind. I believe that is the way you want to be.

So you see, this letter isn't really for you—because you couldn't see the words or comprehend their meaning. It's for me—somehow forming these thoughts and saying these words makes me understand. And in understanding, I hope there is healing.

Hope. There is a word that is rarely in my thinking and talking. What you did to me left me without hope. Without hope there is nothing to strive for and nothing to live for. One who doesn't hope has no goals or dreams. He has no purpose. If someone has no purpose, there is no reason to exist. That is how I felt for as long as I can remember.

You never talked to me when you were "hurting" me, but your deeds screamed to me in unheard voices—unworthy, unwanted, guilty, garbage—I heard all these things and hundreds more. I've heard those words and voices as long as I can remember. They caused me untold misery and agony. The pain that I've existed with—not lived but merely existed—is so deep and black that it is indescribable.

You are guilty. Your actions and deeds have made my life agony. I've thought of destroying you, literally of killing you—but your pain would be gone and mine would continue. I've thought of publicly exposing you to all of the family, to all of your friends and business associates, but would that be enough? Somehow I don't think it would. I don't think there is anything I could do to you that could cause you the agony I've had. But believe this—if there was a way to get even, to repay, to revenge myself and be rid of you, I would do it.

I realize that your actions caused me to believe many lies. Those lies caused me to believe very destructive, hurtful things. These things I've believed have caused me to make many pitiful decisions in life. You not only affected me but you hurt my son by the things I came to believe.

But all is not lost for me because there is God. Somehow for some reason God has wanted me to live. He not only wants me to live but to live with peace and joy. How is this possible? It's possible because God loves and cares for me, and as much as I want to be healthy and whole—He wants it even more.

I believe God wants me to forgive. Why? You don't deserve it—God knows that. All the demons in hell know it. You don't even want it. So why would I forgive you?

For me! As I forgive you I let go of you—the sorrow, the rage, the memories, and gain peace—imperceptibly, minute bits at a time. I do not forgive because you deserve it, but because I deserve it and God asks it of me. I cannot live with my bitterness any longer, for it has nearly destroyed me.

I forgive you. I ask God to forgive you. I release you.

Beth

Beth's letter provides powerful insight into a process of forgiving. It is obvious from Beth's letter that forgiveness is not the first issue that was addressed in her recovery process. Following two years of therapy, group discussion, and personal reading to acquire information about abuse, she established a foundation from which to forgive her offender.

Her first paragraph highlights the significance of revealing the "secret" of the abuse. As the letter continues, she is re-experiencing the memories of her childhood, once hazy but now clearly before her. The feelings are very deep and expressive of her torment, revealing her utter despair, agony, and hopelessness. She sees with harsh reality her own desire for vengeance.

She has also accomplished the tremendous task of establishing that the offender is responsible for the abuse. With her words "You are guilty," she expresses her understanding of the part he played in damaging her life. She also demonstrates the confidence of knowing that she did not cause the abuse. This is an essential turning point, laying groundwork from which to build on in the process of forgiveness. Once she has assessed his responsibility and emotionally "given" it to him, she is being freed to see areas of her personal responsibility to move toward forgiveness.

Forgiveness involves taking time to assess the fullness of the emotional damage, the false belief systems that have developed, the poor choices that have been made, and the anger and bitterness that remain. This assessment is almost always followed and accompanied by intense grieving over the many losses that have been experienced. (See also grieving process, chapter 12.)

Once a survivor has a personal awareness of a need to forgive and has identified all that needs to be forgiven, it is essential to know what authentic forgiveness is and is not.

In *Forgive and Forget: Healing the Hurts We Don't Deserve,*

Lewis Smedes shares several insights into scriptural forgiveness. Often victims are told by others that if they truly "forgive," then they will "forget" the abuse. Smedes writes that individuals forget only what is too trivial or too traumatic to remember. Forgiving will enable survivors to experience healing from the lingering pain of the abuse, but will not result in forgetting that the abuse ever happened.[8]

In "The Possibility of a Healed Memory," Kevin Huggins writes:

> *Escape* from memories of the past was not scripturally advocated. Biblically, there was no warrant to believe that memory of its impact could be "healed" by forgetting or erasing the recollection of the event from one's mind. Paul's statement in Phil. 3:13, "Forgetting what lies behind, and straining toward what is ahead," is often misinterpreted. By "forgetting," Paul was not implying obliterating from the memory "what lies behind." In verses 4–8 of the same chapter, Paul clearly recalled some traumatic events from his own past (i.e., "persecuting the church"). It is clear "forgetting" these things for Paul amounted to a choice to reevaluate them (i.e., "But whatever was to my profit I now consider . . .") in such a way as to render them insignificant to obstruct movement toward his new goal of deepening his relationship with God. . . . Paul's own prescription for peace involved making one's anxieties and concerns known to God, rather than refusing to think about them at all (Phil. 4:6, 7).[9]

Neither does forgiving mean "excusing" the other person by being mushy and understanding. Smedes writes that excusing is the *opposite* of forgiving. It takes only a little insight to excuse, but it takes grace from God to forgive. Before survivors can forgive, they must stiffen their spine and hold the other person fully accountable. Precisely because there was no excuse for the abuse, the act of forgiveness requires a supernatural act.

Unhelpful Help

The process of forgiveness is sometimes short-circuited by well-meaning "helpers" who try to rush the abuse survivor. Sometimes this comes in the form of simple slogans, such as "You have to get on with things," "What's done is done," or "Let bygones be bygones." The process of forgiveness can also be short-circuited by quoting Bible verses ("All things work together for good"), by moralizing ("There's a lot to be learned from this"), or preaching ("God means this for your good"). None of these shortcuts are helpful to survivors because there are no shortcuts to forgiveness.

When survivors and their "helpers" experience an urgency to forgive, it is often an attempt at pain reduction or to smother conflict. The intense pain of the abuse recovery process is difficult for both survivors and "helpers" to endure. However, pushing a survivor to forgive demonstrates a considerable lack of insight into the depth of another's pain, an intrusion into the sanctity of another's journey, and can even discount the work of God in an individual heart that is inwardly being prepared for the grace to forgive.

Equally unhelpful are assurances to survivors that instantaneous healing will occur if they "simply" forgive. If and when a survivor struggles with residual emotional residue, the recurrent feelings are used as "evidence" that the abuse survivor did not "really" forgive the offender or, perhaps more destructive, that a survivor has an "unforgiving spirit." Ironically, this makes the abuse survivor responsible for any continued emotional distress. The survivor is shamed and consequently re-victimized.

Jan Frank gives a vivid illustration of help that misses the mark. Donna came to one of Jan's support groups and shared the following experience:

> I became depressed last week after a counseling session with my pastor. I'd finally gotten the courage to share with him all the events surrounding my background. I'd been molested from age 7 to age 15 by various men my mother brought home. I'd been raped repeatedly by my uncle and several cousins and eventually forced to have an abortion at age 15. I shared with my pastor how devastating these events had been on my marriage and about the depression that, at times, seemed insurmountable. When I told him about the anger I had toward my children and husband, the nightmares, and my inability to trust my husband, he stopped me short. He abruptly stated, "Donna, the problem is obvious. You have not forgiven those people who have in some way offended you. If you will right now forgive those people who in some way damaged you, you will be healed of all those symptoms you are describing." I wanted to forgive—in fact, I thought I had— but I was still experiencing those same difficulties. I went away in a state of defeat. I thought I was just not spiritual enough. I was destined to live my life in bondage.
>
> As I went to work the following Monday I asked the Lord if He might show me something about forgiveness. Boy, was I surprised when He answered that very day! I'm a nurse and I

work in the emergency room. A young man came in that day. He had just been run over by a truck and suffered a compound fracture of the leg. The bone was protruding, broken in several pieces. It took three doctors and two nurses four hours to get the man's bone set in a position to heal. The healing process would take anywhere from four months to a year. Even then, the young man might experience some difficulty in walking, and it could take several months more to obtain the full use of his injured leg. As I looked at this boy with his leg in a cast, I realized the Lord was using this to illustrate something profound to me. No one at any time approached the young man and said, "Son, I have good news for you. All you need to do is forgive the man who was driving the truck and you will be instantaneously healed." No one would be so foolish, and yet, how many of us approach emotional brokenness in that same simplistic manner?[10]

Sometimes abuse survivors are told that if they truly have forgiven their offender, they should trust the offender once again and restore the relationship. This is neither true nor helpful. Forgiving someone does not include restored trust. While a hopeful situation might include reconciliation of a survivor and an offender over time, realistic factors must be taken into consideration. A return to a safe relationship is based entirely on trust. Because trust has been so gravely violated, it can only be rebuilt over time, if at all. A survivor of abuse must ask the question, "How will I know if or when I can legitimately trust my offender not to abuse me in any way, ever again?"

FORGIVING OURSELVES

One of the most sensitive areas of forgiveness involves abuse survivors forgiving themselves. Sexual abuse is unspeakably hurtful to survivors, and because it is so damaging, the abuse experiences influence many poor choices made by survivors regarding themselves and others. Hurtful choices are often reflected in self-abuse or abuse of others, whether emotionally, physically, or sexually abusing one's own children or spouse, or abusing self with chemicals, sex, food, workaholism, or perfectionism. The scars of these past wrongs must not be allowed to haunt survivors in the present and in the future.

For abuse survivors to forgive themselves means being honest about their own humanness and acknowledging that choices were influenced by sins committed against them. While this is not intended to minimize or "justify" hurting themselves or others, forgiving themselves requires courage, compassion, and the ability to view themselves the way God does. Abuse survivors must forgive themselves for repeating their victimization or for not knowing how to protect their own children. They might feel as though they need to forgive their bodies for responding physiologically to abusive touch or for "betraying" them. Forgiveness should be sought for specific actions and for one action at a time. Survivors do not ask God to forgive them for being cruel, hateful, or stupid, but rather for actions of cruelty, hatefulness, or wrong choices. This distinction differentiates between true guilt, which is about behavior, and shame, or false guilt, that attacks one's identity and value as a person. Smedes writes that if you should dare to forgive yourself, it would be a signal to the world that God's love is a power within you.[11] When abuse survivors can forgive themselves, personal healing is energizing and provides momentum for moving forward in the healing journey.

FORGIVING GOD

At some point, most abuse survivors struggle intensely with anger and bitterness toward God, because he is blamed for allowing the abuse. Just as Elizabeth prayed in chapter 4, many child victims begged God repeatedly to intervene in the abuse but the abuse continued. A tremendous sense of betrayal can accumulate over the years and culminate in rage against God. Such inner turmoil creates agony within Christian abuse survivors who feel they "should" love God, but feel they cannot. Survivors will often suppress their true feelings toward God. Overtly hating God can take the form of flagrant violations of a survivor's moral values and outright defiance of scriptural truth. Sometimes feelings are expressed indirectly to God by hating his gifts, his world, or self.

Smedes illustrates a passive hatred toward God to be indicated by signals such as resenting good things happening to friends, stifling every happy impulse, or shutting our eyes to every reason we have for being glad to be alive. Often Christians behave like Jeremiah, who, when he felt really let down by God, turned his hatred on himself. Hating God's most precious gift of life can be a Christian's way of hating God.

To help relieve abuse survivors of hidden rage against God, counselors can, first of all, acknowledge these feelings—whatever they are at the present stage. Counselors would be helpful during this time by accepting a survivor's expression of intense feelings without judgment or feeling a need to "defend" God. Survivors can be encouraged to express feelings about God in a sexual abuse support group and directly to God in prayer. Philip Yancey addresses this issue in his book *Disappointment With God*: "Knowledge is passive, intellectual; suffering is active, personal. No intellectual answer will solve suffering. Perhaps this is why God sent His own Son as one response to human pain, to experience it and absorb it into himself. The Incarnation did not 'solve' human suffering, but at least it was an active and personal response."[12] Dr. Paul Brand, responding to the question "Where is God when it hurts?" replies, "He is in you, the one hurting, not in it, the thing that hurts."[13] "Would it be too much," writes Yancey, "to say that, because of Jesus, God understands our feelings of disappointment with Him? How else can we interpret Jesus' tears, or His cries from the cross . . . that dreadful cry, 'My God, my God, why have you forsaken Me?' "[14]

Within helpful and supportive relationships, an abuse survivor may discover rage or even hatred toward God that has remained hidden for years. Because this is a critical time in a survivor's spiritual journey, these feelings should not be stifled by counselors, group facilitators, or group members who might feel a need to "defend" God, "fix" the spiritual relationship, or avoid being immersed in a survivor's intense emotions. Forgiveness—even "forgiving" God!—begins with the honest expression of authentic emotions. The fullness of the forgiveness process—identifying and expressing feelings about the abuse, looking at the command to forgive, seeing the need to forgive, making the decision to forgive, and experiencing progressive changes in feelings—will be completed in time. One member of BECOMERS, a daughter of missionary parents, and abused by an elder in the church, was inwardly struggling with hate toward God. She wrote in response to a homework assignment:

> Thank you so much for this group. It is so freeing to have a place where people accept me, and I can say all these feelings out loud, and no one is going to condemn me, or better yet, no one is going to throw verses at me or try to argue with me. Thank you for saying it's OK to be where I am—that makes me want to change more than anything.

Suggested Personal Application Questions to Accompany Step Seven

- What does the word *forgiveness* mean to you at this time?
- What part do you feel forgiveness plays in your healing process?
- Who has hurt or offended you, treated you unjustly, violated you? Are you beginning to identify how you feel toward them?
- What do you do with those feelings?
- What happens inside you when you consider forgiving those who have offended, abused, or rejected you?
- What are some of the basic needs of children? How were those needs met or not met for you as a child? Who was responsible for meeting those needs?
- How do you feel toward those persons?
- Could you consider forgiving those persons?
- What have you been taught about forgiving those who have offended you?
- Have you tried doing what you have been taught? What happened?
- How would you respond to the statement "Forgive and forget"?

Forgiving self

- What actions of yours do you think have been hurtful to others?
- What choices have you made that might require you to ask forgiveness?
- In what areas are you unable to forgive yourself? What is it about these areas that makes them difficult for you to accept God's forgiveness?

Body image

With a focus on forgiveness, work through the following questions as they relate to body image.

- What parts of your body do you have difficulty accepting?
- Who were the people in your life who "put down," shamed, or caused harm to certain parts of your body? How did they accomplish this?

- Are you experiencing anger, fear, sadness, disgust, or other feelings toward certain parts of your body?
- If you were to speak to those parts of your body, what would you say to them? What would those body parts answer back to you?
- Do you think God has regard for your body?
- What would help to enable you to forgive those parts of your body that have caused you shame or pain?
- What would help to enable you to forgive the people who shamed or hurt your body?

Forgiving God

- Write a letter to God expressing past childhood feelings about him.
- Write a letter to God expressing current adult feelings about him.
- What would God write back to you?
- What are some issues in your Christian walk that cause you concern and which might be related to your feelings about God?
- What seems to get in the way of your "forgiving" God?
- What might help or enable you to "forgive" God?

15

Step Eight: Maturing in Relationship With God and Others

Step Eight: I have determined to mature in my relationship to God and to those around me.

Maturing: a process of experiencing restorative relationships with God, others, and self in creative new ways.

MATURING: REVITALIZING A RELATIONSHIP WITH GOD

To mature in a relationship with God means, in part, experiencing God in new ways, in new images. Images are more than just concepts or thoughts; they are prevailing pictures weighted with emotions—for good or ill.

Images of God are connected to emotional experiences from earliest stages of development in powerful combinations of thoughts and feelings woven together. At this step, it may be helpful for survivors to reread stages of identity development in chapter 11 and reflect again on the early relational foundation upon which trust or mistrust was built. Early images and emotional impressions have formed a "template," or a basic sense of what can be expected from all other relationships, including one with God. Children who experience a negative attachment in interactions with others will tend to, on the one hand, conclude they are unlovable, and on the other hand, tend to "sense" others are unloving toward them. From this earliest root of disconnection, intimacy with others and God can be significantly blocked.

Such basic "expectations" about relationships are deeply rooted and are not often elevated to conscious awareness. This is precisely why they are so influential, shaping and molding attitudes and beliefs from within, with profound impact on spiritual well-being. Juanita Ryan is a mental health nurse specialist in private practice. She notes that when inner images of God differ greatly from doctrinal beliefs, the disconnect generates spiritual distress. Ryan observes that for "every distortion a person has of God, there is usually a corresponding self-distortion."[1] For example, images of God as vengeful and punishing often correspond with images of self as bad and deserving punishment. This has also been our experience with adult survivors in BECOMERS support groups.

To this point, group members will have discovered at least some links between their images of God and their perceptions of themselves. Group members have been encouraged to pay attention to how images of God have been woven into their life story, which includes sexual abuse and also includes *more* than sexual abuse. They have been encouraged to look at messages they received from their family about God—not for the purpose of assigning blame, but to begin to sort out who God is from who God is not.[2] In Step Eight, we encourage group members to look at new and creative ways of continuing on the healing path.

Maturing in relationship with God might be accomplished through many approaches, a few of which are offered here. At a very personal level, Ryan encourages survivors to remind themselves that God is on their side. "We cannot fix our distorted images of God by some single act . . . but we can risk asking God to personally reveal his grace to us . . . and to give us the capacity to take in divine love."[3] It might be instructive for group members to return to chapter 9 and examine their images of God for any subtle changes in those images.

Another approach to maturing with God is through a spiritual discipline of Scripture reading to intentionally foster new images. However, abuse survivors will need to be attentive to the kinds of Scriptures they select, choosing those that embody healing images. In *Healing of Memories,* David Seamands has noted that many emotionally damaged people find themselves "consistently selecting Bible passages which emphasize wrath, punishment, and the unpardonable sin. Unless Christian workers truly understand the dynamics of this, they will not be able to help these damaged persons. They will actually harm them, overloading more oughts and guilts upon them by giving them the spiritual disciplines of Bible reading and prayer."[4]

The following illustration, adapted from David Seamands,

illustrates how extremely important it is to understand the connection between what one *hears* about God and what one actually *feels* about God. As God's truth is "funneled" into the cognitive intellect, we often expect the mere transmission of that truth to penetrate the heart directly and produce changes in someone's life. However, the relationship with God "funnels" through a "shame filter" and is distorted. A person with a shame filter will not experience the truth directly due to "interference" put in place through unhealthy interpersonal relationships, usually in childhood or adolescence. Distorted truths about God are first transmitted from the outside, but are later generated from within. Such distortions become "blueprints" for interpreting meaning. Seamands asserts that "We could liken their condition to a kind of spiritual paranoia. Paranoid persons can take the most loving, affirming statements and twist them into insults, rejections, and even threats."[5] The good news becomes the bad news—the loving, caring God of Scripture becomes, at best, indifferent, and at worst, hateful.

Receiving God's Truth

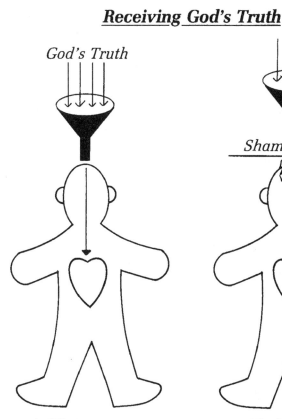

What we expect
to happen . . .

God's truth
produces fruit

What happens . . .

Damaged reception of
truth due to the
shame from unhealthy
interpersonal relationships

Seamands writes that in spite of our "most rigorous Christian disciplines," we will "never find lasting 'righteousness, peace, and joy in the Holy Spirit' (Rom. 14:17) until we find a Christlike God, the kind of God who, like Jesus, tells us He no longer considers us 'slaves' but 'friends' (John 15:15)."[6] We have noted this in our BECOMERS groups as well. When God becomes "friend," abuse survivors have experienced changes in their images of God through a wide range of creative and revitalizing images from Scripture, including Light, Refuge, Rock, Shepherd, Mother Hen, Father of the Fatherless, and many others.

Another approach of maturing with God is through trusted personal relationships. Previous images of God have been damaged in untrustworthy relationships and they will be significantly healed in trustworthy relationships. An increasing capacity to trust others will also affect one's level of trust with God.[7] Survivors are reminded to be gentle with themselves in this process. It may be realistic to expect that, at first, new images of God may be fragile and might just "compete" with old images rather than supplant them. Over time, through continued trusting relationships, old images can gradually be replaced. The ultimate Healer of distortions is God, who desires to be known as he really is.

Another approach to foster the maturing process could include finding a grace-based church family. Survivors are encouraged to find a church that provides a context of God's grace for spiritual nurture. Spiritual authorities have a great deal of power to shape images of God, especially when survivors are in times of vulnerability while taking risks throughout the healing process.

We offer the following image of God as the namesake of BECOMERS. It is attributed to the apostle John, who personally walked with Jesus and experienced being one "whom Jesus loved" (John 13:23). The tone of John's letter implies that he is an old man, mature and secure in his faith:

> Consider the incredible love that the Father has shown us in allowing us to be called "children of God"—and that is not just what we are called, but what we are. Our heredity on the godward side is no mere figure of speech—which explains why the world will no more recognize us than it recognized Christ. Oh, dear children of mine (forgive the affection of an old man), have you realized it?
>
> Here and now we are God's children. We don't know what we shall become in the future. We only know that, if reality were to break through, we should reflect His likeness, for we should see Him as He really is. (1 John 3:1–2 PHILLIPS TRANSLATION)

BECOMERS group members are encouraged to creatively engage with Scripture by taking a passage that is meaningful to them and personalizing it. This can be a valuable exercise in renewing damaged images of God. Below is an example of creatively personalizing 1 Corinthians 13:4–8:

BECAUSE GOD LOVES ME

- Because God loves me, he is slow to lose patience with me.

- Because God loves me, he takes the circumstances of my life and uses them in a constructive way for my growth.
- Because God loves me, he does not treat me as an object to be possessed and manipulated.
- Because God loves me, he has no need to impress me with how great and powerful he is because *he is God*, nor does he belittle me as his child in order to show me how important he is.
- Because God loves me, he is for me. he wants to see me mature and develop in his love.
- Because God loves me, he does not send down his wrath on every little mistake I make, of which there are many.
- Because God loves me, he is deeply grieved when I do not walk in the ways that please him because he sees this as evidence that I don't trust him and love him as I should.
- Because God loves me, he rejoices when I experience his power and strength and stand up under the pressures of life for his name's sake.
- Because God loves me, he keeps on trusting me when at times I don't trust myself.
- Because God loves me, he never says there is no hope for me; rather, he patiently works with me, loves me, and disciplines me in such a way that it is hard for me to understand the depth of his concern for me.
- Because God loves me, he never forsakes me even though many of my friends might.
- Because God loves me, he stands with me when I have reached the rock bottom of despair, when I see the real me and compare that with his righteousness, holiness, beauty, and love. It is at a moment like this that I can really believe that God loves me.

Yes, the greatest of all gifts is God's perfect love.[8]

MATURING: RECONSTRUCTING RELATIONSHIPS WITH OTHERS

Maturing relationships with others build upon on a foundation of increasing security in one's sense of belonging to Christ, concurrent with emergent strength in self-identity. In the past, abuse survivors have experienced deriving a sense of identity from the approval of others. Responses of passivity or aggression were often strategies of life and death emotionally or physically and should not be devalued for their usefulness at the time.

However, in Step Eight we turn to the development of creative new ways of experiencing interpersonal relationships. Adult survivors have already experienced the intentional and difficult back-and-forth progression of their restorative journey. New opportunities are available to move away from passive, dependent, aggressive, or hostile responses within significant relationships and toward more stabilizing assertive interactions. As before, trustworthy friends and a helpful support group can provide a safe setting in which to experiment and "practice" with unfamiliar and sometimes frightening new relationship patterns.

Passivity

A style of relating that is familiar to many abuse survivors is one of giving in and letting others make choices for them. This pattern of relating actually violates one's personal value by declining to express honest feelings, thoughts, and beliefs. This style of relating often permits others to violate them. Passivity is expressed in communicating thoughts and feelings in an apologetic or self-effacing manner that others can easily disregard. Some of the "messages" communicated through passive relationships are: "*I don't count; you can take advantage of me,*" or "*My feelings don't matter; but yours do,*" or "*I'm nothing; you are superior.*" These patterns also contribute to physical symptoms of depression, stress, headaches, insomnia, and body pains.

Passive relationships are hurtful because they are dishonest, often in the name of being "nice." The following excerpt adapted from *Creative Aggression* explains what is meant by "nice" in this context:

> "Nice" behavior eventually has a "price" for both "nice" people and the person or persons involved with them. It is alienating, indirectly hostile, and self-destructive because:
>
> 1. The "nice" person tends to create an atmosphere that causes others to avoid giving honest, genuine feedback. This blocks emotional growth.
>
> 2. "Nice" behavior will ultimately be distrusted by others. That is, it generates a sense of uncertainty and lack of safety in others, who can never be sure if they will be supported by the "nice" person in a crisis situation that requires an assertive confrontation with others.
>
> 3. "Nice" people stifle the growth of others. They avoid giving others genuine feedback, and they deprive others of a

real person to assert against. This tends to force others in the relationship to turn their aggression against themselves. It also tends to generate guilt and suppress feelings in others who are intimately involved and dependent on them.

4. Because of their chronic "niceness," others can never be certain if the relationships with "nice" people could endure conflict or sustain an angry confrontation if it occurred spontaneously. This places great limits on the potential extent of intimacy in the relationship by putting others constantly on their guard.

5. "Nice" behavior is not reliable. Periodically, "nice" people explode in unexpected rage, making those involved with them shocked and unprepared to cope with it.

6. The "nice" person, by holding aggression in, may pay a physiological price in the form of psychosomatic problems and alienation.

7. "Nice" behavior is emotionally unreal. It puts severe limitations on all relationships, and the ultimate victims are "nice" people themselves.[9]

Aggression

Aggression is a style of relating that violates the rights of others through verbal or physical attacks in order to dominate others. This is a win/lose style of relating in which the one who loses is humiliated, degraded, belittled, or overpowered and subsequently becomes less able to express feelings or needs. Those who relate aggressively in relationships are usually dishonest about their own inner feelings, attempting to reduce their own anxiety by blaming others. Aggressive relationships communicate such messages as "This is what I think—you're stupid for believing differently," or "This is what I want—what you want isn't important," or "This is how I feel, and your feelings don't count." Two people interacting with aggression can lead to conflict that spirals out of control.

Passive Aggression

A passive-aggressive style of relating appears to give in, but does so to "get even." Being negative, acting disinterested, intentional procrastinating, or sullenness can be passive attempts to cover aggressive feelings. Passive aggression is dishonest because trickery, seduction, or manipulation is used. Others are criticized or sabotaged behind their backs, causing spiraling antagonism, reprisal, and ill-will. Because a passive-aggressive style is so indirect, the other person is usually unaware of the anger or the intent to "get even."

Assertiveness

The most constructive style of relating in mature relationships is assertiveness. Two components of assertiveness are honesty and respect, for self and others. Assertiveness involves expressing one's thoughts, feelings, and beliefs in a direct, honest, and clear way that does not violate another person's rights or show disrespect. The use of "I" statements helps to avoid unnecessary conflict and can defuse tense interactions. "I" statements more clearly communicate boundaries, wants, and needs in a manner that is self-respecting and respectful of others.

In order to respond assertively, adult survivors will need to learn to think of themselves and others differently. Learning assertiveness skills can be a difficult, trial-and-error learning process for those victimized by sexual abuse. Most survivors are passive in some relationships and aggressive or passive-aggressive in others.

Many adult survivors do not have a *no* in their vocabulary, because *no* never meant "no" when they said it, or because their *no* was overruled. Marge had been sexually abused by her grandfather as a child. As an adult, difficulties arose in her marriage, her husband left her, and she remained separated from him for five years without finalizing a divorce.

Marge's husband made a practice of coming to "visit" her about every six months. He would call one of Marge's friends and tell her to inform Marge that he was coming. Marge would dutifully leave the door open at the appointed time. He would return to the house, verbally and physically abuse her, sexually use her, and then leave, only to return again in a few months to repeat the cycle.

Marge had adopted a passive role in this abusive relationship and was honestly unaware that she could say no to such demeaning and hurtful actions. It took many months of counseling and BECOMERS group sessions to strengthen her to the point where she valued herself enough to say no and not allow him to misuse her so disrespectfully.

Assertiveness is also a difficult skill to learn for those who use aggression in relationships. Maturing in relationships involves taking responsibility for the inappropriate use of power in attempting to control others. (See also "Abuse of Power," chapter 6.) Sam had been severely abused by several significant father figures during his childhood. He had "learned" that to show emotions was perceived as weakness and that to be truly masculine he had to be macho, physically aggressive, and always "win" in any relationship. In group sessions, Sam found it almost impossible to relate to the other men who were sharing feelings of hurt or fear. He even threatened some of the men with physical violence if they showed signs of emotion.

A group exercise helpful in learning assertiveness skills involves two persons in a role-play. This can be conducted with a large group, broken down into pairs. One of the pair attempts to "sell" a product to their partner in the exercise. The partner's task is to refuse to buy the product by calmly yet persistently refusing without becoming argumentative or angry. This might necessitate repeating statements such as "No, thank you. I'm not interested." When asked again, the buyer simply repeats in a calm manner, "No, thank you. I'm not interested." After several minutes, the roles are reversed, so that each experiences what it feels like to be buyer and seller.

This rather arbitrary exercise may seem awkward and stilted at first, but practice of this principle as a communication skill will allow individuals to feel comfortable in ignoring manipulative verbal exchanges and irrelevant logic while maintaining their original point. Once group members have learned about this skill and have gained a little confidence by practicing using it in their support group setting, they can then begin to apply it in real-life situations.

Another assertiveness exercise, again using pairs of individuals, is a role-play involving another response skill. In this exercise, the "seller" tries to manipulate the "buyer" with negative criticism. Instead of simply repeating the same answer over and over, this time the "buyer" acknowledges that even though there may be some truth to what the seller is saying, the decision to decline remains the same. For example, the buyer says calmly, "Yes, I do believe the product is worth the price. However, I am not interested." When the seller persists, the buyer might respond, "It is probably true that my children could benefit from your product, but I am not interested."

After practice in simulated situations, and learning to feel relaxed using this skill, group members can become more comfortable in receiving criticism without feeling defensive or pressured to give in. Group members demonstrate personal integrity and honesty by not doing something they do not want to do. They demonstrate respect for themselves and others as equals by not allowing others to be in control of their personal decisions. Practical skills such as these are invaluable tools for adult survivors to use in maintaining a sense of self-respect and self-control in everyday situations.

PERSONAL BOUNDARIES: BEING A PART AND BEING APART IN RELATIONSHIPS

Adult survivors of abuse have often experienced many violations of personal boundaries in their lives. Thus as adults, they are often unaware of what appropriate personal boundaries might mean to them. Two dimensions of mature intimate relationships are reflected in boundaries of connectedness and separateness. The first dimension is a capacity for *connection*, that is, *being a part* of a relationship. The second dimension is a capacity for *separateness*, that is, *being apart* in a relationship. In a maturing intimate relationship, participants are able to set clear boundaries with assertive interactions. That means persons in the relationship are free to have different opinions, ideas, or preferences, but such individuality does not disturb the underlying connection of being "rooted and grounded" in love (Ephesians 3:17 KJV).[10]

Adult survivors of abuse can feel distressed when they are encouraged to "take responsibility for yourself" in relationships. Those who have a stable sense of self-identity "hear" that respectful autonomy is what is meant by such a statement. However, those who have been raised in hurtful families or who have suffered abuse "hear" something quite different. According to Carmen Berry, wounded persons hear "taking personal responsibility for yourself" to mean being abandoned because no one else is interested or cares about you.[11] This kind of independent "taking care of yourself" is not based on a positive sense of autonomy, knowing you are still connected meaningfully to others. This kind of "taking care of yourself" is related to fears of abandonment, which often present themselves as "clinging" behaviors to those close to them, desperately wanting them to meet needs beyond what they are capable of. Maturing and growing through these fears requires great effort and consistent, non-shaming support while "practicing" alternative relationship interactions.

Boundaries are important. One purpose for adult survivors to learn about and establish clear boundaries is to protect and care for themselves in respectful ways. Boundaries will emerge as adult survivors continue to mature in valuing themselves. Setting boundaries means that one is taking responsibility, being adult, and expecting to be respected in a relationship. Setting boundaries reflects a survivor's right to say *no* and have *no* mean "no."

One specific and important boundary is learning to say no to physical expressions of affection when touch is not desired. While touch can be very affirming and supportive, adult survivors can mature in their relationships to the point that they can say yes or no to physical touch, such as a hug, based on their self-worth and their wishes rather than on the requests or needs of other people.

There are different extremes in boundaries with regard to physical touch. Some survivors touch, hug, or kiss *others* without regard to the boundaries of others; some allow others to touch, hug, or kiss *them* when they don't want to. Some have boundaries that are rigid and isolating, out of fear of any touch or closeness. Maturing toward healthy boundaries is recognizing when others are crossing into one's personal space, recognizing when one is violating another person's space, or when one is isolating oneself by refusing even nurturing contact from trustworthy others.

Suggested Personal Application Questions to Accompany Step Eight

- What is your understanding of differences between assertiveness and aggressiveness?
- What does passive-aggressive mean?
- What are some of the reasons people are hesitant to share their thoughts, beliefs, or feelings in their relationships with others? In what kind of situations do you find yourself hesitating to share your thoughts, feelings, or opinions?
- In which of your relationships do you seem to take
  (a) a passive role
  (b) an aggressive role
  (c) a passive-aggressive role
  (d) an assertive role
- You are involved in many different relationships, such as spouse, friend, co-worker, parent, child, boss/employee, group member. In which of these relationships do you feel most comfortable to
  (a) ask for assistance
  (b) refuse a request
  (c) express your feelings about something important to you

In which of these relationships do you feel least comfortable to
(a) ask for assistance
(b) refuse a request
(c) express your feelings about something important to you

- Can you identify what it is in those relationships that makes them seem more/less comfortable for you? Write one specific event from this week.

Boundary issues

- Recently, my personal boundaries were violated by _____
  I felt . . .
  I did . . .
  Next time, I could . . .
- Recently, I violated the personal boundaries of _____
  I was unaware of . . .
  I felt . . .
  He/she felt . . .
  Next time, I could . . .

Relationships

- What are your current significant relationships like?
- How have you changed in these relationships along your healing journey?
- Are you involved in any unhealthy relationships? If so, what is one thing you could change?
- When you find yourself sensing a desire to approach God, what seems to influence you to draw closer?
- When you find yourself avoiding God, what thoughts/feelings seem to be causing you to pull away?
- What do some of your behaviors and relationships tell you about how you see God in your life at this time?

ASSERTIVENESS INVENTORY[12]

The following questions are helpful to reveal to you a sense of your assertiveness. This tool is not designed to be "scored" but rather to highlight areas of strengths and challenges to maintaining assertive behavior. Be honest in your responses.

Draw a circle around the number that best describes your responses. For some questions the assertive end of the scale is at 0, for others at 4.

Key: 0 means "no" or "never"; 1 means "somewhat" or "sometimes"; 2 means "average"; 3 means "usually" or "a good deal"; and 4 means "practically always" or "entirely."

1. When a person is highly unfair, do you call it to his/her attention?   0 1 2 3 4

2. Do you find it difficult to make decisions?   0 1 2 3 4

3. Are you openly critical of others' ideas, opinions, behavior?   0 1 2 3 4

4. Do you speak up when someone takes your place in line?   0 1 2 3 4

5. Do you often avoid people or situations for fear of embarrassment?   0 1 2 3 4

6. Do you usually have confidence in your own judgment?   0 1 2 3 4

7. Do you insist that your spouse/roommate/partner take on a fair share of household chores?   0 1 2 3 4

8. Are you prone to "fly off the handle"?   0 1 2 3 4

9. When a salesman makes an effort, do you find it hard to say no even though the merchandise is not really what you want?   0 1 2 3 4

10. When a latecomer is waited on before you are, do you call attention to the situation?   0 1 2 3 4

11. Are you reluctant to speak up in a discussion or debate?   0 1 2 3 4

12. If a person has borrowed money (or a book, garment, something of value) and is overdue in returning it, do you mention it?   0 1 2 3 4

13. Do you continue to pursue an argument after the other person has had enough?   0 1 2 3 4

14. Do you generally express what you feel?   0 1 2 3 4

15. Are you disturbed if someone watches you at work?   0 1 2 3 4

16. If someone keeps kicking or bumping your chair in a movie or a lecture, do you ask the person to stop?   0 1 2 3 4

17. Do you find it difficult to keep eye contact   0 1 2 3 4
    when talking to another person?

18. In a good restaurant, when your meal is   0 1 2 3 4
    improperly prepared or served, do you ask
    your server to correct the situation?

19. When you discover merchandise is faulty,   0 1 2 3 4
    do you return it for an adjustment?

20. Do you show your anger by name-calling or   0 1 2 3 4
    obscenities?

21. Do you try to be "unnoticed" in social sit-   0 1 2 3 4
    uations?

22. Do you insist that your landlord   0 1 2 3 4
    (mechanic, repairman, etc.) make repairs,
    adjustments, or replacements that are his/
    her responsibility?

23. Do you often step in and make decisions   0 1 2 3 4
    for others?

24. Are you able to openly express love and   0 1 2 3 4
    affection?

25. Are you able to ask your friends for small   0 1 2 3 4
    favors or help?

26. Do you think you always have the right   0 1 2 3 4
    answer?

27. When you differ with a person you respect,   0 1 2 3 4
    are you able to speak up for your own
    viewpoint?

28. Are you able to refuse unreasonable   0 1 2 3 4
    requests made by friends?

29. Do you have difficulty complimenting or   0 1 2 3 4
    praising others?

30. If you are disturbed by someone smoking   0 1 2 3 4
    near you, can you say so?

31. Do you shout or use bullying tactics to get   0 1 2 3 4
    others to do as you wish?

32. Do you finish other people's sentences for   0 1 2 3 4
    them?

33. Do you get into physical fights with others,   0 1 2 3 4
    especially with strangers?

34. At family meals, do you control the conver-   0 1 2 3 4
    sation?

Another self-awareness tool that has been helpful to many has been the Myers-Briggs Type Indicator, a temperament assessment tool used by many professionals. Completing the questionnaire and attending workshops where temperament types are explored and applied in a friendly setting can be a positive step in developing maturity in relationships with others. Myers-Briggs Type Indicator workshops not only assist in self-awareness but in understanding differences with others and ways to work through conflicts arising from those differences. Myers-Briggs resources are available at many churches, organizations, and online.

16

Step Nine: Ministering to Others

Step Nine: I am willing to be available to God in the healing and restoration of others.

Willingness: a process of actively listening to God with an attitude of personal readiness to respond.

Sensing God's calling to a "helping" ministry involves a process of discernment. For some, that calling may mean becoming involved in support groups with adult survivors of sexual abuse. An important part of the discernment process is to reflect on the underlying desire to serve others and examine the fit of timing, personal gifting, and current life circumstances.

There are many motivators for involvement in "helping" ministries. BECOMERS group facilitators are most often trained peers, gifted "helpers" who are screened for their personal readiness to commit to a ministry of restoration. Adult survivors who wish to be group facilitators must have identified effects of sexual abuse in their lives, and must have healed sufficiently to be able to "step back" from their personal experiences in order to "step in" to the pain of those entering the healing process. Those who have not experienced sexual abuse can also be involved in a ministry of restoration, and must have a calling of informed compassion about sexual abuse that makes their ministry both sensitive and supportive. "Helpers" do not see themselves as "experts" on situations in the lives of group members. Rather, they consider their role to be one of spiritual companionship and grace-full support. Group facilitators need good active listening skills, along with group process facilitation skills. Self-awareness is a critical component of effective group facilitators. Facilitators must have an awareness of personal limitations in their ability to provide support, and need to know their role is not to "rescue" but to encourage.

If inner motivations are not clear, group facilitators risk burnout when the ministry involvement proves too demanding. In our experience, we have encountered several stumbling blocks to effective ministry. However, many stumbling blocks can become areas of personal growth if they are accompanied by a willingness to learn from mistakes and an openness to feedback and support from others. A saying goes that your current safe boundaries were once your unknown frontiers. Being involved in a ministry of deep personal pain and restoration, helpers are likely to encounter "unknown frontiers" in their own lives as they reach out to help others. God's grace can transform those unknown frontiers to safe boundaries in a supportive setting, with an enriched capacity for helping others in constructive ways.

In our experience, a common stumbling block is a desire to "rescue" and to become over-involved in the lives/problems of group members. This may be rooted in patterns of over-responsibility in the "helper." Those who have inner unresolved conflicts with their own parents or siblings may project those unresolved feelings onto group members who are perceived to have the same behavioral characteristics. For example, if "helpers" had passive mothers who did not intervene when fathers abused them, they might experience intense reactions to group members they perceive to be passive. Those who have unresolved issues with their own sexual identity have sometimes encountered difficulties with same-sex attraction to group members. Those who have not walked through a forgiveness process in their own "dark night of the soul" may find it hard to encourage others to move in that direction. Such stumbling blocks do not disqualify anyone from ministry; however, they do require a willingness to address these issues if they arise.

As Christians, we are called to comfort others with the comfort we ourselves have received (2 Corinthians 1:4). The caution is that ministry to others should not be a way to focus on others instead of pursing one's own healing work. Many who have suffered childhood trauma may find themselves in "helping" roles before they are aware of their own losses, and a focus on others is detrimental to their own restoration. After turning to tend to their own healing, however, they often find their ministry to be even more substantial to those they are helping and less costly to themselves. In our experience with BECOMERS, we often encourage recent "graduates" of the program to participate in a ministry of "resting" for a year or two before becoming involved as group facilitators. We exhort them to enjoy their recovery, as it is often the first time in their lives they have experienced freedom to do so.

It is also important for "helpers" to have sufficient personal resources and support systems outside their ministry setting to enable them to successfully engage in the challenges of group process. They will need to draw personal strength from their faith journey, their family, and their support network, and bring all their resources to bear in their "helper" role. Support group ministry has been likened to being inside an embassy in a hostile foreign country. In a foreign country where there is a small United States Embassy, the embassy is not just a safe place—it is actually U.S. soil in the midst of hostile territory. The ambassadors in the embassy are ministers of refuge for U.S. citizens who need safety and rest. In the same way, Christ is our Embassy—a safe place in hostile territory. Those who take refuge in him find safety and rest, in turn becoming his ambassadors—safe people—for others needing assistance.

A "helper" wrote the following poem describing her experience of "ministry."

Ministry

Striving
  Obeying
    Failing
      Growing
        Quitting
Is ministry supposed to be so laborious, Lord?
  Did you intend it to be such a struggle?
    Is there something lacking in me?
Weary
  Hurting
    Fearing
      Inadequate
        Ineffective
It is hard to call others to a life I struggle to
  live.
    Where is the abundance, the joy, the peace?
      Help me, Lord, to persevere.
Forgiven

Learning
Changing
Helping
Sharing
It all makes up ministry, doesn't it, Father?
I desire to help others remove their pain,
but I forget to go to you with my own.
Loved
Adequate
Effective
Accepted
Challenged
I choose to believe all that you say, Lord.
You are sovereign over all.
I will persevere.
Yours . . . Anna[1]

A MINISTRY OF PREVENTION

A specific ministry to which all Christians can be committed is a *ministry of prevention*—that is, protecting children from sexual abuse. A prevention ministry takes many forms. Adult survivors from BECOMERS have made some courageous changes in their lives to equip their children or the children of others with basic preventive skills that were lacking for them. One component of prevention is enhancing children's self-esteem to empower them with confidence to reduce their risks of being victimized. Adult survivors who are in BECOMERS groups have firsthand experience that breaking the cycle of shame is a tremendous challenge. They are encouraged that their hard work in reaching for God's grace to replace shame will help to break generational patterns that contribute to abuse.

Another way adult survivors have ministered to others, especially their children, is by developing active listening skills through their experience of group process. Most adult survivors were raised in hurting families with poor communication skills. Their families were places where thoughts and feelings were unimportant or overruled. Adult survivors know from painful life experience that "it takes two to speak the truth—one to speak and another to hear."[2] With great effort and perseverance, adult survivors have overcome many of the roadblocks to direct communication, and they minister daily to those important to them by developing skills of healthy relationships.

Another significant piece of prevention ministry is in teaching children about "personal body safety." Many adult survivors initially avoid talking about sexuality or sexual abuse to their children, but gain confidence in their group experience to develop an accurate language to speak of body parts and ways to talk about appropriate touch with children.

Adult survivors also minister to others by sharing their awareness that Christian adults can oversimplify children's obedience to authority. Survivors have told us how they have taught their children that it is not always "right" to "obey their elders" if asked to do something uncomfortable. Instead, BECOMERS group members have taught their children biblical examples of those who stood against authority when it was misused, such as Daniel, Esther, and Peter. From their own experience, adult survivors know that teaching children protective education has to be repeated in different ways as children mature. We have seen survivors from BECOMERS notify their family and friends that they have taught their children about personal body safety. This doubly protects children, as it gives permission to trustworthy others to reinforce appropriate boundaries, and it alerts any potential offenders within their families or acquaintances that such children are empowered with knowledge and skills to protect themselves.

There are many ways one can be involved in ministry related to child sexual abuse. The ministry of protection is one that can involve everyone.

Suggested Personal Application Questions to Accompany Step Nine

- Who has been an encourager/support in your life? How were they helpful to you?
- Where have you seen healing in your life—in actions, character, responses, thoughts, interaction with others?
- What are some areas in which you are aware of a need for further healing?
- How might some of your past experiences enable you to offer encouragement and hope to someone else?
- How do you experience actively listening to God? Do you have personal experience with being able to "rest"? If so, write about a specific experience of rest/reflection.

- When you think about being a "helper" to someone, what does that mean to you?

In what ways do you give help/express care? What expresses care to you?

Expanding Territories of Ministry

17

Second Thoughts

When Bethany House Publishers contacted Jeanette and me about revising *Helping Victims of Sexual Abuse,* their request presented an opportunity for us to reflect on the content and ministry impact of the book since its release in 1989. Just as God promised to enlarge Moses' territory (Exodus 34:24), so it seems God has enlarged our territories of ministry over the past two decades.

Thus, Jeanette and I have chosen to write this final section in two voices, offering complementary perspectives in the hope that a twofold approach might "enlarge the territory" of our readers. It is our prayer that these offerings will further equip the church for ministry as, together, we follow in the ways of the Shepherd who gently binds up the brokenhearted.

A MANDATE FOR MINISTRY: SECOND THOUGHTS FROM LYNN

The perspective of time allows for reflection on how my involvement in ministry to adult survivors of sexual abuse has developed since the first edition of this book. As have many others who work with victims of sexual abuse, I concluded over time that prevention is an essential component of effective ministry. Thus, after several years as director of the BECOMERS ministry, my path turned to education with an emphasis on family well-being and sexual abuse prevention.

According to Ephesians 4:12, it is a desire of Christ for his people to be fully equipped to do that which he calls them to do in ministering to and building up the church. For those called to minister to victims of sexual abuse, becoming equipped for such a specific ministry requires many callings, but certainly among them, a call to gain understanding, acquire expertise, practice informed compassion, and exercise discernment. To that end, I invite you on a path of continual learning about sexual abuse that has spanned the last twenty years.

FIRST STEPS

There are at least three influences that have affected ministry related to child sexual abuse. These influences are essentially three different levels of awareness that work together to define how we in the church will attempt to recognize, understand, and prevent child sexual abuse: (1) one's personal awareness about sexual abuse, (2) the degree to which church communities acknowledge sexual abuse, and (3) levels of broader awareness within contemporary society.

First Steps in Personal Awareness: A Little Child Shall Lead

The stepping-off point of my education about sexual abuse was ignorance. I was unaware of childhood sexual abuse simply because I *could* be. My eyes were opened because a wounded child sought sanctuary and healing within our family. The first face of child sexual abuse I had ever "seen" belonged to a child who became our first foster daughter.

My ignorance about sexual abuse rapidly dissipated as we lived with daily effects of the residual damage of child victimization—despairing depression, suicidal periods, outbursts of rage coupled with stony silences, bulimia, precocious sexuality. It was devastating, wrenching, and emotionally and spiritually costly for us to walk alongside this courageous young woman while she lived in our family for nearly a decade. As she left our home and transitioned into independent adulthood, we maintained a relationship with her from the sidelines of her life, anguishing over her involvement with abusive boyfriends, unanticipated pregnancies, and more than one abortion. Her journey would include many dark nights of the soul, although the Light would, in time, overtake the darkness of her path.

Bearing witness to the reality of childhood sexual abuse, I then found myself facing a moral dilemma that could not be ignored. As a witness, and I daresay all who are bystanders are "witnesses" to these grave offenses, I felt compelled to take sides. All that was required for me to take the side of the perpetrators was that I remain unaware and do nothing. On the other hand, believing victims required me to take action—because I would be called to help bear another's burden.[1]

First Steps in the Church: Open Our Eyes, Lord

My first response was to turn to the church. I had expected the church to be able to provide sanctuary and bring light into the darkness of wounded survivors of sexual abuse. However, most churches in my circle of familiarity were not yet ready. Attempts to raise awareness about sexual abuse within church communities were met with comments such as "We don't have that problem here," or "those people" are not in "our church." Similarly, Len Hedges-Goettl, author of *Sexual Abuse: Pastoral Responses*, writes that in the late 1980s during his year of seminary internship working with sexual abuse survivors, he approached congregations to request meeting space for abuse support groups. He encountered similar resistance when a local congregation refused to allow a support group announcement to be posted on the bulletin board because their church did not have "people like that here."[2]

Because something that is "unseen" cannot be addressed, attitudes like these kept child sexual abuse at the periphery of awareness in many church communities. The lack of specialized ministry to and for adult survivors was both appalling and compelling to me. The burden of seeing such need was the impetus God used to provide me with a vision for the BECOMERS ministry. However, the BECOMERS support groups would become viable primarily as a parachurch ministry because adult survivors remained invisible at the margins of the church.

The first BECOMERS group began in 1984. In those early days, requests to start up BECOMERS programs in other locations began to pour in, exceeding any capacity I had to meet those needs. It was at that time that Bethany House Publishers offered an invitation to put the BECOMERS program into book form, essentially multiplying the ministry within the U.S. and beyond. Looking back, it was a significant blessing for ministry to sexual abuse victims when Bethany House took a risk to break the silence at a time when much of the Christian community remained in denial about the existence of sexual abuse in society, let alone in the church.

First Steps in Societal Awareness: A Gradual Awakening

The BECOMERS ministry was established within a social context that had only recently passed laws against child sexual abuse. As I researched the history of societal awareness of child sexual abuse, I was astounded. The first *reported* case of child abuse in the U.S. took place in 1874—the case of Mary Ellen, age nine, in New York City. A social worker tried to intervene in the child's starvation and severe physical torment but was prevented from doing so because there were no laws against child abuse. What was ultimately so astonishing is that intervention was successful only because the social worker made the case that the child was, at the very least, a part of the animal kingdom and therefore should be protected under existing laws for the prevention of cruelty to animals!

In 1962, pediatrician C. Henry Kempe educated us about what he termed the "battered child syndrome," and by 1968, all states in the United States had passed laws requiring professionals to report the physical abuse of children. However, it was not until 1978 that child *sexual* abuse was incorporated into the Federal Child Abuse and Prevention Act. Thus, the formation of the BECOMERS ministry took place only six years after the reality of child sexual abuse was recognized by U.S. law.

NEXT STEPS

Over the years, I have seen ministry to victims of sexual abuse move forward in many directions, continually shaped by the same three levels of awareness—personal, church, and societal. At this revision, my personal awareness has broadened; additional resources exist for ministry within church communities, and societal awareness has contributed to greater knowledge through research in the social and biological sciences.

Next Steps in Personal Awareness: Little Children Still Lead

Throughout the 1990s, I pursued a second undergraduate degree in child development and advanced degrees in family social science. Over time, my ministry to victims of sexual abuse had turned toward a path of *prevention* through an emphasis on family wellness and parent education. Along the way, I was surprised by an increasing interest in cross-cultural studies and overseas missions, and followed my heart across new thresholds of experience. Having become a more global citizen over the intervening years since founding BECOMERS, I must now "bear witness" to child sexual abuse within the international family.

Sexual abuse of children is rampant across continents, and although it wears different faces in different cultures, the damage remains devastating. For example, the spread of HIV/AIDS throughout Africa significantly relates to child sexual abuse. Traditional African beliefs often promote the deadly idea that a person who has any type of sexually transmitted disease, such as HIV/AIDS, can be "cured" or "cleansed" by having intercourse with a "virgin"—even a "virgin" child. Such dark beliefs have targeted even the tiniest of infants, both female and male, for horrendous acts of rape.[3] In addition, more than 14 million children worldwide have been orphaned because of AIDS. That is the equivalent of every child under five in America having no one to look after them.[4] As orphaned children become "heads of household" for younger siblings, they also fall prey to wholesale victimization as a deplorable fact of daily life.

I am compelled to speak up for these little ones because they cannot speak for themselves. In an unanticipated development in ministry focus, my husband and I find ourselves not only entering the "second half"[5] of our married lives together but also sharing a calling together to "look after orphans . . . in their distress" (James 1:27). We currently spend much of our year serving with The Love of Christ Ministries, a South African orphanage that cares for abandoned babies left behind in the wake of HIV/AIDS. This is child sexual abuse prevention at its most basic level—protecting children from almost certain harm.

I share this evolving ministry path with you, our readers, to encourage you that no matter where you are situated in God's world, you are able to be part of the solution to the devastation of child sexual abuse. For example, if you are reading this book, you are involved in ministry to sexual abuse victims, because you are increasing your understanding and acquiring expertise for the practice of informed compassion as you respond on behalf of Christ to wounded souls. Or, perhaps you are called to the prevention of abuse by promoting family well-being, even your own.

Perhaps you wonder whether you have the right to speak out to help survivors of abuse because you are not a survivor yourself. Christian therapist Diane Langberg has worked with sexual abuse survivors for over twenty-five years. As the author of *Counseling Survivors of Sexual Abuse*, she writes about her early work with victims of abuse. Because she herself had not been sexually abused, she initially thought it might be presumptuous or even arrogant for her to write about "what it was like to be molested as a child . . . or to tell abused people what would help them heal."[6] However, she suggests that even though there might be a type of silence that is rooted in feeling inadequate for a given task, "there is also a silence that is a betrayal or a choice to ignore reality because it is too painful. To be silent is to abuse the victim again, to allow others to erase her trauma from their minds."[7]

All of us speak in some way to the issue of child sexual abuse. Becoming a witness defines a mandate for ministry that can take many pathways. Yet the purpose remains focused: Avert future harm to children through ministries of prevention, and offer hope of restoration and spiritual companionship along the healing journey of those who suffer.

Next Steps in the Church: Expanding Territories of Ministry

In addition to an expanding awareness of abuse across the globe, my vision for ministry has expanded as I have become more aware of the complexity and mystery of God's healing work within the interior of wounded hearts. I have encouraged my seminary students to consider an appreciation for the integration of insights from many sources as they prepare for pastoral care and counseling ministries that will include counseling victims of childhood sexual abuse.

With regard to being equipped for ministry, a few students are disinclined to, others are cautious about, making use of insights for healing that are derived from social science—especially if those conducting the research are not coming from a distinctively Christian perspective. However, I am persuaded that it is God who has given humanity a desire to search for truth, whether we search for truth about God in Scripture or search for insights about human relationships through social science. From a vantage point that God is the source of all truth, harmony can exist between the truths of Scripture and insights from the sciences. The following model has shaped my views for expanding our territories of ministry.

Ted Ward, professor emeritus of Trinity Evangelical Divinity School, has conceptualized a way of integrating foundational knowledge from Scripture with helpful insights from scientific disciplines. Aspects of truth can be discerned through views of God as Author and Creator. God, as Author, reveals truth in Scripture, and this search for truth is pursued through the study of theology. God, as Creator, reveals truth through his creation, and this search for truth is pursued through the study of science. By pursuing truth revealed by God as Creator, it is possible to learn about creation through the study of science and to learn about some aspects of interpersonal relationships through the study of social science.[8]

Those of us within the church have greater opportunities than ever before to increase our understandings about sexual abuse and also increase ministry effectiveness by integrating foundational truths of Scripture with gleanings from the social and biological sciences. *Findings* from the sciences can be examined for insight. Although the *application* of those findings requires discernment for biblical application, there is much to be gained from this perspective. Over the past two decades, adult survivors of sexual abuse have been significantly helped through integration of social science research into effective Christian ministry.

Accessible Ministry Resources

When conducting research for this book in the 1980s, there were very few Christian resources available addressing issues of sexual abuse. Today, there are nearly a hundred books to be found through online listings of Christian books related in some way to sexual abuse. Resources address issues of sexual abuse in many specific areas, such as making worship sensitive to abuse survivors in our congregations. The Internet facilitates connections for abuse survivors worldwide to support one another in their recovery, and expands the availability of resources to those with otherwise limited access.

Church staff can go online to Web sites, such as *www. reducingtherisk.org,* to find resources for making church communities safe from child sexual abuse, to understand more about sex offender profiles, and for information about developing screening for staff/volunteers and implementing supervision guidelines.

Resources for pastors offer specific assistance for appropriate pastoral responses to the many aspects of abuse they might encounter in their church settings. Internet Christian resources, such as *www.pureonline.com,* are available for those struggling with sexual addictions, such as to online pornography.

Increased Ministry to Women

Since the first edition of *Helping Victims of Sexual Abuse,* recognition within churches of adult female survivors of sexual abuse has unquestionably increased. The church has made progress in confronting denial about the existence of sexual abuse and has taken significant steps to break the silence by offering help to adult women who have been abused. While many women and children still hold secret tragedy in their hearts, many others have been encouraged to find their voice, and they are speaking out. Large church ministry models, such as Celebrate Recovery, are addressing a variety of recovery issues in corporate worship settings and smaller teaching groups where those who are adult survivors of abuse are reminded that they are not alone.

Inadequate Ministry to Men

The church has not yet come to grips with the degree to which men are also victims of sexual abuse. A beginning awareness is emerging—in response to an increasing chorus of voices of little boys, now men, speaking up about their abuse. The public nature of clergy abuse disclosures has helped to encourage more men to speak up than ever before. Until recently, victims of clergy abuse had no forum in which to disclose abuse because so few had gone to their churches and been believed. Instead, "they suffered alone in silence and the rest of us never knew."[9]

The Department of Justice estimates there are two hundred fifty to five hundred thousand pedophiles in the U.S.[10] While some (Level 1) pedophile offenders molest fewer victims, the National Institute of Mental Health reports that other (Level 3) pedophiles will molest up to two hundred eighty boys during their lifetime. Only 1–10 percent of these offenses will be reported. The most vulnerable age for sexual abuse of boys is seven to thirteen years old.[11] At the very least, these estimates should shake us out of any denial with regard to the reality that a significant number of men in our churches are silently suffering from past experiences of sexual abuse.

Young boys are being abused by both males and females; their offenders are legion. It is poignant and regrettable that it has taken so long for the voices of men who have survived sexual abuse to begin to be heard.

Being invisible to the church and therefore without ministry intervention, adolescent boys and men are often left to fend for themselves to cope with any residual damage from sexual abuse. Social science research informs us about several ways of coping. Some victimized males "cope" by considering sexual abuse to be their fate, in a sense. A tragic outcome may be that a boy who experiences himself as a passive victim will later become a male prostitute "taking refuge in what he knows: a world of dependence, submission, humiliation, even brutalization."[12] While some might think that male prostitution is an extreme outcome of male sexual abuse, the Office of Juvenile Justice and Delinquency Prevention (OJJDP) has found that male juvenile prostitutes outnumber female juvenile prostitutes by 61 to 39 percent.[13] How much more should young men be finding refuge in our churches than on the streets!

Another destructive way of "coping" is that some sexually victimized boys become offenders themselves. Through abusing others, an adolescent or adult man may not only seek a sense of control and dominance but also may target a specific *kind* of child to molest and defile—a child like the *child he would have wanted to be* if he had not been abused.[14] How might our awareness of such destructive intentions inform strategies of detection and prevention in our churches?

Yet another male victim of abuse might present himself to others as a "typical boy next door," going to great lengths to cover up his mistrust, sense of vulnerability, and shame with a mask of normalcy. How might undisclosed sexual abuse contribute to self-imposed isolation of victimized boys and men within our youth groups and our congregations?

As a woman, I cannot speak to the experience of men who have been victimized. However, researchers have conducted in-depth interviews with men who are victims of sexual abuse, and reading personal abuse histories of men offers insight and understanding into some of the inner anguish of men's experience. A next step for churches in ministry to male survivors of abuse might be to examine barriers that could prevent men from seeking restoration from sexual abuse within our congregations. How might the church offer masculine alternatives to "being tough" so that victimized boys don't feel they must resort to violence to prove their masculinity? How might the church assist men who have been abused by other men to relate to Christ as their male role model? How might the church encourage sexually abused men to develop sexual abuse ministries for other abused men and still perceive themselves as "real men"?

Markedly absent are Christian resources for men who have been sexually abused. Christian resources that do target male audiences often present male roles in a context of male/female differences. From reading abuse testimonies of male survivors, it seems that clear-cut masculine/feminine distinctions might further isolate abused men by making it nearly impossible for them to be recognized as "victims" without being considered "weak" or "passive" or "feminine." How might men be enabled to speak up about inner effects related to their sexual abuse in a context of Christian masculinity presented in images of "warriors" or "conquerors"? A masculinity of stoicism, in which distress or fear is ignored, is often the experience of young boys who are abused. In their research interviews, male victims tell us that on rare occasions when they have taken a huge risk to disclose abuse, their sexual abuse experience is often dismissed as trivial or treated as a "joke."[15]

Once again, we in the church stand as witnesses. This time, we are witnesses to the sexual abuse of men in our congregations. The Christian community must begin to integrate what can be learned from current research into effective ministry to men who suffer in silence. We are again forced to choose between ignoring their voices or helping to bear our brothers' burden in light of great injustices that have been committed against them.

Authentic Accountability for Church Leaders

We also stand as witness to further grievous transgressions. Current societal awareness of pastors and priests abusing children has put churches in the spotlight. This focus offers opportunity for greater accountability within the body of Christ for dealing openly and honestly with church staff and volunteers who use their positions of spiritual authority to sexually exploit children and adults in their care.

Although the news media have targeted sexual abuse by Catholic clergy, church staff and volunteers from churches across the country are also implicated. Terry Mattingly, senior fellow for journalism at the Council for Christian Colleges and Universities, writes that according to a 2000 report to the Baptist General Conference of Texas, "the incidence of sexual abuse by clergy has reached 'horrific proportions'" with studies finding that "about 12 percent of ministers had engaged in sexual intercourse" with church members and nearly 40 percent had acknowledged "sexually inappropriate behavior." The report goes on to say that, according to religious journals and research institutes, "the rate of incidence for clergy abuse exceeds the client-professional rate for both physicians and psychologists."[16]

The church's witness for Christ stands in the balance of our acknowledgment of and response to sexual violations committed by those in Christian leadership.

Next Steps in Societal Awareness: Inferences and Insights

Society is in a period of heightened awareness to the issue of childhood sexual abuse. Research began exposing sexual abuse of children as a problem of sizable proportions in the late 1960s and early 1970s. Current research offers us continued insights for increased effectiveness in Christian ministry to victims of sexual abuse.

Links Between Sexual Abuse and Eating Disorders

In the mid–1980s, I became personally acquainted with a connection between childhood sexual abuse trauma and eating disorders when our foster daughter began to struggle with bulimia in her early teens. Over the last two decades, researchers have continued to try to understand possible links between sexual abuse and eating disorders. Some sources report that between one-third and two-thirds of patients who go to treatment centers for eating disorders have experienced some type of abuse in the past.[17]

We now know that the victims of childhood sexual abuse who are most likely to develop eating disorders (particularly bulimia) are those who have experienced sexual abuse before age eighteen, suffered abuse involving a family member, and/or experienced abuse involving the use of force.[18] In one study, a group of undergraduate women not involved in any type of counseling completed anonymous questionnaires. Of the 214 women, 25 reported that they were victims of family incest; they also reported high levels of bulimia. In addition, those twenty-five women scored high on measures of internalized shame, most clearly linked to their incest experience.[19] Thus, a primary "link" between incest and bulimia might be internalized shame. In another study, women who were being treated at trauma clinics for eating disorders disclosed that 93 percent of them had experienced sexual abuse prior to developing eating disorders.[20] Such insights might guide us to a focused ministry on resolving shame as foundational to recovery from incest and as a possible intervention to reduce the risk that sexual abuse victims will develop eating disorders.

The scope of eating disorders within the Christian community is reflected by the development of specialized ministries such as Remuda Ranch, a professional resource for families, health care, and pastoral professionals.[21] The Remuda Ranch professional publication, *The Christian Journal of Eating Disorders*, integrates current social science research with a biblically based approach to develop effective treatment of eating disorders. Whatever the complex connections are between child sexual abuse and eating disorders, intervention into destructive and potentially life-threatening symptoms is essential.

Links Between Sexual Abuse, Trauma, and "Malignant" Memories

Another area for potential ministry insight comes from neuroscience research regarding effects of trauma and the creation of "malignant memories."[22] In acute stress, specific hormones, such as norepinephrine and epinephrine, activate the nervous system to directly increase heart rate and increase muscle readiness for an alarm response, that is, a "fight-or-flight" response. A surge of neurological stimulation sets up a pattern for associating sensory information and emotional states of fear as a "memory." After storing information in the form of a stress-related memory, the central nervous system returns to a pre-alarm relaxed state, with an ability to "retrieve" that stored information for an appropriate response in the case of future threats to safety.

However, this alarm reaction can go awry when stressful events—such as child sexual abuse—are of such intensity or duration or frequency that there is no "return to normal" state experienced. Instead, a child stays in "hyper-alert-expecting-danger" mode or, alternatively, a dissociative "unaware-and-numb-to-danger" mode. In these cases, memories that are stored are more than a record of stress-responses for later retrieval, when needed. These responses become "malignant" memories.

Malignant memories are thought to be made up of neurological functions that integrate complex groupings of survival responses, thoughts, feelings, body sensations, and behaviors. A maladaptive and continual activation of the alarm response can contribute to post-traumatic stress disorder.

Research suggests that the central nervous system in the developing brain is "exquisitely sensitive" to acute stress.[23] Because a young child's brain is still developing, researchers are concerned that the formation of malignant memories, such as traumatic experiences of childhood sexual abuse, may affect not only the alarm response but also affect neurological pathways that influence the child's development. In addition to feeling as if they are in a state of persistent alarm, children experiencing consistent threat are likely to have a "sensitized" alarm response and tend to over-respond to verbal and non-verbal cues that, to them, seem threatening.[24] If intervention to stop the trauma does not occur, research suggests that childhood trauma may be hidden until adulthood.

In adults, when some *external* sensory input or some *internal* thought, feeling, or body sensation "triggers" a malignant memory response, an adult abuse victim experiences tremendous levels of heightened arousal, which may result in behavioral and emotional overreaction or emotional numbness. Malignant memories can emerge in the form of shame, depression, violence, dissociation, or suicidal behaviors.

Through research such as this, we begin to comprehend how violence against children can leave lasting marks on function and structure in the brain as well as in the soul. At the very least, these findings should compel us to strive to prevent childhood abuse in all its forms. At the same time, this type of research can evoke great compassion within us as we begin to appreciate the depth of healing required as those suffering with post-traumatic stress engage in daily struggles to take captive every thought to Christ (2 Corinthians 10:5).

PREVENTING CHILD SEXUAL ABUSE

Over the last two decades, a great deal of effort has gone into evaluating the effectiveness of abuse prevention programs aimed at educating children to recognize unwanted touching that might lead to sexual abuse. In addition, current attention toward prevention is addressing the latest forms of abuse related to newly developed technologies.

Preventing Abuse by Educating Children

In the early '80s, I attempted to interest more than one Christian book publisher in printing a parents' workbook I had written for sexual abuse prevention education. However, consensus was that there was not enough of a need to warrant such a project. The workbook was eventually published by an inexperienced entrepreneur and had only limited distribution. In spite of this personal setback, I felt compelled to encourage parents to raise their children's awareness of the potential risk of sexual abuse. Christian parents seemed willing to raise the idea of stranger abuse with their children but were hesitant to alert their children to the much more prevalent occurrence of abuse by a familiar person or family member. In some respects, current clergy abuse scandals have had a positive effect on addressing this hesitation. Parents have been alerted once again to the need to talk to their children about the possibility of sexual abuse perpetrated by someone they know and trust.

In 2006, most elementary schools routinely incorporate child abuse prevention programs in their yearly curriculum. While there have been mixed reviews about the effectiveness of prevention programs, we are learning more about the specific features of prevention education that actually help children protect themselves.

One national research study evaluated child sexual abuse prevention programs for children over age ten. Children who had been involved in a variety of comprehensive prevention programs were more likely to disclose abuse or attempted abuse, were more likely to feel successful in protecting themselves, and were less likely to blame themselves if they did experience abuse.[25]

Studies of preschool and early elementary age children have found that the most significant component of sexual abuse prevention education programs is providing children with *opportunities to role-play* and *practice new assertiveness skills*.[26] This feature of preventive education grew out of interviews with sex offenders who were asked what they did to engage a child in sexual contact after they had identified a potential victim. Most offenders described a "pre-abuse" period of time to determine how far they could go with sexual advances: "I would initiate different kinds of contact, such as touching the child's back, head. Testing the child to see how much she would take before she would pull away."[27] In light of such insights, the most effective prevention approach is behavior-based curriculum, which gives children an opportunity to learn—and to practice—ways to effectively resist unwanted touch of any kind, even when someone uses tactics of bribery, intimidation, or emotional rejection.[28]

We also should be awakened to the necessity for parents to be as vigilant with boys as they are with girls. Churches should educate parents to be just as concerned about whom their sons are with, where they are, asking them how they are doing—so that families are places where a son could feel safe enough to talk about any sexual abuse or questionable situation that he may have encountered.[29] Families can reduce children's risk of sexual abuse by promoting open communication, respecting each other's privacy, and discussing healthy sexuality. Parents can prevent children's exposure to sexually explicit TV and movies, and, if children are old enough to use a computer, parents can put safety rules in place for the use of the Internet.

Preventing Exploitation by Monitoring the Internet

The Internet was in its infancy when *Helping Victims of Sexual Abuse* was first published. In contrast, there are now nearly twenty-four million children online regularly each month. One in five children currently online is sexually solicited.[30] The Crimes Against Children Research Center contacted a representative sample of children ages ten to seventeen across the U.S. and found that 19 percent of the fifteen hundred children surveyed had received unsolicited online requests to engage in sexual activities, and 15 percent of those cases were "aggressive solicitations" in which online predators tried to personally contact children at their homes.[31] Concern about online sexual predators is further heightened by use of the Internet by pedophiles themselves to access other pedophiles worldwide, receive support for their sexual perversions, share ideas about ways to lure victims, and have instant access to child victims worldwide, including the means to track down a child's home contact information.[32] Families and churches must be attentive to this new form of child exploitation.

However, even more startling than Internet use by pedophiles is the documented use of the Internet by family members and close acquaintances to sexually abuse children! Once again, the stereotype of "stranger danger" does not serve children well. Several new technologies are converging to put children at risk.

Digital photography and the online market for child pornography have made family exploitation of children more lucrative. As well, the Internet offers new opportunities for family members and acquaintances to seduce children into abusive situations and expose children to sexually explicit images.[33]

The National Juvenile Online Victimization Study took place over a one-year period (2001–2002) and examined cases involving arrests of family members and acquaintance offenders using the Internet to gain access to children for the purpose of sexually abusing them. About one-quarter of the offenders lived in suburban neighborhoods, while almost half of the offenders lived in small towns and rural areas. Family offenders most often targeted young girls (six to twelve), while acquaintances of the family tended to target mostly teenage boys. The most common exploitation was to fondle young victims while jointly viewing child pornography to show children how to perform sex acts, as in the case of a forty-three-year-old offender fondling his five-year-old neighbor while showing her pornography on his computer.[34]

A Calling of Caring

Those called to any facet of ministry regarding childhood sexual abuse are called, among many things, to gain understanding, acquire expertise, practice informed compassion, and exercise discernment. While gaining understanding is necessary for protecting children, and acquiring expertise for informed compassion facilitates discernment in helping others along their healing journeys, our education about the darkness of such sin is heartrending and grievous.

Marie Fortune, author of *Sexual Violence: The Unmentionable Sin*, has shaped my views in coming to a broader understanding of the multifaceted sin of childhood sexual abuse. Sexual abuse is

- A bodily sin: Sexual abuse is a sin against the body, violating bodily boundaries of personal space and leaving behind distortions about one's body image.
- A relational sin: Sexual abuse is a sin against relationship, violating the command to love one's neighbor as oneself. It is a sin betraying trust and destroying relationships between victims and those who should have cared for them but instead caused them harm. Consequences of this sin create barriers to trust between victims and their future relationships.
- A social sin: Sexual abuse is a sin against the church as the body of Christ, because when one member suffers, all are made to suffer.
- A sexual sin: Sexual abuse is a sin against God because the blessing of sexuality is used to destroy instead of build intimacy. Sexual abuse sins against God because it violates his most sacred creation, human beings made in his image.[35]

"This is the verdict: Light has come into the world, but men loved darkness instead of light because their deeds were evil. Everyone who does evil hates the light, and will not come into the light for fear that his deeds will be exposed. But whoever lives by the truth comes into the light so that it may be seen plainly that what he has done has been done through God" (John 3:19–21).

Let us live by the Truth and bring others into the Light. Let the church bring together all the resources God has given us so that, as instructed in Ephesians 6:15, we may, having done everything, stand with our wounded sisters and brothers against the darkness they face. As Ezra and Nehemiah worked together to accomplish the holy task of the restoration of Israel, so abuse survivors need those in the body of Christ to work together in the holy task of restoring lives that are suffering damage from destruction inflicted by others.

From within God's grace, let us refrain from dividing healing journeys into separate categories of "sacred" and "secular." Instead, let us bring Ezra's "grounding" resources to the task of rebuilding identities in Christ that are crumbling in disrepair—that is, let us make use of Scripture and worship and obedient "listening" to God's living presence. And let us bring Nehemiah's "brick and mortar" resources—education, research, and therapeutic skills—to the task of rebuilding broken "selves" who cannot hold fast to their Maker's image.

As long as it is day, may the body of Christ follow the example of Christ and continue to do the work of him who sent us (John 9:4).

A Mandate for Ministry: Second Thoughts From Jeanette

In the years since starting the Christian Recovery Center, I have continued to learn and grow in the knowledge of helping sexual abuse victims. I have used various treatment modalities to bring freedom and healing from the life experience of abuse. God has brought victims of many ages and experiences to CRC. There have been children as young as three and adults as old as seventy. Children I have counseled have been abused within their families, at child-care centers, at churches, at schools, and in their neighborhoods. At CRC over one-third of the clients we see are children.

It is heart-wrenching for me to see the young victims who can barely speak and put words to their trauma of sexual abuse walk through the door for help. I have used directive and non-directive play therapy to help these young children. In the play therapy room I have seen children play out their feelings of anger, fear, and powerlessness. I teach them about "good" and "bad" touches, what offenders look like, and that it is okay to tell if abuse happens. I want children to know that the abuse is not their fault and that they are not bad people because abuse happened to them. Hundreds of these children are now living a happy, carefree childhood.

God has given me a heart for adolescents, and I have worked with children who were abused in their families, children in foster care, and children who have been adopted. Some of these children have been abused in orphanages in foreign countries and been adopted by Christian families in the States. All of these children are truly survivors of horrific trauma and have significant psychological damage. I count it a privilege to help these children and to help their families develop a trusting, caring, and supportive environment in which these children can recover and heal.

The BECOMERS sexual abuse program has continued to help many victims at the Christian Recovery Center and throughout the United States. I've had the privilege of conducting BECOMERS sexual abuse workshops throughout the country and at CRC. I have a vision for the BECOMERS groups to network and receive training together. We do have a BECOMERS manual that can be ordered from the Christian Recovery Center to be used in conjunction with the *Helping Victims of Sexual Abuse* book to start BECOMERS groups. I am willing to train volunteers and professionals who want to start a group and want to have a sexual abuse workshop to launch a BECOMERS program.

In the fall of 2004, I was involved in a filming project wherein I taught and facilitated a sexual abuse group using the BECOMERS nine-step recovery material from *Helping Victims of Sexual Abuse*. This project was done in conjunction with Restoring the Heart Ministries, Inc., a ministry started and directed by Julie Woodley, Setauket, New York, under the titles *Into My Arms* and *In the Wildflowers*. The videos and curriculum are available for your church or counseling center from Restoring the Heart Ministries (631-689-6686).

The Christian Recovery Center has seen an increase in clients who are suffering from the life experience of ritual or satanic sexual abuse. I personally have worked with many of these clients. They are diagnosed with Dissociative Identity Disorder and have many personalities (alters) who dissociated because they were forced to be involved in sexual, physical, emotional, and spiritual abuse that included horrific satanic rituals and torture. Sandra Wilson, in her book *Released From Shame*, stated that "Children are subjected to terrifying rituals, mind-altering drugs and techniques, or grisly threats to confuse and control them. Often, adults force the victims to participate in ritualistic murder and mutilation to create a sense of personal guilt and guarantee the victim's silence."[36]

God has given me a real heart to help those wounded by ritual abuse. It's important that alters feel safe so they can develop trust to deal with the difficult abuse they've been through. In their book *Beyond the Darkness,* Cynthia Kubetin and James Mallory say it's important to realize that each alter has a specific role, feelings, and response to the abuse. Each alter needs to know that they are part of a larger whole. The goal of therapy is "to have a healthy integration so the positive traits of the different alters can add up to an improved whole." The alters need to be supported to work together in unity and harmony to bring health and healing to the total person.[37] I have used a form of prayer therapy with ritual abuse victims, where God helps them know the truth, break vows made with Satan, and break down dissociative walls to make them a whole person. Because these clients have so many problems, I've spent years helping them find healing and freedom. God has been faithful to empower these very special people to resolve their childhood trauma.

At CRC we have counseled children who have been sexual abuse victims themselves and who then become involved in sexually offending other children. We see children as young as six or seven and adolescents abusing younger children in the family, neighborhood, or school. Because of the child's past sexual abuse, they have become overly stimulated sexually. They need to be taught how their sexual abuse has led them to abuse other children, how they are going to deal with these sexualized behaviors, and boundaries they need to set up to keep themselves and others safe. The therapist has to understand both sides of the problem. The therapist needs to have empathy and understanding for the "victim," but also be able to confront the "victimizer." I have helped these children learn the reasons for their abuse, learn appropriate boundaries, and receive help and healing. What I have learned is that if these children do not receive help, they could go on to become adult offenders.

I have also been involved in working with sexual offenders through Christian Recovery Center's Project Restoration Program. Part of my original vision at CRC was not only to help victims of sexual abuse but also to help offenders break the cycle of abuse, thereby stopping any more little children from being abused. You can look under the sexual offender's section of *Helping Victims of Sexual Abuse* to learn more about this program. It has been exciting to see how God has transformed not only the offenders who have spent two to three years in group and individual therapy getting help but also their victims, marriages, and families. God is truly restoring the years the locusts have eaten (Joel 2:25).

For further information about RESTORATION PROJECT, contact Christian Recovery Center, 6120 Earle Brown Drive, Suite 200, Brooklyn Center, Minnesota 55430 (763-566-0088).

Conclusion

The process of restoration from childhood sexual abuse is not random—it is an intentionally chosen path. However, a healing journey will not be experienced in a series of steps as they are written in any book. Most adult survivors envision their healing process as a spiral. They return again and again to the same circular cycle of "steps," but often at a different level and with new insights and perspectives.

Initial stages in this process often precipitate a sense of "crisis" for abused adults. Dealing with repressed feelings can wreak havoc in their lives and result in what feels like a state of emergency. They fear they might "go crazy" or harm themselves. The benefit of crisis is that it can motivate a desire to seek help.

Most survivors involved in BECOMERS are also involved in intense individual counseling/therapy for a significant length of time. And then many experience a season of rest from the intense emotional work. Feeling somewhat strengthened and stabilized, they feel ready to disengage from dealing with past abuse issues and focus on their present daily life. At times of transition—engagement, marriage, childbirth, death of a parent, career change, or return to school—something triggers unresolved memories and old feelings are activated. This is not regression. Rather, each spiral back through steps of healing provides opportunities to integrate new experiences into the self, to feel, to develop deeper relationships with God and others. These circular journeys represent levels of personal growth that require tremendous effort and resilience.

The best teachers about the healing journey are those who are traveling it. Adult female abuse survivors from several BECOMERS groups agreed to participate in an extensive research project to identify and prioritize issues in relation to their significance to the healing process. The issues reflect what this group of survivors considered to be the biggest challenges of their healing. After identifying the most significant issues, they then ranked them in order of what they felt needed to be dealt with early on and later on in the process. For example, forgiveness was considered to be a significant issue in recovery, and at the same time BECOMERS group members deemed several other issues to have priority before concerns about forgiveness could be addressed.

Issues identified as most important in the process were:

1. Looking at the area of victimization
2. Dealing with shame, guilt, and fear
3. Honestly dealing with issues and taking responsibility for change
4. Support of BECOMERS group and group leaders
5. Individual therapy
6. Sharing and letting go of feelings
7. Looking to God as the source of help
8. Dealing with issues of sexuality
9. Forgiving self and/or the abuser
10. Being of help to others

The women and men whose stories are told in this book are people of great courage and integrity. They have graciously ministered to the body of Christ by allowing their pain to be exposed so that others might learn of the grievous sin of child sexual abuse both in and outside the church. In so doing, they have demonstrated the possibility of restoration through God's grace.

At the same time, damaged lives of adult survivors often appear to others to be in disarray. Unfortunately, in the past we in the church have been guilty of trying to "fix" them with pat answers, religious clichés, and, perhaps unintentionally but because of a lack of understanding, we have attempted to "heal their wounds lightly" (Jeremiah 6:14 RSV) or have not taken them seriously. In the past, the church has responded much like the Israelites in the time of Hosea (4:6), with the result that adult survivors of abuse "are destroyed from lack of knowledge" within the church about the depth of their trauma and lengthy process of restoration. That is, we have lacked *informed* compassion. With this revision of *Helping Victims of Sexual Abuse*, may the body of Christ be further equipped with increased understanding, may we persist in acquiring supportive expertise, and may our ministries be enhanced with informed compassion.

Suggested Resources

Coates, Jan. *Set Free: God's Healing Power for Abuse Survivors and Those Who Love Them.* Minneapolis, MN: Bethany House Publishers, 2005.

Frank, Jan. *Door of Hope: Recognizing and Resolving the Pains of Your Past.* Nashville: Thomas Nelson, Inc., 1995.

Hedges-Goettl, Len. *Sexual Abuse: Pastoral Responses.* Nashville: Abingdon Press, 2004.

Heggen, Carolyn Holderread. *Sexual Abuse in Christian Homes and Churches.* Scottdale, PA: Herald Press, 1993.

Kubetin, Cynthia A., and James Mallory, MD, *Beyond the Darkness: Healing for Victims of Sexual Abuse,* 1st edition. Dallas: Rapha Publishing/Word, Inc., 1992.

Langberg, Diane Mandt. *On the Threshold of Hope.* Wheaton, IL: Tyndale House Publishers, 1999.

———. *Counseling Survivors of Sexual Abuse.* Longwood, FL: Xulon Press, Inc., 2003.

Mason, Marilyn, and Merle Fossum. *Facing Shame: Families in Recovery.* New York: W. W. Norton & Company, 1986.

Simkin, Penny, PT, and Phyllis Klaus, CSW, MFT. *When Survivors Give Birth: Understanding and Healing the Effects of Early Sexual Abuse on Childbearing Women.* Seattle: Classic Day Publishing, 2004.

Smedes, Lewis. *The Art of Forgiving: When You Need to Forgive and Don't Know How.* New York: Ballantine Books, 1996.

Tracy, Steven. *Mending the Soul: Understanding and Healing Abuse.* Grand Rapids, MI: Zondervan, 2005.

Travilla, Carol, and Joan Webb. *The Intentional Woman: A Guide to Experiencing the Power of Your Story.* Colorado Springs: Navpress, 2002.

VanVonderen, Jeff. *Tired of Trying to Measure Up.* Minneapolis, MN: Bethany House Publishers, 1989.

Wilson, Sandra. *Released From Shame: Moving Beyond the Pain of the Past.* Downers Grove, IL: InterVarsity Press. Revised edition, 2002.

Brain Structure and Function: Handbook From Child Trauma
Academy: to assist parents, caregivers, teachers, and various
professionals working with maltreated and traumatized children. Download at: *www.childtrauma.org/ctmaterials/
brain_II.asp*
Child Prevention Resources
www.prevent-abuse-now.com
www.preventchildabuse.org
National Association for Christian Recovery
www.nacronline.com
National Center for Post-Traumatic Stress Disorder
www.ncptsd.va.gov/facts/
Remuda Ranch: an intensive biblically based inpatient program for
eating disorders
www.remudaranch.com
Resources for making church communities safe from child sexual
abuse
www.reducingtherisk.com
Sexual Addiction Resources
www.pureonline.com/learn-more.aspx
www.christiananswers.net/q-eden/edn-f016.html

Bibliography

Arp, Claudia, and David Arp. *The Second Half of Marriage*. Grand Rapids, MI: Zondervan, 1998.

Augsburger, David. *Caring Enough to Forgive*. Ventura, CA.: Regal Books, 1981.

Benatar, Pat. "Hell Is for Children," *Live From Earth*. New York: Chrysalis Records, 1983.

Berry, Carmen Renee. "Beyond Victimization." *National Association for Christian Recovery*. *www.nacronline.com/dox/library/carmen/beyond.shtml* (accessed November 20, 2005).

Briere, John, and Diana Elliot. "Immediate and Long-Term Impacts of Child Sexual Abuse." *The Future of Children* 4, no. 2 (Summer/Fall 1994): 54–69.

Browne, Angela, and David Finkelhor. "The Impact of Child Sexual Abuse: A Review of the Research." *Psychological Bulletin* 99, no. 1 (January 1986): 66–77.

Carnes, Patrick. *Out of the Shadows: Understanding Sexual Addiction*. Minneapolis, MN: CompCare Publications, 1983.

"Child Molesters and Pedophiles." Rape and Sexual Abuse Center. *www.rasac.org/education/statistics.html#02* (accessed October 27, 2005).

"Concept of Sexual Addiction" in *Sexual Addiction*. *http://rf-web.tamu.edu/security/secguide/Eap/Sex.htm* (accessed November 30, 2005).

Conte, J. R., and others. "What Sexual Offenders Tell Us About Prevention Strategies." *Child Abuse and Neglect* 131, no. 2 (1989): 293–301.

Crewdson, John. *By Silence Betrayed: Sexual Abuse of Children in America*. New York: Harper & Row, 1988.

Donaldson-Pressman, Stephanie, and Robert Pressman. *The Narcissistic Family: Diagnosis and Treatment*. San Francisco: Jossey-Bass Publishers, 1994.

Dorais, Michael. *Don't Tell: The Sexual Abuse of Boys*. Translated by D. Meyer. Quebec: McGill-Queens, 2002: Cited in Sharon M. Valente. "Sexual Abuse of Boys." *Journal of Child and Adolescent Psychiatric Nursing* 18, no. 1 (January-March, 2005): 13.

Diagnosis and Statistical Manual of Mental Disorders IV. Washington, DC: American Psychiatric Association, 1994, 424–29.

"Eating Disorders: Types, Warning Signs and Treatment," in *Help-guide*. *www.helpguide.org/mental/eating_disorder_treatment.htm* (accessed on November 12, 2005).

English, Diana. "The Extent and Consequences of Child Maltreatment." *The Future of Children* 8, no. 1 (1998): 39–53.

"Fact Sheet: Sexual Abuse of Boys." *Prevent Child Abuse America*. *www.preventchildabuse.org* (accessed October 27, 2005).

Faller, Kathleen Coulborn. "Child Sexual Abuse: Intervention and Treatment Issues." U.S. Department of Health and Human Services Administration for Children, Youth and Families. National Center on Child Abuse and Neglect (1993): 1–132. *http://nccanch.acf.hhs.gov/pubs/usermanuals/sexabuse/acknowledge.cfm* (accessed November 1, 2005).

Finkelhor, David. *A Sourcebook on Child Sexual Abuse*. Beverly Hills, CA: Sage Publications, 1986.

———. "Current Information on the Scope and Nature of Child Sexual Abuse." *The Future of Children* 4, No. 2 (1994): 31–53.

———. "Legacy of the Clergy Abuse Scandal." International Child Abuse Network (November 2004), *www.yesican.org/articles/article10–1.html* (accessed November 11, 2005).

Finkelhor, David, and Angela Browne. "The Traumatic Impact of Child Sexual Abuse: A Conceptualization." *American Journal of Orthopsychiatry* 55, no. 4, (October 1985): 530–540.

Finkelhor, David, and others. "Sexual Abuse in a National Survey of Adult Men and Women: Prevalence, Characteristics and Risk Factors." *Child Abuse and Neglect* 14 (1990): 19–28.

———. "Victimization Prevention Programs for Children: A Follow Up." *American Journal of Public Health* 85 (1995): 1684–1689.

Fitzgerald, Helen, and Lana R. Lawrence. "Childhood Sexual Abuse and Loss: An Overview of Grief and Its Complications for Survivors." *Moving Forward* 3, no. 2 (1994) *www.findingmysoul.com/grief.htm*.

Flaherty, Sandra M. *Woman, Why Do You Weep? Spirituality for Survivors of Childhood Sexual Abuse*. Mahwah, NJ: Paulist Press, 1992.

Fortune, Marie. *Sexual Violence: The Unmentionable Sin*. New York: Pilgrim Press, 1984.

Forward, Susan, and Craig Buck. *Betrayal of Innocence: Incest and Its Devastation*. Los Angeles: Penguin Books, 1988.

Fowler, James. *Stages of Faith*. San Francisco: Harper & Row, 1981.

Frank, Jan. *A Door of Hope.* San Bernardino, CA: Here's Life Publishers, 1987.

Genung, Mike. "Statistics and Information on Pornography." *Blazing Grace. www.blazinggrace.org/pornstatistics.htm* (accessed November 30, 2005).

Grunlan, Stephen, and Dan Lambrides. *Healing Relationships: A Christian's Manual of Lay Counseling.* Camp Hill, PA: Christian Publications, Inc., 1984.

Guidry, Harlan M. "Childhood Sexual Abuse: Role of the Family Physician." *American Family Physician* (February 1, 1995): 1–10.

Hagelin, Rebecca. "Overdosing on Porn." *The World and I* (March 2004). *www.worldandi.com/specialreport/2004/march/ Sa23779.htm* (accessed November 30, 2005).

Hall, Michael, and Bobby Bodenhamer. "New Identity in Christ." *www.renewingyourmind.com/Techniques/inchrist.htm.*

Hamblen, Jessica. "PTSD in Children and Adults." National Center for Post-Traumatic Stress Disorder, Department of Veterans Affairs. *www.ncptsd.va.gov/facts/specific/fs_children.html.*

Hanson, R. F., and others. "Factors Related to the Reporting of Childhood Sexual Assault." *Child Abuse and Neglect* 23 (1999): 559–69.

Hedges-Goettl, Len. *Sexual Abuse: Pastoral Responses.* Nashville: Abingdon Press, 2004.

Heggen, Carolyn Holderread. *Sexual Abuse in Christian Homes and Churches.* Scottdale, PA: Herald Press, 1993.

Herman, Judith. *Trauma and Recovery: The Aftermath of Violence.* New York: Basic Books, 1997.

Holmes, William C. "Sexual Abuse of Boys Is More Common Than Believed." University of Pennsylvania School of Medicine. *www.newswise.com/articles/view/?id=SEXABUSE.UPM* (accessed November 7, 2005).

Hopper, Jim. "Sexual Abuse of Males: Prevalence, Possible Lasting Effects, and Resources." *www.jimhopper.com/male-ab.* (accessed October 27, 2005).

Huggins, Kevin. "The Possibility of a Healed Memory." *Institute in Biblical Counseling Perspective* 1, no. 1. A publication of the Institute in Biblical Counseling, Winona Lake, IN, 1985.

"Incest." The National Center for Victims of Crime. *www.ncvc.org/ ncvc/main.aspx?dbName=DocumentViewer&Document ID=32360* (accessed October 27, 2005).

Janssen, Martha. *Secret Shame: I Am a Victim of Incest.* Minneapolis, MN: Augsburg Fortress, 1991.

Kaufman, Gershen. *Shame: The power of caring.* Cambridge, MA: Schenkman Books, 3rd edition, 1992.

Keck, Gregory, and Regina Kupecky. *Adopting the Hurt Child: Hope for Families With Special-Needs Kids.* Colorado Springs: Pinon Press, 1995.

Kia-Keating, Maryam, and others. "Containing and Resisting Masculinity: Narratives of Renegotiation Among Resilient Male Survivors of Childhood Sexual Abuse." *Psychology of Men & Masculinity* 6, no. 3 (July, 2005): 169–85.

Kraiser, Sherryll, and others. "Child Sexual Abuse Prevention Programs: What Makes Them Effective in Protecting Children?" *Children Today* (Sept.–Oct., 1989). *www.findarticles.com/p/articles/mi_m1053/is_n5_v18/ai_8153035* (accessed October 29, 2005).

Kubetin, Cynthia A., and James Mallory, MD, *Beyond the Darkness: Healing for Victims of Sexual Abuse.* 1st edition. Dallas: Rapha Publishing/Word, Inc., 1992.

Landorf, Joyce. Cited in Stephen Grunlan and Daniel Lambrides, *Healing Relationships: A Christian's Manual of Lay Counseling.* Camp Hill, PA: Christian Publications, Inc., 1984.

Langberg, Diane Mandt. *On the Threshold of Hope.* Wheaton, IL: Tyndale House Publishers, 1999.

———. *Counseling Survivors of Sexual Abuse.* Longwood, FL: Xulon Press, Inc., 2003.

Mackenzie, Tricia. "Survivors of Sexual Abuse: What We Would Like You to Know About Us." Christian Women Support. *www.trickenzie.com/cwrecovery.html* (accessed November 18, 2005).

Maddock, James W., and Noel R. Larson. *Incestuous Families: An Ecological Approach to Understanding and Treatment.* New York: W.W. Norton & Company, 1995.

Mahoney, Debbie, and Nancy Faulkner. "Brief Overview of Pedophiles on the Web" in *Pandora's Box. www.prevent-abuse-now.com/pedoweb.htm* (accessed October 27, 2005).

Mason, Marilyn. "Intimacy." Center City, MN: Hazelden Foundation, 1986.

Mason, Marilyn, and Merle Fossum. *Facing Shame: Families in Recovery.* New York: W. W. Norton & Company, 1986.

Mattingly, Terry. "Where Does the Baptist Buck Stop?" in *On Religion. http://tmatt.gospelcom.net/column/2002/06/19* (accessed November 11, 2005).

Mayer, Adele. *Sexual Abuse: Causes, Consequences, and Treatment of Incestuous and Pedophilic Acts.* Holmes Beach, FL: Learning Publications, 1985.

Melby, Todd. "Baby Steps in Studying an Age-old Problem." *Contemporary Sexuality: The International Resource for Educators, Researchers and Therapists* 38, no. 12 (December 2004): 3–5.

"Mental Health Evaluations of Child Sexual Abuse." New Jersey Department of Human Services. *www.state.nj.us/humanservices/NJTaskForce/mhsae.html.* (accessed October 31, 2005).

Meier, Paul D. *Christian Child-Rearing and Personality Development.* Grand Rapids, MI: Baker Book House, 1984.

Mitchell, Kimberly, David Finkelhor, and Janis Wolak. "The Internet and Family and Acquaintance Sexual Abuse." *Child Maltreatment* 10, no. 1, (February 2005): 49–60.

Murray, Claire, and Glenn Walker. "Reported Sexual Abuse and Bulimic Psychopathology Among Non-Clinical Women: The Mediating Role of Shame." *International Journal of Eating Disorders* 32, no. 2 (September 2002): 186–91.

"Myths and Facts About Sex Offenders." Center for Sex Offender Management. *www.csom.org/pubs/mythsfacts.html* (accessed November 22, 2005).

National Center for Missing & Exploited Children. CyberTipLine. *www.missingkids.com/missingkids/servlet/PageServlet? LanguageCountry=en_US&PageId=169* (accessed October 19, 2005).

"Notes From a Talk About the Book" *When Survivors Give Birth. www.gentlebirth.org/archives/abuseNotes.html* (accessed November 18, 2005).

O'Brien, Michael, and Walter Bera. "Adolescent Sexual Offenders: A Descriptive Typology." *Preventing Sexual Abuse* 1, no. 3 (Fall 1986): 1–4.

Peck, M. Scott. *The Road Less Traveled.* New York: Simon and Schuster, 1978.

Perry, Bruce D. "Brain Structure and Function II: Special Topics Informing Work with Maltreated Children. The Child Trauma Academy. http://www. childtrauma.org/ctamaterials/ brain_II.asp (accessed November 10, 2005).

Peters, David. *A Betrayal of Innocence: What Everyone Should Know About Child Sexual Abuse.* Dallas: Word Books, 1986.

Peterson, Eugene. *The Message: The Bible in Contemporary Language.* Colorado Springs: Navpress, 2002.

"Post-Traumatic Stress Disorders in Children and Adolescents."

Child Trauma Academy. *www.childtrauma.org/ctamaterials/ PTSD_opin6.asp* (accessed October 29, 2005).

Powell, John. *Why Am I Afraid to Tell You Who I Am?* Valencia, CA: Tabor Publishing, 1969.

"Pregnancy to Parenting: A Guide for Survivors of Child Sexual Abuse." Abuse and Violence Helpful Information: Domestic Violence and Incest Resource Center. *www.dvirc.org.au/ HelpHub/PregnancySexualAbuse.htm* (accessed November 18, 2005).

"PTSD in Children and Adolescents." National Center for Post-Traumatic Stress Disorder. *www.ncptsd.va.gov/facts/specific/ fs_children.html* (accessed October 29, 2005).

"Prostitution Facts." *www.rapeis.org/activism/prostitution/prostitutionfacts. html* (accessed October 25, 2005).

"Prostitution Statistics and Quotes." Program Against Sexual Violence Home Page, University of Minnesota. *www1.umn.edu/ aurora/prostitutionstats.htm.* (accessed October 25, 2005).

"Reports & Statistics." Child Lures Prevention. *www. childlures.com/research/statistics.asp.* (accessed on October 26, 2005).

"Respite As a Support Service for Adoptive Families: Fact Sheet Number 33." National Resource Center for Respite and Crisis Care Services. *www.archrespite.org/archfs33.htm* (accessed November 16, 2005).

Richards, Ramona. "Dirty Little Secret." *Today's Christian Woman* (September/October 2003). *www.christianitytoday.com/tcw/ 2003/005/5.58.html* (accessed November 30, 2005).

Russell, Sherry. "Grief and Sexual Abuse." The Bright Side. *www.the-bright-side.org/site/thebrightside/content.php?type=1&section_id=718&id=1221* (accessed November 19, 2005).

Ryan, Dale. "The F Word: Forgiveness and Its Imitations: An Interview With David Augsburger." National Association for Christian Recovery. *www.nacronline.com/dox/library/forgive.shtml* (accessed November 20, 2005).

Ryan, Juanita. "Seeing God in New Ways: Recovery From Distorted Images of God." The National Association for Christians in Recovery. *www.nacronline.com/dox/library/images.shtml* (accessed November 20, 2005).

Sanford, Linda Tschirhart. *The Silent Children: A Parent's Guide to the Prevention of Child Sexual Abuse.* New York: McGraw-Hill, 1982.

Schwartz, Eitan D., and Bruce D. Perry, "The Post-Traumatic Response in Children and Adolescents." *Psychiatric Clinics of North America* 17, no.2 (1994): 311–26.

Seamands, David. *Healing of Memories*. Wheaton, Ill.: Victor Books, 1985.

———. "Healing Distorted Images of God." Minneapolis, MN: National Counseling Conference, Crystal Free Evangelical Church (May 14–16, 1986).

Sgroi, Susanne. *Handbook of Clinical Intervention in Child Sexual Abuse*. Lexington, MA: Lexington Books, D. C. Heath and Company, 1982.

Smedes, Lewis. *Forgive and Forget: Healing the Hurts We Don't Deserve*. New York: Pocket Books, 1984.

———. *Shame and Grace: Healing the Shame We Don't Deserve*. San Francisco: Zondervan Publishing, 1993.

Smolak, Linda, and Sarah Murnen. "A Meta-Analytic Examination of the Relationship Between Child Sexual Abuse and Eating Disorders." *International Journal of Eating Disorders* 31, no. 2 (March 2002): 136–50.

"Socio-cultural Aspects of HIV/AIDS in SA." *www.health24.com/medical/Condition_centres/777-792-814-1762,23100.asp* (accessed October 23, 2005).

Spindler, Regine. "Childhood Sexual Abuse and Its Effects on Childbirth." GentleBirth.Org. *www.gentlebirth.org/archives/abusepaper.html* (accessed November 18, 2005).

Sroufe, L. Alan, and Robert Cooper. *Child Development: Its Nature and Course*. New York: Alfred A. Knopf, 1988.

Stafford, Tim. *Do You Sometimes Feel Like a Nobody?* Grand Rapids: MI, Zondervan Publishing, 1980.

"Statistics on Pedophiles." Counter Pedophilia Investigative Unit. *www.cpiu.us/statistics.php?name=* (accessed October 28, 2005).

Stonehouse, Catherine. *Joining Children on the Spiritual Journey: Nurturing a Life of Faith*. Grand Rapids, MI: Baker Books, 1998.

Strong, James. *Strong's Exhaustive Concordance of the Bible*. McLean, Va.: MacDonald Publishing Company.

Suler, John. "Defense Mechanisms." Rider University. *www.rider.edu/suler/defenses.html* (accessed November 19, 2005).

Terry, Karen, and Jennifer Tallon. "Child Sexual Abuse: A Review of the Literature." *The Nature and Scope of the Problem of Sexual Abuse of Minors by Catholic Priests and Deacons in the United States: A Research Study Conducted by the John Jay*

College of Criminal Justice (2002). *www.usccb.org/nrb/johnjays-tudy/litreview.pdf* (accessed October 27, 2005).

"The Sexual Assault of Boys and Its Aftermath." New York State Coalition Against Sexual Assault. Fact Sheets and Brochures *www.nyscasa.org/* (accessed November 3, 2005).

Thompson, Marjorie. *Family: The Forming Center.* Nashville: Upper Room Books, 1996.

Townsend, John. "Learning to Set Boundaries." *Secrets of Your Family Tree.* Chicago: Moody Press, 1991.

United Nations Foundation and Ad Council. Apathy Is Lethal Home Page. *www.apathyislethal.org* (accessed October 23, 2005).

VanVonderen, Jeff. *Tired of Trying to Measure Up.* Minneapolis, MN: Bethany House Publishers, 1989.

"What Research Shows About Female Adolescent Sex Offenders." National Center on Sexual Behavior of Youth (January 2004). *www.ncsby.org/pages/publications/Female%20ASO.pdf* (accessed November 30, 2005).

Whealin, Julia M. "Men and Sexual Trauma." A National Center for PTSD Fact Sheet. *www.ncptsd.va.gov/facts/specific/fs_male_sexual_assault.html* (accessed November 3, 2005).

Wilson, Sandra. *Released From Shame: Moving Beyond the Pain of the Past.* Downers Grove, IL: InterVarsity Press. Revised edition, 2002.

Wonderlich, Stephen A, and others. "Eating Disturbance and Sexual Trauma in Childhood and Adulthood." *International Journal of Eating Disorders* 30, no. 4 (December 2001): 401–12.

Yancey, Philip. *Disappointment With God: Three Questions No One Asks Aloud.* Grand Rapids, MI: Zondervan Books, 1988.

Endnotes

Chapter 1

1. Pat Benatar, "Hell Is for Children," *Live From Earth* (New York: Chrysalis Records, 1983).
2. David Finkelhor, "Current Information on the Scope and Nature of Child Sexual Abuse," *The Future of Children* 4, No. 2 (1994): 31–53.
3. David Finkelhor, and others, "Sexual Abuse in a National Survey of Adult Men and Women: Prevalence, Characteristics, and Risk Factors," *Child Abuse and Neglect* 14, (1990): 19–28.
4. Diana English, "The Extent and Consequences of Child Maltreatment," *The Future of Children* 8, No. 1 (1998): 39–53.
5. R. F. Hanson, and others, "Factors Related to the Reporting of Childhood Sexual Assault," *Child Abuse and Neglect* 23, (1999): 559–69.
6. James Maddock and Noel Larson, *Incestuous Families: An Ecological Approach to Understanding and Treatment* (New York: W. W. Norton & Company, 1995), 1.
7. Ibid., 3.
8. "Prostitution Facts," *www.rapeis.org/activism/prostitution/prostitution facts.html.*
9. "Prostitution Statistics and Quotes," Program Against Sexual Violence Home Page, University of Minnesota *www1.umn.edu/aurora/prostitution stats.htm.*
10. Ibid.
11. "Reports & Statistics," Child Lures Prevention *www.childlures.com/research/statistics.asp.*
12. Karen Terry and Jennifer Tallon, "Child Sexual Abuse: A Review of the Literature," *The Nature and Scope of the Problem of Sexual Abuse of Minors by Catholic Priests and Deacons in the United States: A research study conducted by the John Jay College of Criminal Justice* (2002), *www.usccb.org/nrb/johnjaystudy/litreview.pdf.*
13. Jim Hopper, "Sexual Abuse of Males: Prevalence, Possible Lasting Effects and Resources." *www.jimhopper.com/male-ab/.*
14. "Reports & Statistics."
15. "Fact Sheet: Sexual Abuse of Boys," Prevent Child Abuse America, *www.preventchildabuse.org.*
16. Finkelhor, and others, "Sexual Abuse in a National Survey of Adult Men and Women: Prevalence, Characteristics and Risk Factors," 19–28.
17. "Reports & Statistics."
18. "Statistics on Pedophiles," Counter Pedophilia Investigative Unit, *www.cpiu.us/statistics.php?name=.*
19. John Crewdson, *By Silence Betrayed: Sexual Abuse of Children in America,* (New York: Harper & Row, 1988), 31.
20. Susan Forward and Craig Buck. *Betrayal of Innocence: Incest and Its*

Devastation. (Los Angeles, CA: Penguin Books, 1988), 85.

21. Maddock and Larson, *Incestuous Families: An Ecological Approach to Understanding and Treatment*, 199–205.

Chapter 2

1. Maddock and Larson, *Incestuous Families: An Ecological Approach to Understanding and Treatment*, 55.
2. Carolyn Holderread Heggen, *Sexual Abuse in Christian Homes and Churches* (Scottdale, PA: Herald Press, 1993), 20.
3. John Briere and Diana Elliot, "Immediate and Long-Term Impacts of Child Sexual Abuse," *The Future of Children* 4, No. 2 (Summer/Fall 1994): 54–69.
4. Angela Browne and David Finkelhor, "The Impact of Child Sexual Abuse: A Review of the Research," *Psychological Bulletin* 99, No. 1 (January 1986): 66–77.
5. "Post-Traumatic Stress Disorders in Children and Adolescents," in Child Trauma Academy, *www.childtrauma.org/ctamaterials/PTSD_opin6.asp*.
6. Briere and Elliot, *Immediate and Long-Term Impacts of Child Sexual Abuse*, 54–69.
7. Jessica Hamblen, "PTSD in Children and Adults," National Center for Post-Traumatic Stress Disorder, Department of Veterans Affairs, *www.ncptsd.va.gov/facts/ specific/fs_children.html*.
8. Ibid.
9. Sheldon J. Kaplan, "When the Past Won't Go Away," *Jacksonville Medicine* (August/September 2002) *www.dcmsonline.org/jax-medicine/ 2002journals/augsept2002/PTSD.htm*.
10. Hamblen, "PTSD in Children and Adults."
11. Ibid.
12. Briere and Elliot, "Immediate and Long-Term Impacts of Child Sexual Abuse," 54–69.
13. Judith Herman, *Trauma and Recovery: The Aftermath of Violence*, New York: Basic Books, 1997), 99.
14. Briere and Elliot, "Immediate and Long-Term Impacts of Child Sexual Abuse," 54–69.
15. Linda Tschirhart Sanford, *The Silent Children: A Parent's Guide to the Prevention of Child Sexual Abuse* (New York: McGraw-Hill, 1982), 162.
16. Briere and Elliot, "Immediate and Long-Term Effects of Child Sexual Abuse," 54–69.
17. L. Alan Sroufe and Robert Cooper, *Child Development: Its Nature and Course*, (New York: Alfred A. Knopf, 1988), 32–33.
18. Stephanie Donaldson-Pressman and Robert Pressman, *The Narcissistic Family: Diagnosis and Treatment*, (San Francisco: Jossey-Bass Publishers, 1994), 13.
19. Adele Mayer, *Sexual Abuse: Causes, Consequences and Treatment for Incestuous and Pedophilic Acts* (Holmes Beach, FL: Learning Publications, 1985), 54.
20. Catherine Classen, Oxana Palesh, and Rashi Aggarwal, "Sexual Revictimization: A Review of Empirical Literature," *Trauma, Violence, and Abuse* 6, No. 2 (April 2005): 103–29.

21. Sanford, *The Silent Children: A Parent's Guide to the Prevention of Child Sexual Abuse*, 162.
22. Ibid., 139.
23. Sroufe and Cooper, *Child Development: Its Nature and Course*, 38–40.
24. Diana English, "The Extent and Consequences of Child Maltreatment," 39–53.
25. Browne and Finkelhor, "The Impact of Child Sexual Abuse: A Review of the Research," 66–77.
26. Ibid.
27. Sanford, *The Silent Children: A Parent's Guide to the Prevention of Child Sexual Abuse*, 139.
28. Marie Fortune, *Sexual Violence: The Unmentionable Sin* (New York: Pilgrim Press, 1984), 15
29. Herman, *Trauma and Recovery: The Aftermath of Violence*, 34.
30. Sanford, *The Silent Children: A Parent's Guide to the Prevention of Child Sexual Abuse*, 139.
31. Finkelhor, "Current Information on the Scope and Nature of Child Sexual Abuse," 31–53.
32. Heggen, *Sexual Abuse in Christian Homes and Churches*, 21.
33. Martha Janssen, *Secret Shame: I Am a Victim of Incest* (Minneapolis: Augsburg Fortress, 1991.) Reprinted by permission.
34. Len Hedges-Goettl, *Sexual Abuse: Pastoral Responses* (Nashville: Abingdon Press, 2004), 30.
35. Kimberly Mitchell, David Finkelhor, and Janis Wolak. "The Internet and Family and Acquaintance Sexual Abuse." *Child Maltreatment* 10, No. 1, (February 2005): 49–60.
36. Browne and Finkelhor, "The Impact of Child Sexual Abuse: A Review of the Research," 66–77.
37. Herman, *Trauma and Recovery: The Aftermath of Violence*, 102.
38. Fortune, *Sexual Violence: The Unmentionable Sin*, 168.
39. Sanford, *The Silent Children: A Parent's Guide to the Prevention of Child Sexual Abuse*, 142.
40. Briere and Elliot, "Immediate and Long-Term Impacts of Child Sexual Abuse," 54–69.
41. Ibid.
42. David Peters, *A Betrayal of Innocence: What Everyone Should Know about Child Sexual Abuse* (Dallas: Word Books, 1986), 21.
43. Sanford, *The Silent Children: A Parent's Guide to the Prevention of Child Sexual Abuse*, 140.
44. Ibid.
45. Finkelhor, "Current Information on the Scope and Nature of Child Sexual Abuse," 31–53.
46. "Mental Health Evaluations of Child Sexual Abuse," New Jersey Department of Human Services, *www.state.nj.us/humanservices/NJTaskForce/mhsae.html.*
47. Mary de Young, "A Conceptual Model for Judging the Truthfulness of a Young Child's Allegation of Sexual Abuse," *American Journal of Orthopsychiatry* (October 1986): 550–59.
48. "Mental Health Evaluations of Child Sexual Abuse."
49. Suzanne Long, and others, *Sexual Abuse of Young Children* (New York: The Guilford Press, 1986).

Chapter 3

1. David Finkelhor, *A Sourcebook on Child Sexual Abuse* (Beverly Hills, CA: Sage Publications, 1986), 182.
2. Kathleen Coulborn Faller, "Child Sexual Abuse: Intervention and Treatment Issues," U.S. Department of Health and Human Services: Administration on Children, Youth and Families. National Center on Child Abuse and Neglect (1993), 22–29. *http://nccanch.acf.hhs.gov/pubs/usermanuals/sexabuse/*
3. *Ibid.*
4. *Diane Langberg, On the Threshold of Hope* (Wheaton, IL: Tyndale House Publishers, 1999), 115.
5. Donaldson-Pressman and Pressman, *The Narcissistic Family: Diagnosis and Treatment*, 36.
6. English, "The Extent and Consequences of Child Maltreatment," 39–53.
7. Browne and Finkelhor, "The Traumatic Impact of Child Sexual Abuse: A Conceptualization," 530–40.
8. Donaldson-Pressman and Pressman, *The Narcissistic Family: Diagnosis and Treatment.*
9. "Fact Sheet: Sexual Abuse of Boys," Prevent Child Abuse America, *www.preventchildabuse.org.*
10. Briere and Elliot, "Immediate and Long-Term Impacts of Child Sexual Abuse," 60.
11. Ibid., 57.
12. Langberg, *On the Threshold of Hope*, 17–21.
13. Briere and Elliot, "Immediate and Long-Term Impacts of Child Sexual Abuse," 54–69.
14. Ibid.
15. William C. Holmes, "Sexual Abuse of Boys Is More Common Than Believed," University of Pennsylvania School of Medicine, *www.newswise.com/articles/view/?id=SEXABUSE.UPM.*
16. Julia M. Whealin, "Men and Sexual Trauma," A National Center for PTSD Fact Sheet *www.ncptsd.va.gov/facts/specific/fs_male_sexual_assault.html.*
17. Harlan M. Guidry, "Childhood Sexual Abuse: Role of the Family Physician," *American Family Physician* (February 1, 1995): 1–10.
18. Langberg, *On the Threshold of Hope*, 115.
19. Briere and Elliot, "Immediate and Long-Term Impacts of Child Sexual Abuse," 54–69.
20. Finkelhor, *A Sourcebook on Child Sexual Abuse*, 180–98.
21. Briere and Elliot, "Immediate and Long-Term Impacts of Child Sexual Abuse," 58.
22. "The Sexual Abuse of Boys and Its Aftermath," New York State Coalition Against Sexual Assault, Fact Sheets and Brochures, *www.nyscasa.org/*
23. Whealin, "Men and Sexual Trauma."
24. Ibid.

Chapter 4

1. Sandra M. Flaherty, *Woman, Why Do You Weep? Spirituality for Survivors of Childhood Sexual Abuse*, (Mahwah, NJ: Paulist Press, 1992), 1.

2. Ibid., 2.
3. Catherine Stonehouse, *Joining Children on the Spiritual Journey: Nurturing a Life of Faith* (Grand Rapids, MI: Baker Books, 1998), 33–35.
4. David Seamands, "Healing Distorted Images of God" (Minneapolis, MN: National Counseling Conference, Crystal Free Evangelical Church, May 14–16, 1986).
5. Ibid.
6. Ibid.

Chapter 5

1. James W. Maddock and Noel R. Larson, *Incestuous Families: An Ecological Approach to Understanding and Treatment*, 72–129.
2. Ibid., 130–172.
3. Ibid.
4. Ibid.
5. Ibid.
6. Ibid.
7. Ibid.
8. Susanne Sgroi, *Handbook of Clinical Intervention in Child Sexual Abuse* (Lexington, MA.: Lexington Books, D.C. Heath and Company, 1982), 251.
9. Ibid., 258.
10. Ibid., 253.
11. Martha Janssen, *Secret Shame: I Am a Victim of Incest* (Minneapolis: Augsburg Fortress, 1991). Reprinted by permission.
12. Marilyn Mason and Merle Fossum, *Facing Shame: Families in Recovery* (New York: W. W. Norton & Company, 1986), 158.
13. Marilyn Mason, "Intimacy" (Center City, MN: Hazelden Foundation, 1986), 8.
14. Mason and Fossum, *Facing Shame: Families in Recovery*, 72.
15. Ibid., 80.
16. M. Scott Peck, *The Road Less Traveled* (New York: Simon and Schuster, 1978), 105.
17. Ibid.
18. David Augsburger, *Caring Enough to Forgive* (Ventura, CA: Regal Books, 1981), 30.
19. Maddock and Larson, *Incestuous Families: An Ecological Approach to Understanding and Treatment*.

Chapter 6

1. David B. Peters, *A Betrayal of Innocence: What Everyone Should Know About Child Sexual Abuse* (Dallas, TX: Word Books, 1986), 27.
2. Rebecca Hagelin, "Overdosing on Porn," *The World and I* (March 2004) *www.worldandi.com/specialreport/2004/march/Sa23779.htm.*
3. Mike Genung, "Statistics and Information on Pornography," in Blazing Grace, *www.blazinggrace.org/pornstatistics.htm.*
4. Ramona Richards, "Dirty Little Secret," in *Today's Christian Woman* (October 2003) *www.christianitytoday.com/tcw/2003/005/5.58.html.*

5. Peters, *A Betrayal of Innocence*, 29.
6. "Myths and Facts About Sex Offenders," Center for Sex Offender Management, *www.csom.org/pubs/mythsfacts.html*.
7. Michael O'Brien and Walter Bera, "Adolescent Sexual Offenders: A Descriptive Typology," *Preventing Sexual Abuse*, vol. 1, no. 3 (Fall 1986), 1.
8. Ibid., 2.
9. Ibid., 1–4.
10. Ibid., 2.
11. Ibid., 3.
12. "What Research Shows About Female Adolescent Sex Offenders," *National Center on Sexual Behavior of Youth* (January 2004), *www.ncsby.org/pages/publications/Female%20ASO.pdf*.
13. Ibid.
14. Ibid.
15. Sanford, *The Silent Children: A Parent's Guide to the Prevention of Child Sexual Abuse*, 101.
16. Ibid., 103.
17. Mayer, *Sexual Abuse: Cause, Consequences and Treatment of Incestuous and Pedophilic Acts*, 20.
18. Ibid., 21.
19. Ibid., 20.
20. Ibid.
21. Sanford, *The Silent Children: A Parent's Guide to the Prevention of Child Sexual Abuse*, 103.
22. "Myths and Facts about Sex Offenders," Center for Sex Offender Management, *www.csom.org/pubs/mythsfacts.html*.
23. Sgroi, *Handbook of Clinical Intervention in Child Sexual Abuse*, 218.
24. Ibid., 225.
25. Program for Healthy Adolescent Sexual Expression (PHASE), East Communities Family Center, Maplewood, MN.
26. Peters, *A Betrayal of Innocence*, 132.
27. Ibid., 153.
28. "Concept of Sexual Addiction," *Sexual Addiction*, Texas A & M Research Foundation, *http://rf-web.tamu.edu/security/secguide/Eap/Sex.htm*
29. Ibid.
30. Patrick Carnes, *Out of the Shadows: Understanding Sexual Addiction* (Minneapolis, MN: CompCare Publications, 1983), 9.
31. Ibid.
32. In recognition of the many Christian men and women who struggle with addictions to pornography, please seek help from the many resources available. For recovery resources written by Dr. Carnes, see *Don't Call It Love* (New York: Bantam Books, 1992). Christian resources on the Internet include sites such as Pureonline.com, endorsed by Chuck Swindoll, Steve Arterburn, and others: *www.pureonline.com/learn-more.aspx*. See also ChristianAnswers.Net for indicators of sexual addiction, stages of addiction, and suggested resources, *www.christiananswers.net/q-eden/edn-f016.html*.
33. "Myths and Facts about Sex Offenders," *www.csom.org/pubs/myths facts.pdf*.
34. Forward and Buck, *Betrayal of Innocence*, 117.

35. Ibid., 75.
36. The development of RESTORATION PROJECT was due, in part, to efforts of Tom Mills, Tom Berscheid, and Dan Beyer.

Chapter 7

1. These steps have been adapted from the original 12-step recovery program of Alcoholics Anonymous.

Chapter 10

1. Gershen Kaufman, *Shame: The Power of Caring* (Cambridge, MA: Schenkman Books, 3rd edition, 1992).
2. John Powell, *Why Am I Afraid to Tell You Who I Am?* (Valencia, CA: Tabor Publishing, 1969), 21. Used by permission.
3. Sandra Wilson, *Released From Shame: Moving Beyond the Pain of the Past* (Downers Grove, IL: InterVarsity Press, revised edition, 2002), 76.
4. Lewis Smedes, *Shame and Grace: Healing the Shame We Don't Deserve* (San Francisco, CA: Zondervan Publishing, 1993), 9–11.
5. Jane Ault, 1989. Used by permission.
6. Adapted from Jeff VanVonderen, *Tired of Trying to Measure Up* (Minneapolis, MN: Bethany House Publishers, 1989).
7. Wilson, *Released From Shame: Moving Beyond the Pain of the Past*, 78.
8. Ibid., 151.

Chapter 11

1. "Respite As a Support Service for Adoptive Families," Fact Sheet Number 33, in National Resource Center for Crisis and Care Services, *www.archrespite.org/archfs33.htm*.
2. Marjorie Thompson, *Family: The Forming Center* (Nashville: Upper Room Books, 1996), 22.
3. Sroufe and Cooper, *Child Development: Its Nature and Course*.
4. Gregory Keck and Regina Kupecky, *Adopting the Hurt Child: Hope for Families With Special-Needs Kids* (Colorado Springs: Pinon Press, 1995), 45–52.
5. Ibid.
6. Ibid.
7. Janssen, *Secret Shame: I Am a Victim of Incest*. Reprinted by permission.
8. James Fowler, *Stages of Faith* (San Francisco: Harper & Row, 1981), 80.
9. Paul D. Meier, *Christian Child-Rearing and Personality Development* (Grand Rapids: Baker Book House, 1984), 25–26.
10. Tim Stafford, *Do You Sometimes Feel Like a Nobody?* (Grand Rapids: Zondervan Publishing, 1980).
11. Adapted from Michael Hall and Bobby Bodenhamer, "New Identity In Christ," *www.renewingyourmind.com/Techniques/inchrist.htm*.

Chapter 12

1. Diane Mandt Langberg, *Counseling Survivors of Sexual Abuse*, (Longwood, FL: Xulon Press, Inc. 2003), 24–25.
2. Wilson, *Released from Shame: Moving Beyond the Pain of the Past*, 100.
3. Donaldson-Pressman and Pressman, *The Narcissistic Family: Diagnosis and Treatment*, 96.
4. Ibid., 72.
5. James Strong, *Strong's Exhaustive Concordance of the Bible* (McLean, Va.: MacDonald Publishing Company), #58 in the Greek dictionary.
6. Kenneth S. Wuest, *Wuest's Word Studies in the Greek New Testament* (Grand Rapids: William B. Eerdmans Publishing Co., 1978), 113–114.
7. Helen Fitzgerald and Lana R. Lawrence, "Childhood Sexual Abuse and Loss: An Overview of Grief and Its Complications for Survivors," *Moving Forward* 3, No. 2, 1994.
8. Joyce Landorf, cited in Stephen Grunlan and Daniel Lambrides, *Healing Relationships: A Christian's Manual of Lay Counseling* (Camp Hill, PA: Christian Publications, Inc., 1984), 113.
9. Tricia Mackenzie, "Survivors of Sexual Abuse: What We Would Like You to Know About Us," Christian Women Abuse Support, *www.trickenzie.com/cwrecovery.html.*
10. "Pregnancy to Parenting: A Guide for Survivors of Child Sexual Abuse," Abuse and Violence Helpful Information: Domestic Violence and Incest Resource Center, *www.dvirc.org.au/HelpHub/PregnancySexualAbuse.htm.*
11. Regine Spindler, "Childhood Sexual Abuse and Its Effects on Childbirth," GentleBirth.Org, *www.gentlebirth.org/archives/abusepaper.html.*
12. Notes from a talk about the book *When Survivors Give Birth*, *www.gentlebirth.org/archives/abuseNotes.html.*
13. "Pregnancy to Parenting."
14. Jan Frank, *A Door of Hope* (San Bernardino, CA: Here's Life Publishers, 1987), 62.
15. Sherry Russell, "Grief and Sexual Abuse," The Bright Side, *www.the-bright-side.org/site/thebrightside/content.php?type=1&section_id=718&id=1221.*
16. Artwork by Delores Selland, MA, psychotherapist. Used by permission.
17. Used by permission of author.

Chapter 13

1. Donaldson-Pressman and Pressman, *Narcissistic Family: Diagnosis and Treatment,* 102.
2. John Suler, "Defense Mechanisms," Rider University, *www.rider.edu/suler/defenses.html.*
3. Powell, *Why Am I Afraid to Tell You Who I Am?*, 139–40. Used by permission.
4. Material adapted from Anna Gates. Used by permission.

Chapter 14

1. Janssen, *Secret Shame: I Am a Victim of Incest*. Reprinted by permission.
2. Pastor Dave Johnson, "Forgiving the Little Ones," based on Matthew

18:21–35, sermon tapes 83 and 84 (Minneapolis: Church of the Open Door, March 1989).
3. Ibid.
4. Dale Ryan, "The F Word: Forgiveness and Its Imitations: An Interview with David Augsburger," National Association for Christian Recovery, *www.nacronline.com/dox/library/forgive.shtml.*
5. Pastor Dave Johnson, "Forgiving the Little Ones."
6. Frank, *A Door of Hope*, 151.
7. Jane McClain, "Overcoming the Trauma of Incest," *Virtue* (October 1988), 20.
8. Lewis B. Smedes, *Forgive and Forget: Healing the Hurts We Don't Deserve* (N.Y.: Pocket Books, 1984), 61.
9. Kevin Huggins, "The Possibility of a Healed Memory," *Institute in Biblical Counseling Perspective*, vol. 1, no. 1 (a publication of the Institute in Biblical Counseling, Winona Lake, IN, 1985), 77.
10. Frank, *A Door of Hope*, 133.
11. Smedes, *Forgive and Forget: Healing the Hurts We Don't Deserve*, 105.
12. Philip Yancey, *Disappointment With God: Three Questions No One Asks Aloud* (Grand Rapids: Zondervan Books, 1988), 192.
13. Ibid., 183.
14. Ibid., 128.

Chapter 15

1. Juanita Ryan, "Seeing God in New Ways: Recovery From Distorted Images of God," The National Association for Christians in Recovery, *www.nacronline.com/dox/library/images.shtml.*
2. Ibid.
3. Ibid.
4. David Seamands, *Healing of Memories* (Wheaton, IL: Victor Books, 1985), 103.
5. Ibid.
6. Ibid., 104.
7. Ryan, "Seeing God in New Ways."
8. Pastor Dick Dickinson, Inner Community Counseling Center, Long Beach, CA.
9. George Back and Herb Goldberg, *Creative Aggression: The Art of Assertive Living* (Wellness Institute, 1974).
10. John Townsend, "Learning to Set Boundaries," *Secrets of Your Family Tree* (Chicago, IL: Moody Press, 1991), 165–86.
11. Carmen Berry, "Beyond Victimization," National Association for Christian Recovery, *www.nacronline.com/dox/library/carmen/beyond.shtml.*
12. Assertiveness Inventory, Dr. Paul Mauger.

Chapter 16

1. Anna Gates, 1986. Used by permission.
2. Thoreau.

Chapter 17

1. Herman, *Trauma and Recovery*, 7.
2. Hedges-Goettl, *Sexual Abuse: Pastoral Responses*, 17.
3. "Socio-cultural aspects of HIV/AIDS in SA," *www.health24.com/medical/Condition_centres/777-792-814-1762,23100.asp.*
4. United Nations Foundation and Ad Council, *Apathy Is Lethal* Home Page, *www.apathyislethal.org.*
5. Claudia Arp and David Arp, *The Second Half of Marriage* (Grand Rapids, MI: Zondervan, 1998).
6. Langberg, *Counseling Survivors of Sexual Abuse*, 6.
7. Ibid.
8. Stonehouse, *Joining Children on the Spiritual Journey: Nurturing a Life of Faith*, 15.
9. Heggen, *Sexual Abuse in Christian Homes and Churches*, 100.
10. "Reports & Statistics," Child Lures Prevention, *www.childlures.com/research/statistics.asp.*
11. "How Common is Childhood Sexual Abuse?" Counter Pedophilia Investigative Unit, *www.cpiu.us/childsafety.php?name=.*
12. Michael Dorais, *Don't Tell: The Sexual Abuse of Boys*, Translated by D. Meyer, (Quebec: McGill-Queens, 2002), cited in: Sharon M. Valente, "Sexual Abuse of Boys," *Journal of Child and Adolescent Psychiatric Nursing* 18, no. 1 (January-March, 2005): 13.
13. Todd Melby, "Baby Steps in Studying an Age-old Problem," *Contemporary Sexuality: The International Resource for Educators, Researchers and Therapists* 38, No 12 (December 2004): 4.
14. Dorais, *Don't Tell: The Sexual Abuse of Boys*, 13.
15. Maryam Kia-Keating, and others, "Containing and Resisting Masculinity: Narratives of Renegotiation Among Resilient Male Survivors of Childhood Sexual Abuse," *Psychology of Men & Masculinity* 6, No. 3 (July, 2005): 169–85
16. Terry Mattingly, "Where Does the Baptist Buck Stop?" *On Religion*, http://tmatt.gospelcom.net/column/2002/06/19.
17. "Eating Disorders: Types, Warning Signs and Treatment" Helpguide, *www.helpguide.org/mental/eating_disorder_treatment.htm.*
18. Claire Murray and Glenn Walker, "Reported Sexual Abuse and Bulimic Psychopathology Among Non-Clinical Women: The Mediating Role of Shame," *International Journal of Eating Disorders* 32, no. 2 (September 2002): 186.
19. Ibid.
20. Stephen A. Wonderlich, and others, "Eating Disturbance and Sexual Trauma in Childhood and Adulthood," *International Journal of Eating Disorders* 30, no. 4 (December 2001): 410.
21. *www.remuda-ranch.com.*
22. Eitan D. Schwartz and Bruce D. Perry, "The Post-Traumatic Response in Children and Adolescents," *Psychiatric Clinics of North America* 17, no.2 (1994): 311–26.
23. Ibid., 315.
24. Bruce D. Perry, "Brain Structure and Function II: Special Topics Informing Work with Maltreated Children," The Child Trauma Academy, *www.childtrauma.org/ctamaterials/brain_II.asp.*

25. David Finkelhor, and others, "Victimization Prevention Programs for Children: A Follow Up," *American Journal of Public Health* 85 (1995): 1684–689.
26. Sherryll Kraiser, and others, "Child Sexual Abuse Prevention Programs: What Makes Them Effective in Protecting Children?" *Children Today* (Sept.–Oct., 1989). *www.findarticles.com/p/articles/mi_m1053/is_n5_v18/ai_8153035*.
27. J. R. Conte, and others, "What Sexual Offenders Tell Us About Prevention Strategies," *Child Abuse and Neglect* 131, no. 2 (1989): 293–301.
28. Kraiser, "Sexual Abuse Prevention Programs."
29. Holmes, "Sexual Abuse of Boys Is More Common Than Believed."
30. CyberTipLine, National Center for Missing & Exploited Children, *www.missingkids.com/missingkids/servlet/PageServlet?Language Country=en_US&PageId=169*.
31. "Online Victimization: A Report on the Nation's Youth, Congress by the Crimes Against Children Research Center" (2000), *www.rasac.org/education/statistics.html#02*.
32. Debbie Mahoney and Nancy Faulkner, "Brief Overview of Pedophiles on the Web," Pandora's Box, *www.prevent-abuse-now.com/pedoweb.htm*.
33. Kimberly Mitchell, and others, "The Internet and Family Acquaintance Sexual Abuse," *Child Maltreatment* 10, no. 1 (February 2005): 49–60.
34. Ibid.
35. Fortune, *Sexual Violence: The Unmentionable Sin*, 86–87.
36. Wilson, *Released From Shame*, 57.
37. Cynthia A. Kubetin and James Mallory, M.D., *Beyond the Darkness: Healing for Victims of Sexual Abuse*, 1st edition. (Houston & Dallas: Rapha Publishing/Word, Inc., 1992), 18.

Index

CHRISTIAN RECOVERY CENTER (CRC),
A NONPROFIT, NONDENOMINATIONAL ORGANIZATION,
IS A MINNESOTA-LICENSED RULE 29 CLINIC.

Our primary mission is to help men, women, children, and families heal from their life experience of sexual, emotional, and physical abuse.

— ❧ —

Our Spiritual Foundation

CRC uses Christian biblical principles to facilitate healing. The scriptural foundation for CRC is:

"For I know the plans I have for you," declares the Lord,
"plans to prosper you and not harm you,
plans to give you hope and a future."
Jeremiah 29:11

— ❧ —

For those who desire to integrate their Christian faith into their healing process, Scripture and prayer are blended into our treatment model and strongly influence our individual, group, marriage, and family counseling.

CRC offers consultation, training, resources, and workshops in the prevention and treatment of physical, emotional, and sexual abuse and domestic violence. General counseling and psychotherapy are offered for individuals, couples, families, and children. These services are independently available as well as in collaboration with one or more of our unique programs designed for victims of domestic violence; survivors of childhood sexual abuse; women who need help setting boundaries; men and women with severe emotional and behavioral disturbances; families who have experienced loss, trauma, stress, or abuse; marriage enrichment; coaching in parenting; play therapy for children with emotional-behavioral issues; and long-term outpatient programs for men who have sexually offended children.